Posters, London Road, Manchester, c1925 (Manchester Local History Library)

Ephemera

A book on its collection, conservation and use

Chris E. Makepeace

Gower   A Grafton Book

© Chris E. Makepeace 1985

Published by
Gower Publishing Company Limited,
Gower House,
Croft Road,
Aldershot,
Hants GU11 3HR,
England

Gower Publishing Company,
Old Post Road,
Brookfield,
Vermont 05036
U.S.A.

British Library Cataloguing in Publication Data

Makepeace, C.E.
   Ephemera.
   1. Libraries – Special collections
   Printed ephemera
   I. Title
   025.17   Z688.P7

Library of Congress Cataloging in Publication Data

Makepeace, Chris E., 1944
   Ephemera.
   (A Grafton book)
   Includes bibliographies and index.
   1. Libraries – Special collections – Printed ephemera. 2. Printed
ephemera – Conservation and restoration. 3. Printed ephemera –
Collectors and collecting. 4. Vertical files (Libraries) I. Title.
   Z688.P74M35   1984   025.2'82   84-13644

ISBN 0–566-03439–5

Phototypeset by Saxon Printing Ltd., Derby.

Printing by Adlard & Son Ltd, Dorking, Surrey

Contents

Acknowledgements

There are a number of people whom I wish to thank for their help, advice and assistance whilst writing this book. Firstly, I would like to express my gratitude to the late Dorothy McCulla, who died so tragically in 1981 and without whose encouragement this book would never have been attempted and whose advice and assistance was invaluable in its early stages. My thanks are also due to David Taylor and the staff of Manchester Local History Library, John Cole and Morris Garratt of Rochdale Libraries, Diana Winterbotham of the Lancashire Library, David Cousins of Kent County Library, Julia Harrison of Essex County Library, Geoff Adams of the Greater Manchester Council's library, Norma Armstrong from Edinburgh City Library, Donald Buttress of the Buttress Langton Partnership, and many others who have provided ideas or examples of ephemera. Special thanks are due to Patrick Baird, head of Birmingham Local Studies Library, and Tony Barrett, conservationist at Birmingham, for reading through the manuscript and providing very useful comments and corrections. Finally, my thanks are due to my wife, Hilary, who has not only read through the manuscript looking for typing errors, but has also made very helpful suggestions and comments, and to young Peter, who despite the love of tearing up and eating paper, left the manuscript untouched.

Illustrations

1   Introduction

The aim of this book is to look at the subject of ephemera and to try, first of all, to define the subject and show how it differs from minor publications with which it is often confused. It will also look at the various types of material that make up ephemera, the way the material can be collected and discuss the extent that contemporary ephemera should be acquired and preserved by libraries, record offices, museums and other collecting agencies.

In addition, it is intended to look at the question of storing and conserving ephemera once it has been acquired by the library. It will include the treatment of both historic and current ephemera as it is important to treat both types of material properly before it is used by the public or displayed.

The book will also look at the problems of cataloguing and classifying the material so that potential users can trace what exists within a particular collection on a particular subject.

Finally, it will look at the use of the material. It is often easier to justify the existence and acquisition of older material than it is of contemporary material as the usage of the latter will not be as obvious as that for the older material. It could be argued that contemporary ephemera should not be deliberately collected or that only certain types should be. There is a simple answer to those who advance this argument. This is that no-one knows what subjects are going to be of interest in the future. Interests change and it is not the duty of a librarian, especially a local studies librarian, to act as a censor and determine what material should be kept and what should not. For example, the failure to preserve some types of recent ephemera is well illustrated by a comment from Mr M. Blanc, Director of the Bankfield Museum at Halifax, on an exhibition staged there on the 'Swinging Sixties'. He commented that 'the sixties ephemera seemed hard to find. We did not have that problem with the forties . . .'[1] In the field of contemporary ephemera, much will be determined by the fact that a large proportion of what is produced today will not survive because it never reaches a repository of any kind.

Although the aim of this book is to look at the whole field of ephemera, its definition, collection, storage, conservation, classification, cataloguing, indexing and exploitation and to try to suggest ways in which its coverage can be improved. It is in the local studies field that ephemera can create the greatest problems as much of the material that is acquired here will be permanently preserved. However, other types of library department use items of ephemera for various reasons. In addition, although the book will look at the subject from the point of view of a librarian, it is hoped that it will also be of interest to the archivist and museum curator whose interests often coincide with those of the local studies librarian. It is also hoped that it will provide a means of encouraging those librarians whose departments contain ephemera, but which is not retained once it has outlived its usefulness to look again at the material which is discarded and to pass it onto the local studies collection for preservation.

Although the position which has been referred to is the ideal one, it is appreciated that there are very often problems which prevent the ideal being attained, problems of lack of staff and staff time, space and ignorance on the part of some librarians of the value and importance of this type of material. However, it sets a target which can be aimed at.

It is also hoped that, in addition to providing helpful advice to those involved with ephemera on a day-to-day basis, it will provide assistance to those engaged in research as to the wide range of material that can be consulted in addition to the recognised sources.

Although the book does not aim to solve the problem of locating collections and their coverage, support is given to ideas put forward by Alan Clinton and John Pemberton in their reports on ephemera. The more the problems of discovering who has what and where it can be found, are discussed, the greater the chance of concrete results being achieved. Until the full extent of these problems is appreciated, little will be done. Clinton and Pemberton have highlighted certain aspects of it and it now requires positive action to implement their proposals.

As Rickards once put it, ephemera is a 'fragment of social history . . . a reflection of the spirit of its time . . . which is not expected to survive, but which can prove to be very useful in research.'[2] 'Ephemera', says Rickards 'represents the other half of history: the half without guile. When people put up monuments or published official war histories they had a constant eye on their audience and their history would be adjusted to suit, whereas ephemera was never expected to survive – it would normally have been thrown straight away – so that it contains all sorts of human qualities which would otherwise be edited out . . . '[3] Who is to say that what is printed today and discarded tomorrow by the majority of people will not fulfil some important role in historical research in the future.

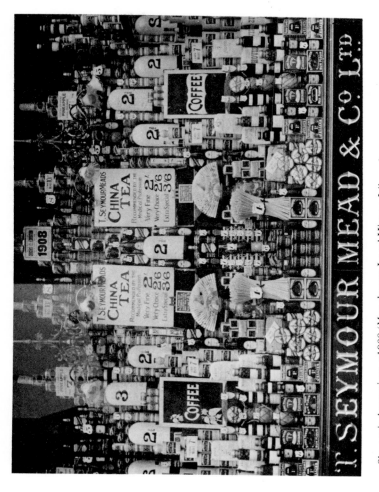

Shop window prices, c1908 (Manchester Local History Library)

　　　　　　　　　　　　　# What is ephemera?

Ephemera means different things to different people. It is therefore very important to establish what precisely is meant by ephemera and to define it as closely as possible, so that there can be no misunderstanding as to what is meant by the word and also to enable it to be compared with other types of material which may be similar or even confused with it, such as minor publications.

The first part of this chapter will look at the various definitions of ephemera that have been put forward and will then attempt to synthesise these to produce a definition which covers all the various attributes of ephemera and which enables it to be distinguished from minor publications, which are sometimes called ephemera.

The following section will discuss, in general terms, the various locations where collections of ephemera may be found, such as libraries, record offices and museums and where preservation and exploitation is the prime objective of collecting the material rather than collecting out of pure interest or for investment purposes or where it is kept, not out of any regard for its usefulness in the future, but for legal purposes.

Finally, this chapter will try to answer the question of why ephemera should be collected and preserved. It will also seek to explain why certain types of material, which fit the definition of ephemera, have been excluded from consideration in this book.

The definition of ephemera

Probably the simplest of the definitions that have been advanced for ephemera are not really definitions as such, but merely alternative names such as 'non-book material', 'fugitive material', 'grey literature' or 'miscellaneous material'. The problem with using such descriptions is that they are not really specific and could be used to describe other types of material, such as pamphlets, maps and illustrations, which do not fall into the category of ephemera. If one wants to use an alternative name for ephemera, then probably the most useful are either 'fugitive material' or 'miscellaneous material' as both descriptions imply that the material does not fit into a particular category, that there may be problems with acquisition, storage, retrieval and that it may have a relatively short life and may not be able to be dealt with in the normally accepted way.

If one looks in a dictionary one discovers that ephemera is defined as something 'lasting only for a day'[1] and that ephemeral is something that is 'beginning and ending in a day; existing only for a day or for a few days'[2]. Another dictionary definition refers to ephemera as 'short-lived or transitory'.[3] These dictionary definitions of ephemera imply that it has an adjectival quality whereas the librarian and the archivist tend to use the word as a collective noun to describe a certain type of material. A similar adjectival quality is to be found in the alternative words which are given in Roget's *Thesaurus*. Although ephemera is not given, ephemeral is and has the following alternatives 'tempor-al,-ary, provisional, cursory, short-lived, deciduous, perishable, mortal, precarious, impermanent'.[4] Although the dictionary definitions and the alternative words are not adequate as definitions for ephemera, they do imply one of the qualities of the material constituting ephemera, namely that it is usually short-lived.

One of the first people to use the word ephemera in a sense similar to that which librarians and others use the word was John Lewis in *Printed ephemera: the changing use of type and letter forms in English and American printing*. Although he does not give a definition of ephemera, the many illustrations of changing type faces used on posters, tickets, trade cards, broadsheets, handbills, menus, invitations etc. by jobbing printers, clearly shows the type of material which Lewis had in mind when he referred to it as ephemera.

In a second book, *Collecting printed ephemera*, Lewis included a definition of the material as this was aimed at the wider market of the general public. He defined ephemera as:

a term used for anything printed for a specific short term purpose; such things as a bus ticket, a circus poster, a Christmas card or a Valentine, a police summons, a tax demand, a pin packet, a soapflake box, a wine label, a beer mat, a cigarette card, an airline ticket, a train timetable or a travel brochure. There is hardly any limit and although books are outside our field, magazines, comics and newspapers are very much part of it.[5]

Lewis's definition contains all the essential elements of what constitutes ephemera, namely that it is short-lived and produced for a specific event or activity. However, he overlooks the fact that not all items of ephemera are short-lived and that some of it does have a considerable length of life and that some items are produced with the collector in mind with the result that their life can be, theoretically, almost infinite. To see exactly the type of material Lewis regards as ephemera, it is necessary to look carefully at the chosen examples in the book. He concentrates on printed items and ignores the fact that there can be manuscript items of ephemera.

Lewis's definition of ephemera appeared in 1976, five years after Pemberton's report for the Social Science Research Council on the *National provision of ephemera in the social sciences* in which he defined ephemera as 'documents which have been produced in connection with a particular event or item of current interest and which are not intended to survive the topicality of their message'.[6]

The type of ephemera in which Pemberton was interested is that which 'could be used by social scientists. This could be interpreted to include such things as cloakroom tickets at one extreme, and perhaps patent specifications at the other'.[7] In order to ensure that those asked about their holdings of ephemera understood the type of material he was interested in, Pemberton prepared a list of thirty-nine different types of ephemera which he circulated with a questionnaire.[8] The list ranged from advertising circulars to aerial photographs and maps. Some of the material which Pemberton regarded as ephemera would not be regarded as such by some librarians. For example, aerial photographs are usually treated as part of an illustrations collection rather than items of ephemera whilst maps are regarded as a separate type of material in their own right. In addition, material such as pamphlets were also included in the list of ephemera, but these, to many librarians, especially those engaged in local studies work, can be treated as book material in that they can be classified, catalogued and shelved although they may require pamphlet cases before they can be shelved and may not be acquired through the usual channels.

Another view as to what is ephemera was published in *The Times Literary Supplement* in an article reviewing an exhibition organised by the Ephemera Society. The reviewer quoted members of the Society as regarding ephemera as 'items specifically designed for a limited useful life and throw away disposal'.[9] The review mentioned a few types of material that were collected, but also pointed out that when it came to such things as rent demands, tax forms, membership cards 'most people collect . . . involuntarily'[10] and that to deliberately collect this type of material 'seems to be making a vice of necessity; that way madness lies'.[11]

Although this is not a full definition it does provide an insight into the type of material which members of the Ephemera Society regarded as constituting the subject. It is a short definition and is similar to the other short definitions that have been produced. However, it does not distinguish between ephemera and other material such as minor publications which some regard as ephemera.

The Ephemera Society was founded in 1975 to bring together those interested in this type of material. Their objectives were stated to be to 'provide a permanent institutional framework as the internationally recognised body for the study, conservation and display of ephemera'.[12] As such it is the only society whose members have an interest in this type of material and its bimonthly newsletter provides information on the Society's activities.

The chairman of the Ephemera Society, Maurice Rickards, has defined ephemera on a number of occasions. In his book *This is ephemera*, he described ephemera as 'the word . . . used to denote the transient everyday items of paper – mostly printed – that are manufactured specifically to use and to throw away'.[13]

Three years later, in 1980, Rickards refined his definition. In an interview published in *Now* he said it was 'the study of the transient minor documents of everyday life . . . everything that would normally go into the waste paper basket'.[14]

Rickards looked at the definition of ephemera from the point of view of a collector rather than an archivist or librarian. In his view a piece of ephemera was ephemera irrespective of whether it was printed or manuscript whereas the librarian and archivist would tend to distinguish between a printed item and a manuscript item. In other words, Rickards looked at the whole question of what constituted ephemera from a very much wider standpoint than the professional collectors and preservers of the material. Despite this recognition that ephemera can be either manuscript or printed, there is still the underlying assumption that it is short-lived. This is not necessarily so as some items, by their very nature, use or purpose have much longer periods of existence than other items.

Probably the most detailed of the definitions of ephemera that has been produced is by ADCEMP, which reflected the views of the professional bodies interested in the collection and preservation of this type of material as a source of information for the future. In its preliminary report it defined ephemera as:

Material which carries a verbal message and is produced by printing or illustrative processes but which is not published in standard book or periodical form.

It thus has one or more of the following characteristics:

(a) it is often produced in connection with a particular event or item of interest and it is not intended to survive the topicality of the message;

(b) it is available often without charge sometimes on a local, specialised or personal basis;

(c) it shows the widest possible variation though it is normally on paper, textile or similar material;

(d) it does not normally lend itself to standard library processes of acquisition, recording or storage. It is however classifiable.

(e) its value can be factual, illustrative, typographical or more broadly aesthetic or a combination of these depending on the terms of reference of the collection.[15]

In addition to being the longest definition that has been produced, it attempts to be the most comprehensive by including characteristics which other definitions have mentioned or implied, thus enabling it to be used to distinguish the material constituting ephemera from other types of material which may be called by the same name. However, one criteria which has been excluded is that of size, that is the length of the item, which means that it is still possible for confusion to arise, particularly with minor publications. Neither is there any reference to items produced for the collector. However, when the definition was published, it was the most detailed that had been produced and went much further than the others in attempting to clarify the nature of ephemera.

The definitions contained in two British Library reports on ephemera and minor publications appear to have been influenced by the definition produced by ADCEMP. The first report by Clinton defined ephemera as:

a class of printed or near print documentation which escapes the normal channel of sale and bibliographical control. It covers both publications which are freely available to the general public and others which are intended for a limited and specific circulation only. For librarians, it is part defined by the fact that it tends to resist conventional treatment in acquisition, arrangement and storage and it may not justify full cataloguing.[16]

Clinton is critical of some of the other definitions that have been produced, particularly those which include the characteristics of the material and argues that librarians and others take a restrictive view of the subject. He points out that the importance and use of different types of ephemera will vary according to the user of the material and that different people will have different ideas as to the type of material that can be included in an ephemera collection. He adds that 'If one considers printed ephemera purely from the point of view of its form then it can be located somewhere on a continuum between printed and bound volumes at one end and small scraps of manuscript at the other.'[17] Whatever the case may be for ignoring the definitions which librarians and others have put forward, the people most concerned with collecting material and preserving it are the librarians and archivists and not the researchers. If the professional collectors did not acquire this material and define the parameters of their collecting policy, then much of the material that exists today in libraries and record offices would not have survived and likewise, if they do not collect contemporary material, there will be little for the researchers in the future to work from.

Clinton's definition contains some of the elements which help to describe what ephemera is and why there are problems with it. However, like other definitions, it fails to enable a distinction to be made between it and other forms of publication such as pamphlets and booklets that are not produced by mainstream publishers as these often have similar characteristics as ephemera. For example, there is no mention made of the length of the document or even of the fact that it is often available free of charge. Perhaps Clinton was taking too narrow a view of what constituted ephemera, based on the three areas which he sampled and on the fact that researchers use certain types of material today, but are unable to ascertain what may be used in the future.

Although the other report by Dixon dealt with minor or local publications, it did include a definition of ephemera so that a distinction could be made between the two types of material. In Dixon's view, ephemera comprises:

> an almost infinite variety of printed items, usually flimsy or insubstantial, designed for an immediate use in the course of some transaction or other. They are in no sense intended to be contributions to knowledge. Only in the eyes of a collector or scholar do they acquire some interest outside the original transaction. They range from bus tickets, and blank forms, to posters to an almost limitless range of other items.[18]

Although Dixon's definition is not dissimilar to some of the others that have been produced, she includes one phrase which is very important, namely that the material is flimsy or insubstantial, implying that it will consist of a single sheet or very few sheets and not be assembled like a newspaper or comic. The other important point which Dixon makes is that the material might be of interest to someone after its topicality has ended, even though this might be restricted to the scholar or collector and that this might not occur until some considerable time has elapsed after its initial publication.

The various definitions that have been presented all contain elements which help to produce a satisfactory definition, but none of them include all the important elements. For instance, all the definitions except one imply that ephemera is short-lived, but this only relates to its topicality or usefulness. Some items may have a considerable life and be designed with that in mind. For example, a bus or railway ticket may have a usefulness of only a few minutes whilst the journey is being undertaken, although it must be pointed out that some do have much longer periods of validity. Invitations, on the other hand, may have a useful life of several weeks from the time they are first issued until the actual event takes place. Other types of ephemera, such as share certificates or bank notes, may have a long period of validity and usefulness. Finally, there are those items of ephemera which are specifically designed for the collector and as a result may be sold or passed on from one person to another, theoretically existing indefinitely.

A satisfactory definition of ephemera would contain elements from all these definitions which have been quoted. For the purposes of this book, the following definition is suggested as one which contains all the essential elements associated with ephemera and which can be used to distinguish it from minor publications:

> Ephemera is the collective name given to material which carries a verbal or illustrative message and is produced either by printing or illustrative processes, but not in the standard book, pamphlet or periodical format. It has the following characteristics:
> (a) it is usually flimsy or insubstantial;
> (b) it is a transient document produced for a specific purpose and not intended to survive the topicality of its message or event to which it relates. Consequently, most items have a limited useful life, although the life of an item will vary according to the purpose for which it is produced and may well be of interest to scholars and collectors after its topicality has expired;
> (c) its acquisition, storage, classification and cataloguing may not fall within the conventionally accepted methods of treatment within libraries and record offices and consequently, may require special consideration. It is, however, classifiable;
> (d) its availability will depend on where it was produced, by whom and for what purpose and where it is available from;
> (e) it can be either primary or secondary source material.

Minor publications

The main type of material that is confused with ephemera is one which is called minor publications or local publications. It is, therefore, important to distinguish between the two types of material. The reason why minor publications may be called ephemera by some institutions is simply because they are not emanating from the main stream of publishing and therefore may not be available through the usual channels. In other words, a special effort has to be made to trace and acquire such material.

ADCEMP defined minor publications in its preliminary report as:

> material in book, pamphlet, newspaper, news-sheet or other multipage form, produced by printing, duplication or illustrative processes, being sometimes an isolated publication, sometimes an occasional publication, sometimes a periodical publication, and having one or more of the following characteristics:
>
> (a) it is produced 'uncommercially', i.e. either for free distribution or for a cost covering charge only, or if intended to produce a return, sold through casual, uncertain outlets on a haphazard basis.
>
> (b) it is produced for distribution either to members of a particular society or organisation with or without some surplus for casual disposal, or within a limited local area, or to publicise a specific place, business, organisation, activity or cause, or to accompany a specific event or occasion.[19]

In her report on local publications, which are akin to minor publications as the two are often the same, Dixon described them as consisting of:

> that large quantity of material in certain forms, mainly pamphlets, leaflets, newsletters and other kinds of informal serial, which contains information of value to research. This material, for a variety of reasons, such as appearing irregularly, in small format and not through regular trade outlets, tends not to be collected at the national level and not to be easily accessible to potential users.[20]

If these two descriptions of what constitutes minor publications are taken together, they do provide a framework which enables minor publications and ephemera to be distinguished. It also provides a position from which to decide whether something is a minor publication or the product of mainstream publishing.

Minor publications can be divided into two basic groups: serials and pamphlets. Irrespective of which group an item fits into, minor publications make up a large proportion of the stock of any local studies library as much local studies material is not published by main-stream publishers, but by local publishers and individuals. It must also be remembered that other specialist departments may also have a large proportion of their stock in minor publication format.

Serials

Although many serial and periodical publications are published by major publishing houses and national societies and are, consequently, readily available in bookshops, newsagents or by subscription, there are a great many others which are published by societies and organisations specifically for their own membership, employees or those residing in a particular area which thus have a restricted circulation. For example, with a few exceptions, parish magazines will be circulated only within the parish which publishes them and may only be available to subscribers, although copies may be available within the church for casual visitors or in the local shop or newsagents. The same restricted circulation also applies to house journals of firms and newsletters of societies. Despite this apparently restricted circulation it does not mean that libraries are not able to obtain copies for their collection. Arrangements can often be made for libraries to receive a copy of each issue as a donation or if that is not possible to take out a subscription as these are usually relatively inexpensive. Most church magazines cost less than £5 a year for a subscription.

With this type of minor serial publication, it is possible that the only complete set may be in the records of the originating organisation. This, however, may not always be the case as it will depend to a large extent on the person responsible for their production ensuring that a copy is placed in the official records. However, if the person is not interested in keeping back-copies or if there is a change in the person, gaps in the series can result and, in some cases, there may be complete destruction of the back copies. For instance this can happen when a new incumbent takes over a church and is not particularly interested in what happened before his arrival, as happened with one church in Coventry in the mid–1960s. The safest way to ensure that as complete a set survive as possible is to try to persuade the organisation to donate the back copies to the library for safekeeping. Often gaps are not noticed until it is too late to fill them. For example, just before St Thomas's Church, Ardwick was declared redundant, several piles of parish magazines were noticed at the back of the church. Manchester Local History Library had some issues whilst there were others in the official records of the church deposited in the Diocesan Record Office. Before anything could be done, vandals entered the building and did a fair amount of damage. Fortunately, it was possible to rescue some of the magazines and when the various holdings were checked, it was discovered that neither organisation had copies of the ones left lying around. As a result, the missing copies were passed on and this helped to fill in a few of the gaps in the holdings. It can be seen from this example, that it is important to take all necessary precautions to ensure that at least a copy of all issues reaches the library.

Pamphlets and booklets

By far the largest number of minor publications are pamphlets and booklets published by bodies such as historical societies, businesses, pressure groups, churches, local authorities and individuals. Usually such publications seek either to explain a particular point of view, describe an area or a building, provide a biography of a local personage, are accounts of the history of a town, village or suburb, firm or organisation or publicise the results of the author's research. For example John Short's biography of John Gulson[21] was privately published and available only from the author or certain bookshops in Coventry. It was only reviewed locally and did not have an ISB number or appear in the *British National Bibliography*. Similarly, *Birch Church: a short guide*[22] was only available from the church and no copy has found its way into the Manchester Local History Library.

Amongst the biggest publishers of minor publications are local authorities, central government and the nationalised industries, although one might expect these bodies to be classified as mainstream publishers. Often, their publications are extremely difficult to trace, particularly those of local authorities and individual government departments. Many do not appear in the *British National Bibliography* or contain an ISB number. Not only are such publications difficult for librarians to trace but quite often they can be difficult for members of staff in other parts of the same department to trace. When it comes to the question of legal deposit, many departments in local authorities are not aware of their obligations, thinking that it does not apply to them. Sometimes, the librarian can persuade the authority to comply with the legal requirements, but it is not an easy task as many authorities do not have a centralised publications system, each department publishing on its own.

The failure of local authorities and other similar bodies to ensure that a copy of their publications reaches the British Library, let alone the local library, can result in the complete disappearance of all copies within the space of a few years. In many cases not even the local library is considered as a place for deposit of a publication. For example, in

Election posters, Lancaster, 1895 (Lancaster Museum)

1931, Manchester Corporation Rivers Department published a pamphlet about two local sewage works[23] in the preface to which it was claimed that the booklet would provide 'an adequate and understandable description of the works and thus be useful not only to technical and scientific visitors, but to the general visitor'.[24] It appears that this booklet was given to visitors to the two sewage works and sent to those who wrote in asking for information about the way Manchester treated its sewerage. In view of the claims made in the preface, it would have been expected that a copy would be found in Manchester Central Library. However, there is no copy to be found there and this at a time when Manchester was following a very active policy of building up its holdings of local material. The implication must therefore be drawn that the Rivers Department did not consider depositing a copy with the Library or even informing them of its publication. As a result, it appears that the only copies that exist today are in private hands.

In addition to the difficulties encountered in tracing what minor publications exist and distinguishing between minor publications and ephemera, there are also difficulties in saying whether something is a minor publication or the product of normal publishing activities. If the size and format of the publication is one of the criteria which is used to distinguish between minor publications and normal publications, then there can be blurring between the two types. For example, Shell published a substantial paperback in Holland entitled *Nederland van de weg af gezien*,[25] which was only available through the company's garages. As a result of its restricted availability, it fits the criteria of a minor publication, but the length and content of the work give the impression that it is the result of normal publishing activity. Thus size or format cannot be used solely to distinguish between minor publications and the normal publishing activities of mainstream publishers.

If size was the only criteria which was used, then some items which are definitely minor publications would be excluded. For instance, *Greater Manchester: international conference and exhibition centre 1982*[26] would also be regarded as normal publishing. In actual fact, some might even regard this as an item of ephemera despite its length. Ideally, it is a minor publication because it can be treated by libraries in the conventional manner.

The confusion between minor publications and ephemera

In the past, there has been confusion as to what actually constituted ephemera and what were minor publications. For example, in the early 1970s, the British Library tended to refer to all minor publications as 'ephemera', in other words, publications that were peripheral to those publications by the larger, nationally orientated publishers and which were, as a result, not easy to trace and record. The confusion can probably be accounted for by the fact that there were no acceptable definitions of either type of material and that the word 'ephemera' tended to be used haphazardly. It is to be hoped that this problem has now been overcome and that when ephemera is referred to, people know the type of material that is involved.

The fact that there has been confusion in identifying what is exactly meant by ephemera and what is meant by minor publications is in part understandable as both types of material have certain features which are common, namely that the means of production, availability, level of production and circulation patterns can be similar. The main point of similarity between the two types of material is that they are both produced by people or organisations who are not involved with the mainstream of publishing and therefore may not be fully conversant with the question of legal deposit and that their circulation is, in the main limited to a small area around their place of production. Consequently, there is no means of knowing what has been produced, by whom and where.

Another complicating factor which affects both types of material is that print-runs may be very small. Consequently, they may go out of print very quickly, even before the British Library gets to know of their existence.

The situation is further confused by the treatment libraries give the material, especially that which will fit into either category. For example, a leaflet on Rochdale Town Centre Conservation area[27] is a single sheet with a number of folds. As a result, it can be opened up to be consulted. However, in one library it has been treated as a minor publication, being given a pamphlet case and catalogued in the normal manner whereas by definition it fits the category of ephemera. This can also apply to other material where it is possible to put it in a pamphlet or slip case and treat it as a normal publication within the library system.

However, there are clear differences between the two types of material, which can be summarised as follows:

1 Format.
2 Treatment within the library system.
3 Means of production and distribution.
4 Period of validity or topicality.
5 Level of production within a given time span.
6 Objectives behind publication.

When it comes to format, it should be relatively easy to distinguish between ephemera and minor publications. In the case of ephemera, it is usually printed on a single sheet of paper, possibly only on one side, although it may be folded several times. For example, a leaflet advertising the Britannia Hotel, Manchester[28] is printed on both sides and folded five times, but opens out into a single sheet. Likewise *Britain: Manchester the City and the County*[29] appears at a glance to be a minor publication, but when it is investigated further, it is discovered that it is a single sheet, printed on both sides, folded so that it appears like a booklet. First impressions can give the wrong impression as to which category an item fits into. As a rough rule of thumb it could be said that anything that exceeds four pages, that is two sheets stapled together, should be regarded as a minor publication and that items which are folded and open up into a single sheet are ephemera. Thus, the order of service for the enthronement of the Bishop of Sheffield[30] is a minor publication whilst the admission ticket is an item of ephemera although the latter may have been preserved inside the order of service.

Treatment within the library system

One of the reasons why ephemera and minor publications are confused in the minds of librarians is that the same item will be regarded in a different light in separate departments. For example, a glossy advertising brochure published by Pickfords[31] might be regarded as an item of ephemera in a commercial library as it merely is advertising material showing the type of work that the company undertakes, but it gives very little other information. As a result its usefulness is limited and may not be regarded as worthwhile cataloguing, classifying and pamphlet casing. In this situation, it is possible that it will be filed in a cabinet with other general material either under the company's name or more generally under removal firms.

A local studies library, on the other hand, may regard this type of brochure as a minor publication and ask for it to be catalogued, classified and pamphlet cased so that it can be shelved as any normal publication. Although the amount of information in written terms may be small, the large amount of illustrative material will provide some information for the researcher in the future if the firm is of local significance.

The contents of such publications are often the criteria which are used by non local studies departments to decide whether an item is ephemera or is worthwhile treating as a normal publication. For example, a commercial library may well treat *The bluebook of brushware*[32] as a normal publication as it contains information on the price of paint brushes as well as other general information on the company's products. The same course of action would also be taken by the local studies library which covers the area of London where the firm was based.

As a result of this divergence of views as to whether an item is to be treated as a minor publication or a piece of ephemera, much will depend on the use that a particular library or department will make of it and how it regards its future usefulness. Where a potential future use is recognised, it is more likely to be treated as a minor publication by those departments which are more interested in current awareness than if it has no apparent interest in the future.

The decision as to which type of material it is will affect the way it is treated once it is received into the library. If it is a minor publication it will receive the full cataloguing, classifying and binding treatment. It will also be shelved with the remainder of the library stock rather than in its own special sequence.

Ephemera, on the other hand, will tend to be dealt with by the staff of the department concerned on an *ad hoc* basis. A local studies library might give it some limited form of classification and cataloguing, but the amount will depend on the time and staff available to undertake such work. Alternatively, it may be just filed away under a general heading or under the firm's name and no further record of its existence in the library made, except in the memories of the staff of the department where it is located.

Means of production

On the surface, it may appear that both ephemera and minor publications are similar in that they are usually produced by someone or an organisation which is not heavily involved in publishing. This is, however, where the similarity ends. To produce a minor publication, it is necessary to have some understanding of book production to ensure that the text reads consecutively and that the finished product has a reasonable appearance. To this end, it often means that minor publications are printed by small firms of printers who are able to deal with the problems that are posed by booklet and pamphlet production.

In the case of ephemera, it is not so necessary to understand the problems of book production as most items are very simple and could be produced on a duplicator. For example, Salford Museum of Mining has issued a duplicated leaflet entitled *An appeal to preserve the local mining heritage*.[33] Duplication is a means of production which is well suited to this kind of leaflet. Where something is wanted to impress, then normal printing methods will be used. Often this type of ephemera is aimed at attracting members of the public to attend an event or visit a specific place. For instance, the leaflet issued by Manchester Publicity Department on the craft village[34] has been printed and contains illustrations and a map as well as details about the craft village. Thus, the methods of production of ephemera will vary according to the purpose for which it is intended. In some cases, items of ephemera are only produced when there is a demand for them. Such items are usually receipts for a transaction such as a railway or theatre ticket where money changes hands.

The distribution of both minor publications and ephemera can be on a very haphazard basis. Many minor publications circulate in a relatively small area which is well defined by the interest in the publication. Despite this, they are usually available through some formal type of outlet as often their acquisition requires the payment of a sum of money by the purchaser which in turn requires some means of accounting for the money and the numbers sold. With ephemera the situation is somewhat different. Although some items require a monetary transaction to take place, many items of current ephemera are available free of charge and therefore can be handed out at will to passers by, left in public places for members of the public to pick up or pushed through letter boxes. Go into any public place where people gather and there is a strong possibility that there will be items of ephemera around to be picked up. To give an indication of the level of this free distribution of material, a check was made on the main reception desk of Manchester Central Library on 23 July 1979 which revealed that there were twenty different items of ephemera available there for the public to take away ranging from leaflets advertising events in the area to educational courses being held at various adult education centres throughout the city.

Period of validity

Another basic difference between minor publications and ephemera is the length of time each type is valid for. Minor publications are often available for a considerable period of time after their initial publication whereas an item of ephemera will probably disappear once the event has taken place. For example, a history of a church published to commemorate its centenary may be available for a decade after it was first published and may also be reprinted once the initial print-run has been sold if there is sufficient demand for it. An item of ephemera, such as a poster, ceases to have any interest once the event is over, except to the collector, although it may remain visible for some time afterwards if it is pasted onto a notice board or hoarding.

This is a general distinction as there are examples of both types of material which have the opposite characteristics. For example, a serial publication like the Lincolnshire and Humberside Arts Diary[35] is of little use once the events referred to it have taken place, although the articles will be of continuing use and interest far into the future. Some guides are in appearance ephemera and these will have a much longer life than other types of similar material. For instance, a short guide to Christ Church, Moss Side, Manchester [36] is a duplicated sheet folded in half. This will probably still be available a decade from now unless it is revised and expanded into a booklet.

Level of production

The level of production of a particular item also distinguishes minor publications from ephemera. Not only is there a physical limit to the number of books, booklets and pamphlets that can be produced in a given period of time given the need to set the type, check the proofs, bind and distribute them, but in addition, there is also the fact that there is a limit to the number of publications which can be absorbed by the market and the demand or need for such publications. Consequently, print-runs for minor publications can vary from a few copies to several thousand, depending on the market aimed at.

In the case of ephemera, it is not necessary to have a printing-press or a photo-litho machine or even a typewriter. Material can be handwritten and produced on a duplicator. Thus, the potential for the production of ephemera is very much greater than with minor publications. Neither is there the need for the working capital which is often required for the production of a minor publication as many items of ephemera are advertising or publicity material, the costs of which can be written off or they are a receipt for money paid. Thus, it is possible to produce large numbers of the same items and to distribute them widely.

From the point of view of bibliographical control, it is far easier to ascertain what minor publications have been published than it is with items of ephemera simply because of the diversity of the field and the vast amount that is published each year. In addition, the number of outlets for minor publications is limited as there is often a need for some form of accounting whereas with material that is given away, there is no requirement to account for money.

Objectives behind publication

One distinction between minor publications and ephemera which is often overlooked is that of the different objectives of the publishers. Minor publications can be divided into two broad categories. Firstly, there are those works which are the product of research by the author or compiler into a specific subject and may be regarded as a personal interpretation of the facts. The other group consists of those

An enamel sign of the early 1900s (Rochdale Museum)

publications presenting information or facts about a subject. This type of material can be regarded as either advertising material, publicity material or as propaganda. Included in this type of material are transcripts of original documents, published eyewitness accounts, statements of boards of companies, party political manifestos and the like. Where comment has been added to the facts, the material should be regarded as fitting the first type as it will be expressing a personal or a corporate view.

Ephemera, on the other hand, often provides information that is not available elsewhere. In this sense, it can be regarded as an item of primary source material. For example, a railway ticket will not only be a receipt for the fare that has been paid, but it will also give the following information: point of departure, destination, the fare paid, the routing of the journey, such as 'via Sheffield and Bristol', the class the traveller travelled, the type of fare, that is a day return, an ordinary return, or a single, and the date the ticket was issued. This information will be available nowhere else except on this ticket and other tickets issued for the same journey, and even on these the day of issue will probably be different. Similarly, some theatre tickets will give the name of the theatre visited, the title of the production, the date of the performance and its time, the seat number and its price such as those issued by the Royal Exchange Theatre in Manchester. Many items of ephemera are, in effect, advertising in some form or other and hence the item will give information on the product which is being advertised or the shop which is trying to attract customers. For example, a highly coloured leaflet by Vertikaseal[37] shows the products of the firm, states the benefits using them brings and gives details of the location of their firm's showroom and opening hours. This information will almost certainly be available nowhere else, except possibly in the company's own records, and this item of ephemera may be the only item on the company which survives into the future. Thus it can be seen that ephemera can be used for research purposes. This applies not only to historic material, but also to contemporary material.

The fact that ephemera does give details and information does not mean to say that it cannot also express a personal point of view on a particular issue or subject. It can do and very often does this when it has been issued by an organisation or a person feeling particularly strongly about an issue and wishing to publicise their personal point of view. For example, in an election, an independent candidate may stand because he disagrees with the policies of the main political parties or because he believes in something which he wants to achieve. Thus, his election literature will be a personal statement of his views and the solutions to the problems which he sees. The election literature of the candidates of the main parties will in part be personal views, but in the main they will be the views expressed by the headquarters. Similarly pressure groups will produce material which is distributed to members of the public explaining their views on a particular issue and seeking to gain support from the general public for their stand. Although some may regard this as secondary source material, it can be argued that it is really primary material as it helps to complete a picture on that matter. To the person issuing an item, or an organisation publishing ephemera, anything that is put out will be primary material which can be used for research.

A simplistic way which can be adopted to distinguish between minor publications and ephemera is to say that minor publications are, on the whole, secondary sources of information, interpreting the facts according to the author's point of view. Ephemera, on the other hand, consists mainly of primary source material which can be used by scholars and others for the purposes of research into a particular subject.

The types of ephemera collection

Collections of ephemera that are found in libraries, record offices, museums and private ownership can be divided into two broad groups: general collections and collections relating to a specific subject or on a specific theme. Which type of collection is built up will depend to a large extent on the *raison d'être* for the existence of the collection. General collections of ephemera tend to be found in libraries, particularly local studies libraries, although other general collections are also to be found in record offices, academic libraries and museums. The general collections are general in the sense that they will include as much as possible on every topic relating to the field in which they are interested whether it be a particular type of organisation or a city. Thus, it should be possible to find a wide range of different types of ephemera such as railway and bus tickets, invitations, menus, broadsheets and so forth as well as material on a diverse range of subjects from politics and religion to transport and ethnic minorities. The common link between this material is that it relates to a particular locality or subject or does not concentrate on one particular type of material or a detailed subject. It is very unusual for a private collector to concentrate on a general collection of material relating to a specific area. Private collectors prefer to deal with a particular type of material or subject in depth.

Probably the most famous collection of general ephemera that exists is the John Johnson Collection in the Bodelian Library at

Oxford. This collection was the result of the work of one man in the nineteenth century who bequeathed it to the library on his death. It is still maintained by the staff at the library and new material is constantly being added to it with the result that it is unique in not only its size, but also in the range of material that is to be found there.

It is difficult to ascertain the number and size of general collections of ephemera that exist specifically as ephemera collections. In many cases they form part of the general library holdings of material or are merely recorded as part of the holdings of a specific department. In addition, all the ephemera may not be housed in the same place. Some of it may be treated completely differently from the bulk of the material due to the form it has been acquired by the library in. For instance, some may be mounted in scrapbooks and treated as normal books by the library and have no detailed references to the type of material in the volumes. It can be assumed that all local studies collections have substantial amounts of ephemera within the collection and that other material will be found in commercial departments. Beyond this general statement, it is difficult to say what exists. The only way to discover what exists is either to write to every library with specific questions as Pemberton did, or to visit them personally and look at the individual collections.

Thematic collections of ephemera are capable of being divided into two groups which can, and very often do, overlap. Firstly, there are those collections which relate to a particular type of material such as railway tickets, cigarette cards, posters or bill heads. Such collections may include material from many different parts of the world. Secondly, there are the collections which relate to a specific subject. For example, someone may collect railway ephemera on a general level whereas someone else might do it for an area, a company or just a single line. Similarly, someone may collect theatre material generally or material relating to a single theatre or even a single artist. Rickards in his book *This is ephemera* gives examples of different subjects which have been collected as well as examples of the type of material which can be found in other collections which have a thematic base.[38]

It could be argued that all ephemera collections are in fact thematic in one way or another. Even the so called general collections in libraries and record offices are to some extent thematic in that their themes are the specific locality in which they are interested and for which related material is collected. However, such collections contain such a wide range of material on an equally wide range of subjects that it is easier to refer to them as general collections rather than as thematic collections.

Where are ephemera collections to be found?

Although ephemera is to be found everywhere, the amount that is actually preserved in collections in one place or another is only a small proportion of that which has been and is being produced. The most obvious locations to find ephemera that has been specifically collected with a view to preservation is in libraries, record offices and museums, but increasingly material is also being collected and preserved by the private collector either as a hobby or as an investment. However, it is the ephemera collections that are to be found in public ownership that are most likely to be used by the private individual for research rather than those in private hands or in collections which form the part of the official record of an organisation or the working documents of a firm or official body.

The size of collections will vary widely. If the collection is one which deals mainly with what might be termed 'historic ephemera', then the size will be determined by the amount which has survived either within the organisation itself or in private hands which ultimately finds its way onto the market. If the collection, however, also includes contemporary material, then it will be much larger due to the fact that it is possible to acquire new material relatively easily.

The size of the collection will also be influenced by whether the collection is an 'active' one or a 'passive' one. An active collection is one where there is a deliberate policy of seeking out and adding fresh material, usually contemporary material, to the collection. A passive one is a collection where there is no such policy of going out and acquiring new material, but only adding to it when material is donated or is acquired by chance. Consequently, an active collection will grow much faster than a passive one.

The size of the collection will also be determined by the type of material collected or the subject specialised in. If these are areas where there is only a relatively small amount of material produced, then this will be reflected in the size of the collection. However, in such collections, there is likely to be a greater degree of comprehensiveness than in a general collection covering an area or a subject which has much published material.

Libraries

Libraries are probably the largest preservers of ephemera, especially those which have large reference sections and which consider themselves to be research libraries. This not only applies to public libraries, but also to academic libraries and special libraries, especially

3   25

those connected with a particular firm or specialising in providing information on a particular product or subject. It is in special libraries that ephemera and minor publications, rather than the traditional bookstock may play a large role in providing information.

Within the public library field, it is within local studies departments that the largest amounts of ephemera are to be found. The reason for this is very simple, namely that it is incumbent on those responsible for maintaining such collections to ensure that as much as possible of what has been and will be produced about the area is collected and preserved. This is because it is not possible to say whether an item is going to contain information which will be of interest in the future because research interests and demands change with the passage of time. In addition to systematically trying to collect current ephemera, tracing and acquiring historic material, local studies departments sometimes receive donations of ephemera from private collectors who wish to ensure that their collection is kept together and is properly looked after and fully utilised.

Not only are the collections of ephemera in local studies collections amongst the largest that are to be found in public libraries, they are also the most varied as almost every type of ephemera that has been and is being produced may be found there. Pemberton recognised this fact in his report when he claimed that 'there can be little doubt that some public libraries are conscientiously collecting far more printed ephemera than the universities. A high proportion of the contents of their local collections falls into the category and staff are actively engaged on a continuous basis in identifying and acquiring material'.[39] Pemberton should not have been surprised by this fact for anyone involved with public libraries would probably have realised this from the beginning. However, his standpoint was from the academic library and, presumably, he regarded public libraries as not really being involved in acquiring material for research purposes. A few minutes looking through the non-book material, excluding illustrations, newspapers and maps, in a local collection will give a clear indication of the range of material which is collected and preserved. For example, it is possible to find invitations, timetables, broadsheets, handbills, posters, leaflets, prospectuses, election literature, theatre and cinema playbills and advertising material within the same collection and all having one thing in common, other than the fact that they form part of ephemera, namely that they relate to life in a particular community. Such material may not be referred to as an ephemera collection and may not be housed in a single place, but scattered throughout the holdings of the department. For example, a collection of invitations to civic functions may be mounted in a guard book and treated as a normal book for the purposes of cataloguing, classifying and storage whilst broadsheets and posters may have a system of storage and classifying which is completely different. The use of different ways of dealing with ephemera can result in material being overlooked unless it is indexed and catalogued fully. As much ephemera tends not to be given the full bibliographic treatment, it is important that members of staff know the extent of the non-book holdings extremely well so that they can advise readers accordingly.

Although local collections may contain a great deal of the ephemera found in public libraries, similar material can also be found in other specialist departments, which will concentrate on material which is of interest to their subject. For example, in Manchester Central Library in addition to the ephemera which is housed in the Local History Library other ephemera can be found in the Watson Music Library, the Arts Library and the Commercial Library. In some cases, problems can arise when these specialist departments also take and preserve local material. For instance in Manchester material on local music and musical activities is to be found in the Music Library whilst material on local theatres is in the Arts Library. This can create problems for readers when the departments are physically separated and a reader wants to use material from one department in conjunction with that from another. In addition, unless there are entries in the local catalogue, a reader who is not familiar with the system might think that the local collection has no interest in these other aspects of local life.

Outside the local history field, it is the commercial library which probably has more ephemera than any of the other departments which exist. A commercial library may not regard ephemera of any consequence once its current usefulness has passed and may discard it without giving a second thought as to its potential use in the future by those engaged on research. In some libraries, local material is passed to the local collection whilst other material might be processed in the normal way and be found in the permanent library stock. However, in a great many cases, the material is discarded and lost forever. The problem is that those working in such departments are trained for current awareness and not to think of long-term use of non topical material. A further point that has to be borne in mind is that much of the ephemera which is to be found in commercial, and other subject departments, may not be of merely local significance, but of regional or national interest. For example, it is to be wondered whether any library or museum has acquired and preserved a copy of the Hunter-Penrose catalogue[40] of stereo typing machines, a copy of which was discovered in Manchester, but which is not in any library or museum in the area despite its interest to an area which has a relatively large printing and newspaper industry. Unfortunately, there is no way of knowing how much of this type of material is preserved and how much is lost because no-one has taken the trouble to preserve a copy. It is to be hoped that libraries which have large firms with headquarters in their area make an effort to collect material put out by that firm and preserve it, and that companies themselves have an enlightened attitude towards this type of material and preserve at least one copy in their archives, as it appears that Colman's, the mustard manufacturers do.[41]

Not only do libraries have material which is specifically for reference purposes, but also they have much material which is sent to them for distribution to members of the public, to be picked up and taken away as well as displayed within the library building itself. If this is of local interest, it should be arranged that the local collection obtains a copy or is automatically given a copy as soon as the material is received for its files. If it is a poster and only one copy is received, then arrangements should be made to ensure that this will be passed to the local collection as soon as its topicality has passed.

Away from the public library field, there are other libraries with collections of ephemera, although, as with public libraries, such collections might not be called ephemera collections. There are collections in academic libraries although if Pemberton is to be taken as a guide line, their activity appears to be limited. In many cases, ephemera is to be found forming part of specific collections of material. For example, the collection of trade union material at the University of Warwick Library[42] contains material which could be described as ephemera.

The libraries and information offices of research institutes also maintain collections of ephemera. Pemberton believes that it was in such institutions that 'the collection of printed ephemera are most highly developed'[43]. This is probably because much of the material they are called upon to use is to be found only in ephemera form rather than in the traditional book format. The same may also be true of libraries in firms where material on the company's products, as well as on the products of companies making a similar range, will be found only in a leaflet or other similar type of format and not written up into book form.

Record offices and archive departments

Record offices and archive departments are another important location for ephemera, although in many cases it will not be identified as such as it will form an integral part of an archive. For example, a collection of material from an estate agent may not only include material relating to the operation of the firm, but may also include copies of handouts on properties which the firm handled as well as copies of free newspapers and so on produced to advertise property in a specific area or region. This type of material might not exist anywhere else, although some of the information might be found in local newspapers, but to trace it would involve much time-consuming research. Similarly, collections of documents relating to organisations, local government and country estates will contain a great deal of ephemera, such as leaflets, notices and sale posters, which might not survive anywhere else. Although these items are technically ephemera, they will not be described as such in archive calendars and will be treated as part of the archive. Where ephemera is found as part of an archive, it should not be treated separately or split off from the archive, but retained there. To split it off would leave the archive incomplete and destroy the significance of the material. There is no harm, however, in making a photographic copy of some material and placing it with like material provided that the user's attention is drawn to the fact that it comes from an archive and that to discover its proper significance and importance, the archive itself should be consulted.

Businesses

Business organisations may also have substantial collections of ephemera. This is often material which has been used for advertising and publicity purposes, although instructions on how machines should be operated may also be in a format which could be described as ephemera. Ideally, every company should keep at least one copy of everything that it prints in the company's archives. Unfortunately, this is not often the case for once the material has passed its useful life, it tends to be discarded unless there is a legal reason for its continued existence or it is forgotten about or there is an active archivist/company librarian who appreciates that there may be some use in the future for it. Some material, however, does survive, but more by accident than by chance, only to be discovered when a company moves premises or wants additional space and sorts or clears an area which has not been looked at for a period of time. An example of the type of material which might survive in a company's paper store is afforded by the now defunct firm of Craven Brothers of Reddish, near Manchester. Before the firm closed down, Dr R. L. Hills, Director of the North Western Museum of Science and Industry[44] was invited to see if there was any material in which the museum might be interested as there was a growing collection of archival material on industrial firms in the area. In addition to the official company records, there was a large paper store in the basement of the office building in which were found quantities of back numbers of the house journal, photographs, drawings and publicity leaflets on the various machines which the company had produced, sales literature and some technical information leaflets on machines. A check was made of the holdings of this type of material in libraries in the area. It was discovered that Manchester's Technical Library had some copies of the house journal, but the set was far from complete. The upshot of the visit by Dr Hills was that the Museum was able to acquire a complete set of everything that had survived and the holdings of Manchester's Technical Library were also made virtually complete, including copies of the technical literature, some of which had appeared as parts of the house journal in the company's latter years. If the Museum had not undertaken this rescue attempt, most of the material would have been sent either to the local tip or pulped with the resultant loss of important information on the company.

Local government

Local government produces a great deal of ephemera, often in the form of leaflets and posters. Although copies may be put on departmental files, it is more than likely that no attempt will be made to ensure that there is a single collection of all this material within the authority itself. Thus it is very difficult to trace some of the material issued by local authorities which include leaflets on conservation areas, summaries of local plans, trails, information on events in local parks, educational facilities, evening classes, posters announcing smoke control zones and dates of council meetings as well as details of clearance areas and official notices relating to elections. The problem is that no-one knows who is producing what and when, sometimes not even the authorities' own information departments will know so that there is no means of discovering this information. The cause of the problem is the failure of those concerned with the production and distribution of this material to appreciate the fact that there will be an interest in the future about what has been carried out and that libraries are the ideal place where this material can be preserved. Sometimes, the library can provide evidence to support the fact that an item has been issued. For example, when Manchester was clearing the Hulme area of the city, certain notices had to be posted on site and remain there for a statutory period. In one instance, these had been vandalised shortly after they had been put up. The Local History Library had had these photographed as part of a survey of the area. When it came to making a decision on the site, there were claims that the notices had not been posted, but the photographic evidence proved that they had, thus saving much time and money.

Societies

Societies and clubs also produce ephemera which should be kept with the official records of the organisation concerned. This type of ephemera might include copies of leaflets, circulars to members, newsletters and newsheets, programmes, membership cards and notices about meetings and so on. For example, the records of a sports club, such as Disley Amalgamated Club, not only include the minutes of the committee running the club, but also those of the various section committees, invitations, balance sheets, agendas for meetings, rules and newsletters as well as newspaper clippings. This type of information can prove to be invaluable when researching into the history of such a body as it gives more information on activities than do the official minutes. Although some material might survive, it is rare that a complete record will survive as much depends on the conscientiousness of the officers in ensuring that copies of the material are put in the official record.

The problem with society records and the material they contain is that they are built up over a period of time, often on a haphazard basis and no-one takes much notice of how complete they are until the back material is required for some reason or other, such as an anniversary. It is important to ensure that where such records have survived, they are kept in a safe place where they will not be damaged by dampness or lost or destroyed by an accident. The loss of material by an accident, such as a flood or fire can be as catastrophic as deliberate destruction.

Private collectors

Individuals have always collected things such as stamps, cigarette cards or theatre posters and as such, some of these collections are quite extensive, containing material which might not have survived elsewhere. Today, people are becoming aware that items such as posters, railway tickets, commemorative serviettes, cigarette cards and such like have not only an interest value, but also a monetary one and so there are those who are collecting material as an investment. Often, an individual will collect material on a particular subject or a particular type of material. The range of these collections is growing constantly with virtually every type of ephemera on every subject conceivable being collected by someone.

A poster for a lecture in Rochdale, 1851 (Rochdale Local History Library)

It is foolhardy for librarians and archivists to ignore the existence of private collectors as the private collector is often able to acquire material far more easily than an institution if the two are in competition for it on the open market. Not only are they sometimes prepared to pay large sums of money for an item but they can often buy it before the library has had a chance to try and order it due to the relatively slow methods which are used to order items and the procedures that are followed before an order can be placed. In addition, institutions tend to have a limited budget and this has to be spread throughout the year so that an expensive purchase might mean that something else will have to be ignored or not acquired. The arrival of the private collector and his ability and willingness to purchase material also means that libraries, who in the past might have been offered ephemera very cheaply, no longer get the first look at the material or if it is an individual disposing of material, it will be sold rather than donated to the library or record office. It is, therefore, important that the librarian, archivist and museum curator get to know the private collectors and their particular interests. It may be that at some future date, the collection will be donated to the library or record office. It is important, however, to remember that not all material has a monetary value, but purely an interest one to someone in the future.

Sometimes, the private collector will develop his interest to such an extent that it will result in an institution being established to collect material on the subject. For example, Colin Harvey developed an interest in the ephemera of social work through his job which resulted in the establishment of the Museum of Social Work[45]. Thus, what was originally a private collection has now become a public one, available to be used by those interested in social work and allied subjects as well as by those interested in ephemera generally.

The individual

The individual person is, perhaps, the largest single collector of ephemera, although most people would not recognise this fact. This is because many of the items which are to be found in an individual's household and personal files are in fact ephemera. For example, a guarantee or a rate demand is as much ephemera as a theatre playbill or a invitation to the Lord Mayor's reception. Few people realise that this material contains information which historians and social scientists in the future might find useful. Many is the time that material is thrown away without a second thought being given to its future usefulness and often it only takes a few words of explanation to make people realise that someone might be able to use this type of material and to educate them into thinking in terms of passing it to a record office or library or even to a private collector. For example, a collection of rent books covering a thirty-year period was saved from destruction because the person disposing of them had been made aware of their potential usefulness in the future as the rent books contained information of rents, payments and conditions which was available nowhere else.

The wastepaper basket is the usual home for much of this material once its usefulness is finished with or when someone dies. The same also applies to material which arrives through the letter-box either as unsolicited mail or as part of a leaflet drop in an area. Such material includes free advertising newspapers, leaflets advising of a coffee morning or a scouts' jumble sale. Many people do not realise the amount of this material that is received but it can be ascertained quite easily by placing it in a box when it is received and at the end of a given period checking to see how much there is. It is also worth checking to see how much of it has found its way into library collections during the same period of time.

Even members of local history societies sometimes do not realise the importance of this material. At one local society meeting, the question was asked as to how much of this type of material was being collected as the society was trying to bring together everything it could trace on the history of the area and collect current material for the future. Out of 25 people present, only one person had endeavoured to collect some of this material, but then only on a selective basis. Members in general had not realised that what they regarded as 'rubbish' today could in fact be tomorrow's source material.

Few libraries have anything but a few items of household or personal ephemera in their collections. For example, how many libraries have acquired copies of the leaflets which accompany the rates demand each year or the leaflets which are included with gas and electricity bills when the tarrif is raised or the leaflets trying to persuade customers to install showers or buy new gas fires? The answer is that probably very few libraries have bothered to ensure that there is a copy of this type of material in their files, yet every household in the country receives this type of material at least four times a year.

Why collect ephemera?

For those not involved with libraries, archives departments, record offices and museums and who are not aware of the demands made for material on a very wide range of subjects, the question must be asked as to why bother to collect material from the past and preserve it and also why collect contemporary material and preserve this, particularly as it is virtually impossible to achieve what might be called a completely comprehensive collection of material and that there are difficulties to be encountered in trying to collect certain types of material. To this question, there is a simple answer, namely that anything that is published, whether it is illustrative, the printed word or manuscript will add to the store of information that is available for future generations to consult. In an ideal situation, a copy of everything that is published, whether it be a book, minor publication, serial or a piece of ephemera should be sent to the British Library as well as to the local library or record office and also copies should be retained in the originating bodies' files. Although this would add considerably to the problems of storage, conservation and treatment within the library field and probably require an increase in staff to handle it, it is vital that some attempt is made to achieve as comprehensive a coverage as possible. It is not for the librarian, archivist or curator to act as a censor and to determine what future researchers are going to require or have access to. Nobody knows what subjects are going to be of interest in the future. Who is going to say that something that is discarded or not collected in 1982 will not be of interest to someone in 1984 or 2004. A very good example of this changing attitude towards history and our forebearers is to be found in the Victoria County Histories of English counties. This monumental series was started at the end of the nineteenth century and is still being completed today. The early volumes of the series concentrated on the established order of things: the church, landed gentry and stately homes when dealing with individual areas and with only a few references to such subjects as non-conformity, social conditions, industry and transport. These subjects were relegated to the general chapters which were contained in the first two or three volumes for each county. In the more recent volumes, however, some attempt has been made to redress the balance, but the emphasis is still on the established order of things as seen at the beginning of the twentieth century. Attitudes and interests in history change, the present generation is not able to predict future areas of interest no more than Edwardian historians could predict the interests of the late twentieth century historians.

If the librarian tries to act as a censor, deliberately excluding material from his collection, then he is doing a disservice to the future. In the local studies field, it is particularly important that the librarian should try to ensure that the library's collection is as complete and as comprehensive as possible. Judgement on the material and its usefulness should be left to those consulting it in the future. Thus, a local studies library should aim to preserve a copy of everything that relates to the area whilst other subject departments should aim to be comprehensive in their own field, although they might not accept that the preservation of historical material is part of their remit.

The above is the ideal situation. In actual practice, the situation is somewhat different. Because of the difficulty in ascertaining what ephemera has been produced and in collecting it, a form of selection takes place which is imposed on the librarian. Ephemera, by its very nature, is difficult to collect and it is virtually impossible to ensure that a copy of everything reaches the library. The most comprehensive collections are those which are maintained by societies or other organisations which systematically add a copy of everything they produce to their archives. This usually occurs because there is someone interested in preserving a complete record for the future and who is aware of its potential.

Probably the most important reason why ephemera should be collected, and is collected, is that it helps to provide a complete picture of life at a given point in time. It is sometimes able to answer questions which other surviving sources cannot and to fill in gaps which might otherwise remain unfilled. If a local studies department does not collect both historic and current ephemera relating to its area, then part of the source material for the history of that place will be missing as it is very unlikely that anyone else will bother with it. A good example of how the survival of ephemera has been able to provide additional information is shown by the general election campaign that was conducted in the Gorton constituency at the end of 1910.

In this particular election in Gorton, leaflets played an important part in the campaign. There were only two candidates standing: Conservative and Labour. Labour held the seat and were supported by the Liberals in the area. On the surface, there appeared to be nothing unusual about the campaign, but if the reports of it in the local newspapers are read carefully, there is a slight indication that it was not as straight forward as it seemed at first. Both the *Manchester Guardian* and the *Manchester Courier* carried detailed reports of the campaign of the party they supported, but they do not directly mention what can only be described as a 'leaflet war' which both sides engaged it. Neither paper elaborated on the leaflet campaign or the issues which had provoked it, although it was obvious that it was a local rather than a national matter. However, it is possible to discover what the cause of it was as by good fortune some of the leaflets have survived[46] and have been preserved. For example, one of the leaflets published and distributed by the local Labour Party opened with the words:

36

White says he 'ONLY WANTED A YOUTH'
This speaks for itself!

The leaflet then went on to quote an advertisement which had appeared shortly before in the *Manchester Evening News* and to comment upon it in the following manner:

YOUNG MAN as Jeweller's Porter, thor'ly honest and respectable: knowledge of arc lamp pref., refs.:18/– 104, Market-St.
FANCY! An electrician for 18/-
Also thoroughly honest, respectable, and good references. It is said that Mr White's employees worship him. May be this is a case of mutual interest, for these men are in no Union, and the Shop Assistant's Union have made repeated efforts to get them organised, but they absolutely refuse.

Mr White, the Conservative candidate, replied with the following leaflet:

Workers! Do not be Deceived and Bluffed by the last LIE of the Socialist Party.
Leaflets are being circulated throughout the Division in which Mr White is charged with having tried 12 months ago to engage a 'MAN' for the post of 'ELECTRICIAN' (i.e. a skilled workman) at 18/– per week . . . THIS IS A LIE!
What was really wanted was a youth to run errands and clean lamps and 18/– per week is the very highest wage paid for this work anywhere.
WORKING MEN!
An Ounce of Truth is worth a Ton of Lies. Resent this barefaced attempt to Deceive and Bluff you.

In all, over thirty different leaflets are known to have survived from this particular general election campaign in the Gorton constituency. These leaflets show very clearly the tactics used by both parties to persuade the electorate to support their candidate and the pressures to which the local electorate were subjected and the issues which could raise local passions. If it had not been for this chance survival or the enthusiasm of some unknown person or librarian in collecting together and preserving these leaflets, the Gorton election campaign of December 1910 would have appeared to historians to be similar to the campaign fought in any other constituency, despite the hint in the press of the 'leaflet war'. Historians would have been forced to speculate on the content of the leaflets and what had arisen to excite such local passions.

A second reason why it is important to collect ephemera is that it can sometimes provide information that is not available elsewhere or if it is available, is difficult to trace. For example, in 1906, the Master Cloggers of Rochdale issued a leaflet[47] giving new prices to be charged from 23 January 1906. Information on prices is always difficult to trace, especially when it is something which affects the man in the street. This leaflet provides information that is available nowhere else. In addition, it gives an indication of the type of work which cloggers undertook: the manufacture of new clogs, old backs, new fronts, old tops, reclogging and re-ironing. At the end of the handbill there is the following statement 'All work to cease at ONE o'clock on Saturdays, and EIGHT o'clock other days'. This throws some light on the working hours of those engaged in clogging in Rochdale in the early twentieth century. It is probably the only source of this information unless the cloggers' trade association records have been preserved somewhere. It is also important as cloggers are representative of small tradesmen and craftsmen, often working for themselves, or with a very small labour force, about whom information is difficult to trace.

Similarly, the survival of what may be termed 'domestic ephemera', such as gas and electricity bills, guarantees for household equipment, rent and rate demands and so on, also come into this category of material providing information which is difficult to trace and may not be found anywhere else.

A third reason why ephemera should be collected and preserved is that it provides information on life at a given point in time, or in a given situation. Each different item of ephemera will give different information and, therefore, it is only possible to generalise as to the information that each item gives. The most effective way to discover the type of information which can be obtained from ephemera is to study individual items carefully and then consider the use that may be made of that information. This is the only way that the full potential of ephemera can be discovered, by using it in some way or other.

Exclusion of certain types of material

So far, the discussion has centred on the type of material that is referred to as ephemera, and to a lesser extent on minor publications. As the definition implies, ephemera covers a wide range of material a large proportion of which could be termed 'non-book material', often it is little more than a single sheet of printed paper. It is, however, important to explain why certain types of material, whose format would lead one to expect them to be called ephemera, have been excluded from consideration in this book.

Firstly, it is not intended to deal with minor publications although some people might regard them as ephemera. They are a class of material in their own right. However, as certain of the acquisition techniques required for ephemera can also be applied to the acquisition of minor publications, it is possible to substitute minor publications for ephemera.

Secondly, maps and illustrations also fit the definition of ephemera. However, both these types of material have been excluded from consideration as they are separate subject areas in their own right and deserve much fuller treatment than one can give them in a book on ephemera. The only illustrations that might be included in a work on ephemera are photographs of posters which have been painted or stuck on walls and hoardings which would otherwise be difficult to acquire for the library, if not impossible in certain cases. For example, the demolition of a building in the Moss Side/Greenheys area of Manchester revealed a painted poster on a wall for a livery stable. To have tried to add the original to the library collection would not have been feasible for it would have involved taking the wall down brick by brick and then reassembling it. Clearly, the only practical solution was to photograph it. Similarly, old photographs may show posters and notices which can be read either with the aid of a magnifying glass or even without the aid of one. Sometimes, these posters can be used to date the photograph when all other means have failed.[48] In cases where there are posters on photographs, it may be possible to have additional copies made, enlarging the relevant portions until the text is legible, thus making a valuable addition to the ephemera collection of the library. If copies are not made for the ephemera collection, then any material which is likely to be useful should be cross-referenced in the index which contains entries for the other ephemera in the library or collection.

Records and tape-recordings are the most recent forms of non-book material to make their appearance in libraries. These, too, have been excluded as they are neither printed nor illustrative, although the sleeves of records could be classified as ephemera. Transcripts of tape-recordings, however, are often regarded as ephemera yet they can be very substantial documents which warrant treatment either as minor publications or as manuscripts.

Publications on ephemera

It is important that something should be mentioned on the bibliography of ephemera. It is relatively easy to trace books which have been published on ephemera generally and it is also relatively easy to trace articles on the subject. It is, however, much more difficult to compile a complete bibliography of everything that has been written on the different types of ephemera because the subject is so fragmented and there are so many different types of material and different people use ephemera for different purposes. For example, a brief check of the main catalogue in Manchester Central Library under the name of one of the authors of a general book on ephemera, Rickards, produced seven titles on ephemera, a majority of them on posters[49].

In many cases, the books that have been written or compiled on ephemera are of the 'glossy' or 'coffee-table' type dealing with a particular subject, like Osborne and Pipe's book on beer labels, mats and coasters does,[50] or of a particular aspect or type of material, as are Rickard's on posters. The same also applies to articles on ephemera, many deal with a specific type of material and indicate potential uses or refer to the holdings in just one area of the country like that on the Manchester ballad collection[51] or playbills and programmes in the Manchester Arts Library.[52] What is required is a comprehensive bibliography of ephemera and the material which makes up the subject field, but this would be a long task.

Conclusion

Ephemera forms an important part of everyday life as well as providing valuable and useful information for those engaged on research. It is a term which is used to cover a wide range of material and is especially important in the field of local studies. However, local studies libraries and other organisations connected with the history of a particular area or organisation are not the only places where ephemera can be found, other subject departments in libraries will also have their own holdings of ephemera. It is important, therefore, that library staff know something about ephemera in general and the material that there is in the department in which they work so that they can advise the readers accordingly. At the same time, they should also be aware of the holdings of other departments of this type of material. There is no easy way for them to discover what constitutes ephemera except by experience and by looking at those publications they find on the shelves which deal with the various aspects of the material.

The different types of ephemera

The definition of ephemera is such that it enables the word to be used by librarians, archivists and museum curators as a kind of umbrella to cover a wide range of non-book material all of which have similar characteristics and which present similar problems yet which can be very dissimilar in appearance, origins, use and in the information they contain. For example, posters and broadsheets are very different from tickets and invitations and may require different treatment when it comes to acquisition, conservation and storage, yet all four types of material form part of that nebulous field of non-book material which is called 'ephemera', or in some cases 'miscellaneous material'.

One relatively easy way to discover the wide variety of material which makes up ephemera is to look through the non-book material, excluding maps and illustrations, in a library, especially in a local studies or commercial department and to look at the type of material which is displayed on notice boards within a library or left on information desks or at reception desks for members of the public to pick up and take away. If a list is compiled of the various types of material which is found, a lengthy, although not exhaustive list can be compiled. It will not be exhaustive simply because there will always be some types of material which have not been collected for one reason or another, which have escaped detection and therefore collection or which have been overlooked because they have been treated differently from other types of similar material and housed in a different part of the library.

This chapter will look at the different types of ephemera, their format, the information which may be obtained from them and their potential use by those engaged in research. It does not pretend to be a fully comprehensive list of material as there is always material which has been overlooked or very recently produced. An attempt at a comprehensive list of material is to be found in Appendix 1. It is not intended to deal with methods of acquisition in general, which will be covered in the following chapter. However, where specialist means are required, or where a particular method has been successful in acquiring material, these will be dealt with under the relevant section.

PRESTWICH UNION.

TO BE SOLD

(A BARGAIN)

BY PRIVATE CONTRACT,

That thorough-Bred Entire Horse,

LUCIFER NIGHTINGALE,

Long known in Manchester and the Neighbourhood.

Lucifer Nightingale was got by Duplicity, out of Impudence;

And is considered by the Jockeys who know him to be the most perfect specimen of his breed in England. He is a light brown, bald-faced nag, high in the withers, with short legs, and of great physical power. Goes at a devil of a pace and STICKS AT NOTHING. Is a capital fencer, and will leap at aught he is put to, however high, wide, or impracticable. Is especially adapted to a dirty country, as his wonderful animal powers can be brought to the test only in a muddy district. On rotten ground no competitor can live with him. For the last two years he has headed the winner of the Newton Steeple Chase, over a boggy course on Chatterton Moss. Is fit for any kind of Stable, as *he will* LIE *on any thing*. With a man of no *metal* he is apt to shy, bolt, and run away,—but with a *golden curb* in his mouth he may be led, ridden, or driven to a certainty, in any direction, and by any person.

For performances see the Manchester papers.

Up to the summer of 1839, Lucifer Nightingale, along with a well-known fast *trotting* horse named WNOX, plied in a hired Cab round about the Old Church. He then ran as one of the leaders in "*The Chartist*" heavy Coach, from "*The Church and State Inn*," in Manchester, to the "*Universal Suffrage and no Taxation Inn*," on Kersal-Moor, in opposition to *The Queen*, and the 79th *Highlanders*. His employers failing

He was Sold for 30 Sovs.,

in January, 1841, (with a string of others,) to the Duke of Buckingham, who sent him to Walsall, where he ran with another of the Duke's purchases called CHARLEY WILKINS, as a leader in the old crazy five-wheeled Coach, *Protectionist*, then in opposition to Mr. J. B. Smith's New Omnibus *The Free Trader*. On the Duke of Buckingham breaking down, and his Establishments breaking up, LUCIFER NIGHTINGALE was once more sent into the Market, and was bought by the Corporation of Manchester, who after cropping his ears, and docking his tail, muzzled him and kept him privately (in a Stall out of sight) as an occasional Hack for the Council. Subsequently being considered *safe* he was parted with and put by his new owners into the Manchester Union, as an outside wheeler, but proving to be a desperate kicker and a confirmed roarer, with too tender feet for *public* roads, he was turned out to grass.

Latterly he has been working in a *Match* Cart, at Newton Heath, and as he has improved lately in apparent condition, his present owners intend, unless they meet with a customer, to work him as *leader* for a short time in the new Three-Horse Coach, *The Prestwich Union*, which will commence running on or about the 10th of May, instant. Should he have recourse, however, to his former vicious habits, the inhabitants of Newton-Heath need not feel alarmed as measures are already in progress for castrating him before the end of the present season.

Principals without principle, only need apply.

Application to be made to BRIMSTONE, LUCIFER & Co., Newton-Heath.

PRINTED BY W. IRELAND & Co., NEWTON-HEATH.

A sale poster relating to the Prestwich Union, 1841
(Manchester Local History Library)

Advertising leaflets, brochures and handbills

Advertising has existed for a long time, certainly since man has engaged in trade with his neighbours or has entertained them. Initially, it would be by word of mouth, but with the advent of printing, it became possible, although not necessarily feasible and economic, to produce advertising literature on a large scale, reproducing the same item many times, and distributing it over a wide area. However, it was not until there was increased literacy and improved communications that advertising on a large scale came into its own. It could be said that advertising is a feature of a complex urbanised and industrialised society rather than one which is based more on agriculture and to some extent self-sufficient. Advertising in the late twentieth century is big business with the public being bombarded from all directions – radio, television, hoardings, billboards and fly-posting in the streets, material thrust into hands as one walks down the street and unsolicited mail received in the post – irrespective of whether the recipients are interested in the contents or not. How much of this material ever survives and finds its way into libraries, record offices or museums and is permanently preserved is uncertain, but the percentage cannot be high when compared with the amount that is actually produced each year.

To many people, advertising material is material which is aimed at selling a particular product, such as soap powder or a car, persuading people that one particular product is better than another, encouraging members of the public to use one shop as opposed to another, informing the public about the products of a firm or its new address. However, advertising has a much wider usage than trying to sell a product for it can be used to inform people about what is going on in the entertainment field and as such will overlap with theatre playbills.

Advertising material is intended to have a limited life and to be thrown away as soon as its usefulness is over. Its appearance and format will depend on the market it is aiming at and the type of product that is being marketed. Sometimes it is merely a duplicated sheet, produced by a local shop and circulated in a restricted area around the shop. Sometimes, however, advertising material is more elaborate and expensively produced, often in colour and intended to impress the potential customer, such as that produced by various car manufacturers. Despite the fact that the usefulness of advertising material may be limited to the period of its topicality, such material that has survived in collections, will have an interest for those engaged in research. For example, a supermarket in the village of High Lane, between Stockport and Buxton, produced a series of leaflets in 1977 which were distributed in High Lane and the nearby village of Disley.

In all, about a dozen leaflets were produced at fortnightly intervals listing the prices charged for various items of food. For example, one list included the price per pound of twenty-eight different cuts of meat[1] whilst another listed the price charged for twenty-eight grocery items together with the manufacturers' recommended price[2]. The type of information contained in these leaflets may only be of limited interest to those who receive them, but to those engaged on research at some point in the future, the prices will be extremely useful as they provide information on the prices which people actually paid rather than on prices quoted in government or other official statistics. However, the survival of such detailed information is not at all common.

It is difficult for libraries, particularly local studies libraries which are usually to be found in the central library in the centre of a town and which are often the most interested in such items as price lists issued by local shops, to obtain even a few examples, let alone a comprehensive collection, of such material which usually circulates in a very localised area. At the same time, it is equally as difficult to ascertain what has exactly been published and by whom due to the very localised nature of the material. To try to obtain at least a sample of this type of material if possible is important. One way of doing this is to ask shops and shopkeepers to keep a copy of any leaflets they circulate and to forward them to the library or to collect them at certain intervals. However, this requires the co-operation of the shops and will rarely be successful unless the person concerned has an interest in local history or history generally and is aware of the potential usefulness in the future of this type of material. Alternatively, members of staff, not only in the collecting department, but throughout the whole library system in the area, can be asked to save copies they receive through their front doors and to bring them into the library. Sometimes members of the public may well assist, particularly if they have been at a talk where the importance of ephemera and this type of material is pointed out to them. At the same time, their society may also build up a 'private collection' of local material, in which case, it is important that the local studies library knows of its existence and keeps an eye on what is happening to it in case it is decided to throw it away.

Not only do shops produce leaflets which are distributed within a locality, but they also produce ones which are left outside the shop for the public to pick up as they pass. This can frequently happen at specific times of the year, such as Christmas, to encourage people to purchase certain goods. For example, the branch of Dixon's in the Zudplein Centrum, Rotterdam had such a pile of leaflets outside its shop in November 1980 suggesting possible presents for the St

Nicholas celebrations and Christmas[3]. This four page leaflet was displayed outside the shop where passers-by could pick it up and was designed so that it could be folded easily and fit into a pocket or handbag.

Advertising material left for members of the public to pick up as they pass is not restricted to shops. It can also apply to organisations which are selling services. For example, hotels and restaurants may leave leaflets giving details of their services, such as conference facilities, the various restaurants that can be used and special menus which are available on certain nights as well as general details about the hotel, tariffs and possibly other hotels in the group. The Britannia Hotel in Manchester has a good selection of this type of material which can be picked up and taken away. Not only does this material provide current awareness for the visitor, but it also provides information on the facilities and activities which the hotel provided for the historian in the future. Amongst the leaflets that were on display in late June 1983 were 'Swing in and get lit up for the brightest Christmas and New Year'[4] and 'Curtain up on Special Nights at Special Prices'[5]. In both cases menus were given and the price charged and in the case of the former, details of a special overnight accommodation charge. Sometimes, restaurants produce leaflets giving their specialities which can be taken away. That produced by Whitegate Taverns gives the main dishes and wines as well as details of special coffees and on the reverse, a list of the restaurants and their opening times[6].

Sometimes, leaflets produced by hotels are very glossy and are intended to impress potential customers as well as to be circulated over a wide area. For instance, a leaflet advertising the Manor Hotel at Leamington Spa has a brief account of the facilities available and several coloured photographs of public rooms and a location plan together with a short history of the town and nearby attractions[7]. Other leaflets advertise the hotel's other facilities such as those for conferences and banquets[8]. In a similar vein, the Midland Hotel, Manchester also produces literature on facilities available for conferences. Their leaflet includes sample menus, conference rates and a wine list together with a plan of the building showing the location of the various facilities[9].

Another useful item produced by hotels relates to their tariff lists. Sometimes these are incorporated in their brochures, but on other occasions, they are separately produced. That issued by the Packhorse Hotel at Allerford, near Porlock included information on the terms for the summer season, amenities and the price of extras. Unfortunately, this item is not dated and one can only guess that it was issued sometime between the wars or just after 1945 by the style of the drawing on the front of the leaflet[10].

Many leaflets issued for advertising hotels and other attractions are intended to be circulated very widely to attract the widest possible attendance. For instance, the leaflet produced by the Manchester Air and Space Museum[11] was not only circulated in Manchester, but in the whole of the north-west and further afield as well so that those people visiting the city could visit the Museum. This type of leaflet is often issued when a new attraction opens to the public in order to make the public aware of the opening and what it has to offer. The Air and Space Museum leaflet not only gives details of the collections which can be seen, but also its location and opening times. Often, this information might not survive in any other form except possibly in the official records of the body and often it is not even recorded there in an obvious manner.

Another form of advertising leaflet is not aimed at selling a particular product but is related to informing the public of the location of a particular firm or business premises. These are often associated with firms when they move from one location to another. Sometimes they are in the form of posters in the window of the old premises, but other material may be made available for members of the public to take away with them. Sometimes in addition to the address, the leaflet will give the date of the move and the telephone number of the new premises. Sometimes even the products of the company are recorded as was the case in a leaflet issued by T. Armstrong[12] in 1807 when he moved from Long Millgate, Manchester to Press House Steps, Manchester. In addition to the firm's products, the notice also gives one advantage of the move, namely that the new premises are 'completely removed from the noise and bustle of a street'[13]. More recently, when Gibb's Bookshop moved from Mosley Street to Charlotte Street, Manchester, a series of leaflets were produced before and after the move, including a sketch map showing the location of the new premises. In total, five different leaflets were produced in addition to the one which appeared in the window of the old premises showing the route between the two shops[14].

Advertising goods and services is not restricted to those organisations and firms selling a particular product or service, professional bodies also advertise their activities, although in some cases this has to be in an indirect manner to overcome restrictions on advertising placed on some professions by the members' professional body. For instance, the Royal Institute of British Architects prevents its members from advertising, although this restriction is to be lifted in 1984. One firm of architects has overcome this problem by producing a leaflet showing the work it has done in the field of refurbishment and restoration[15]. The leaflet not only indicates the type of work that can be undertaken, but also gives a brief account of the practice and illustrations of the type of work that has been done by the firm. How widely this leaflet was circulated is uncertain, but it was sent to certain architects and may well have been sent to prospective clients.

Acquisition of advertising material is not at all easy. Where the material is on display in a public place, it can be picked up and taken away, but if it is circulated only in a specific locality or is available within the shop or office, then the situation is much more difficult. For example, a new domestic appliance firm opened on Kingsway in Manchester. The leaflet that was produced was distributed within the area of the shop and was only available after that within the shop itself. The leaflet is a useful item in that it indicates the type of work that the owner dealt with as well as the address and telephone number of the premises[16]. Further problems can be created where material only circulates through mailing lists to selected customers as with a leaflet produced by M. and N. Haworth (Manchester) Ltd[17], who took over an old established philatelist's business in the city. The leaflet was only mailed to regular customers of the old firm and gave details of the stock the shop carried and its opening times.

How can such leaflets be obtained for a local collection? The ones that are publically available and which can be picked up in information bureaux, enquiry desks and so on are easy enough to acquire. All that is needed is a systematic system of visiting such places in order to pick up material which has been placed on display since the last visit. It may also be possible with some firms, organisations and professional offices to arrange for such material to be forwarded to the library at regular intervals. In addition, one would expect, although it is not necessarily achieved, for a copy of everything to be placed in the firm's records or archives.

Where the material is restricted to a particular locality or to distribution by mailing, it is necessary to recruit the support of members of the staff to bring in this type of material rather than throw it away. This not only means staff within the department concerned, but also throughout the whole library system within the area.

In addition to advertising material that is aimed at the general public, there is also material that is intended to influence a particular profession or branch of industry. This is technical information and sales literature. It can vary in size and content widely and will also vary in its format. Sometimes, it will be glossy material whilst other material may be produced in an unusual format or even as a large catalogue, the latter really being a minor publication. For instance, the catalogue of printers' machinery, joinery materials and so forth produced by Wright and Co. of London consists of sheets bound together to form a book[18] and although it may be regarded as trade literature, it is in fact a minor publication in all senses of the definition. On the other hand, the leaflet produced by TAC Building and Insulation Division is in the form of a dart board with details of the various products on the reverse[19]. Although libraries may receive copies of catalogues, it is rare for them to receive copies of trade leaflets unless they relate to products which are of interest to the library and then only a small amount is passed on for preservation. Where a library has a collection of trade literature, it has usually been accumulated more by accident than as a result of a systematic collection of material. For example, copies of trade literature relating to some of the products of Craven Brothers of Reddish only survived and reached the North Western Museum of Science and Industry archives and Manchester Central Library because the Museum Director was allowed to take what he considered to be useful when the firm closed down. These leaflets were, on average, two pages long and included an illustration of the machine as well as technical information on such aspects as size and capabilities. These leaflets, although forming part of the company's house journal were only available to those interested in purchasing the machine or attending a trade exhibition where they were on display.

Sometimes trade literature and advertising material is sent in bulk to people as a result of a membership list being sold. For example, architects often receive packets of pre-addressed cards for up to thirty firms inviting the recipient to send for further details. These cards will often contain a brief description of the product and sometimes the address of the firm. It is not suggested that all those which are received or donated to the library should be kept. It is, however, important to try to collect those which relate to the area in which the library is interested as it may be the only information which will survive into the future. To obtain copies of trade literature the most successful way is to try to contact the company concerned, but failing that, someone who receives it may be prepared to pass it onto the library. However, there is always the very real possibility that the person will forget and the material will not reach the library's files.

Although advertising and publicity material issued by commercial firms may be difficult for the public library to acquire, it is to be hoped that firms do arrange for copies to be deposited in the company's own archives or records. If a company fails to do this, then its records will be incomplete and problems might be caused for someone trying to produce a company history or tracing the development of a particular product or line of advertising in the future. It can be argued that in business, space is at a premium and large amounts of paper take up space which could be better used for production. Consequently, there is pressure to discard material that is no longer current or required to be retained for legal purposes. However, this pressure can be countered by the fact that it is possible to reduce the original to a microform, which requires considerably less storage space and allows the originals to be discarded. Often a company will throw out material only to realise that it is required for some purpose or other in the future, such as the compilation of a company history or for an exhibition. Wedgwoods at Barleston, have used many examples of ephemera relating to the history of the company in their factory where there is a permanent exhibition on the company's growth and development.

Sometimes, a firm's collection of material will contain leaflets and other items which relate to the products of rival companies or similar products. Such collections can often help to provide a more complete picture of a particular product's development than otherwise might be possible. It will also enable the position of the company to be established in relation to other firms in the same industry. It is fortunate that companies are now beginning to develop an awareness of their history and the need to preserve more of their records than was previously the case. In this there is much active encouragement from the Business Archives Council who encourage firms to deposit their records in an approved repository rather than discard them and it is amongst these records that ephemera will very often survive.

Advertising ephemera can be found in many sizes, but the most obvious feature about it is that it is designed to be picked up and put into a pocket. Usually important information is placed so that it can be easily seen at a glance and further details are contained inside. For example, an item printed for the Harrow Inn at Enstone has a drawing of the building on the front, a location sketch map on the rear and details about the inn and its telephone number inside.[20] Even single sheets tend to be folded so that there is a word or an illustration which attracts the eye. A leaflet on go-carting issued in Torquay was folded so that the word 'go-carting' was on the front to attract attention[21] whilst information produced by the Contemporary Music Network has the names of the performers in large letters and is clearly visible[22]. Other material has a coloured illustration on the front to attract attention as the leaflet produced by the Exeter Maritime Museum does[23] and inside there is information on the museum and its admission charges and opening hours. Sometimes, advertising literature is designed to double up as a poster. The go-carting leaflet is one example of this, being printed only on one side, but even some material which is printed on both sides can be used in a similar manner. For example, 'What's on'[24] opens up to provide a poster listing events for a specific month.

Although not regarded as advertising material in the usual sense of the word, literature produced by estate agents can be regarded as advertising – advertising that a property is to let or for sale. These leaflets can contain details about the property on offer, the size of the rooms, attractive features, rent and sale or rateable value and the price being sought. For example, Adam Geoffrey and Company produced a very attractive leaflet on Conavon Court[25] which had a drawing of the premises on one side together with the address of the property and on the reverse brief details about the building, the size of the suites that were to be let and an indication of the price being sought per week by way of rental. It is not particularly easy to get copies of this type of material as estate agents appear to be reluctant to pass copies to libraries. Neither is it easy to wander into an estate agent's office and pick up copies of material, as frequently it is not generally available to be picked up. It might be possible to come to an arrangement with a firm for some material to be passed on, as Manchester Local History Library did in the early 1970s, but this relied on a single person and when he left, the material ceased being sent. On the other hand, if someone is looking for a house and is being sent material, it might be possible to arrange for that which is not required to be passed onto the library as the information contained in such leaflets is not generally available elsewhere.

Advance publicity advertising often results in the production of leaflets of various types. For example, theatres may produce leaflets giving information of productions to be staged in the forthcoming season as well as other events being held in the building. The Royal Exchange Theatre, Manchester, for example, publishes a monthly list of events taking place within the theatre whilst Manchester's Library Theatre Company publish a complete list of their productions for a season together with the price of seats, the venue of the production dates of performances, a plan of the seating accommodation and where the different priced seats are located. Sometimes, several different editions are issued of this type of material. For example, in the spring of 1983, the Royal Exchange Theatre produced two leaflets which looked the same, except one had the additional words 'Spring & Summer Season 1983' on it[26] which could be very easily overlooked by someone glancing at the material.

Entertainments are not the only sources for advance pubicity. It can relate equally to new shops, trips, tours and books. For example, a new hair dressing salon opening in an area may well organise leaflets to be delivered in the locality as well as to be left in local shops in advance of its opening. Likewise, information on a new book may be circulated to subscribers to particular journals and left in bookshops so that potential purchasers know the price and something about the contents. For example, Shercliff, Kitching and Ryan's book on Poynton[27] not only gave details of the contents and the price, but as the book was privately printed, it also gave information on where it was obtainable. This advance publicity was distributed around the village, left in the library and sent to people whom the authors thought might be interested in it. Travel is another subject for advance publicity. British Rail often issue leaflets for excursions like the one from Buxton to Scarborough on 1 October 1983[28] which gives the times of departure and return as well as the fare. Sometimes these leaflets contain information on more than one excursion or promotion as that issued by Wallace Arnold for coach trips in the Torbay area does[29]. This appears to cover a week at a time and lists various types of trip and the price as well as telephone numbers for booking.

To obtain copies of advance publicity easily depends on who is producing it, the reason why it is being produced and the way it is distributed. In the case of material relating to entertainments, it will probably be distributed over a wide area and be available in a number of places. With material advertising new publications, it may well be sent to the library or be found inside another publication as was the advance publicity for Taylor's book 'Village and farmstead'[30]. With material relating to transport and tours, this is often available in information offices as well as at coach and railway stations. Sometimes, it will involve a special trip to get this material, although it may be possible to combine it with another visit or to pick material up as one passes through the railway or coach station. One can try to arrange for this material to be forwarded to the library, but much of the success of this type of operation depends on the co-operation of the issuing body and often on the work of one person.

Other types of advertising ephemera that can be overlooked include that issued by various stately homes. Usually only one place is advertised on a leaflet although on some there are two, particularly if they are located close together. For example, a single leaflet has been produced for Haddon Hall and Belvoir Castle[31]. The leaflet extols the virtues of visiting the halls, gives details of how to get there, opening times and in the case of Belvoir Castle, special events held there and a catering tariff.

Educational courses are another source of ephemera which may be overlooked, especially as the material is often on display within the library itself. Some of this material is printed whilst other material is duplicated. In both cases, details of the courses are given together with details of enrolment procedures, the dates and times of the course and the fee payable. Often, the same institution will produce a number of different leaflets so care has to be taken to ensure that all possible ones are collected. For example, the outer sheet of the leaflets produced by Manchester University Extra Mural Department contain the same illustrations, but they vary slightly in colour and in title.

Inside, the contents also vary widely. The leaflet relating to certificate courses issued for the session commencing in October 1983[32] includes full details of the courses, the tutors and the requirements for successfully completing the course. Another leaflet, issued on the subject of education and training for social workers, lists all the courses that are being organised on the subject, a brief synopsis of each course and who is taking it, the venue and duration of the course as well as the starting date and fee.[33] Sometimes, education leaflets will include details of the timetable to be followed and any special qualifications required of those wishing to attend. For example, details of a bridge summer school held at Horncastle Residential College gives details of the type of person the course is aimed at together with a timetable[34] whilst that for a course on Japanese Ribbon Flowers indicates what equipment should be taken by someone attending[35].

Advertising material which is found in unusual formats should not be ignored either. For example, some companies issue packets of matches containing information about the company and its services. It must be pointed out, however, that it is not advisable to keep the matches inside as they can cause a fire risk. North Sea Ferries, for instance, give details of the routes the company operates on the outside of the packet, whilst inside there are the times of sailing, the duration of the crossing, the addresses, telephone numbers and telex numbers of the ports from which the ships sail and where bookings can be made. Although this information can also be found on booking forms and in publicity brochures, a packet of matches which someone carries around with them is a constant reminder and is more easily carried than a leaflet or brochure. Some packet matches contain less information than the example already quoted. Those issued by the Worsley Old Hall near Manchester show a drawing of the building, its telephone number and a list of the various restaurants whilst that issued by the Auberge de Dreef at Rockanje in Holland gives only the name, address and telephone number of the hotel and the information that it is available for receptions.

Advertising material comes in many different forms and the amount of useful information contained in it will vary accordingly depending on the reason for its production. No two items are the same and contain the same information so it is necessary to check each item carefully to see what useful information can be gathered from it by someone engaged in research. The common attribute, as far as libraries, record offices and museums are concerned, is the difficulty in obtaining copies for preservation as circulation may be restricted to a specific section of the community or it may be so widely available that it is overlooked or its full value to researchers in the future is not

1950s posters on a railway viaduct wall in Manchester (Author)

fully appreciated and the material is treated as so much more waste paper.

Agendas

Agendas for meetings, whether they are meetings of societies, companies, local authority or professional bodies, are frequently discarded once the meeting is over as being of no further use, although there should be a copy in the official records of the organisation concerned. Some agendas will be confidential documents, but others will be publically available as they relate to annual meetings and other meetings to which members of the public are admitted. Such documents will contain information on where the meeting is to be held, its time and date as well as matters to be discussed and may also include the names of proposers and seconders to motions on the agenda. In the case of regular meetings, agendas may be distributed with the minutes of the preceding meeting, but where the meeting is annual, agendas may be distributed separately.

Usually, where the library, record office or museum subscribes to an organisation, it receives notices for annual meetings, but not for committee meetings, unless a member of staff is on the committee either representing the body for whom he or she works or in his or her own right. It must be remembered that it may be necessary to keep some material like this sealed for a period of time to preserve confidentiality. This particularly applies to agendas for committees where the number circulated may be limited to committee members only. In such cases, it is appropriate to allow a record office or archives department to collect the material of these bodies and to preserve it as they have recognised procedures for dealing with situations where material has to be sealed for a specific period.

Appeal leaflets

Leaflets issued in connection with local appeals for donations for local causes, such as the restoration of the parish church or to raise funds for a hospital or charity, will often only circulate in a relatively small area. The library may acquire such material from people living in the area or it may be included in a publication which the library receives. Appeal organisers rarely think to send the local studies library or record office copies of such leaflets as they are not potential donors. This is unfortunate as appeal leaflets can often provide useful information on why an appeal has been launched, its objectives and the amount required. For example, in November 1980, St Mary's Church, Disley launched an appeal to raise money to help towards the cost of restoring the church's schoolroom to enable it to be let to outside bodies to produce an income to assist with its regular maintenance. In addition, money was also required to resurface the private road leading to the church. The leaflet that was produced explained what was proposed, the total amount required and the amount already raised. In addition, it gave the names and addresses of the vicar and churchwardens. These latter names provided an interesting sidelight on the usefulness of ephemera as one of the names of the churchwardens was different from that which appeared in the parish magazine, indicating that he had either died or left the district since the general information in the magazine had been prepared and that it had not been updated[36]. Where the restoration of a building is involved, it is possible that the leaflet will include a brief history of it, as did the leaflet produced for St Mary's Church at Eccles[37].

Sometimes, there are appeals which are regional in their catchment area with the result that the information contained in the appeal leaflets and documents is much greater. Although these leaflets may not be pushed through letter boxes, they will probably be circulated to businesses and the press so that the man in the street will probably learn about the appeal through news items rather than as a result of something delivered directly to him. As with localised appeals, copies of the relevant material may not always be sent to the library, although there is a great likelihood of this happening for a regional matter as compared with a purely localised one. Sometimes, however, libraries are sent copies of appeal material for their files as happened in 1978 when an appeal was launched to restore the Albert Memorial in Manchester. Attractive leaflets were produced[38] which were to be found in many places including copies deposited for permanent preservation in Manchester's Local History Library. Another example of a regional appeal is that organised by the Ancient Monuments Society in 1932 for funds to complete the excavation of Chester's Roman Amphitheatre[39] which included details of why the appeal was being made, the importance of the site, a plan of the proposed new road as well as details of the officers of the Society and how to join. This leaflet, however, does not appear to have survived in any library collection yet the information it contained is as important as that contained in the one on the Albert Memorial.

In addition to local and regional appeals, there are national bodies which made appeals on a regular basis, usually annually. In many cases, it is assumed that the general public know why such appeals are being made. Often, they involve house-to-house collections or envelopes through letter boxes which are collected at a later date.

Sometimes, there is information on the organisation contained on the envelope or in an accompanying leaflet. It is a matter of speculation how much of this material is preserved either locally or on a national scale. It is possible that the organising body keeps a copy of everything that is issued and that some local libraries, where the organisation has its headquarters, may have decided to collect material as it represents a local 'industry'. Where such collections exist, not only should the accompanying leaflets be kept, but also the envelopes as these can vary from year to year and the information on the reverse may also vary. Unfortunately it is the most widely circulated ephemera which is often not kept as everyone else thinks someone else is doing it. It may be that the British Library should consider taking responsibility for collecting ephemera produced by national bodies who make national appeals.

Not all appeals are for money or give details of why the collection is being made. Some are for things like wastepaper or old clothes. For example leaflets produced by Marple Ridge Parents Association for wastepaper merely give the dates of collection and what to do with the paper that is for collection. There is no information as to why the paper is being collected or what the money raised from its sale is to be used for. It is possible that it is assumed that everyone knows the reasons and its use, but this is not the case today and certainly will not be the case in the future when all that survives is an isolated leaflet in a private collection which the library might acquire.

As for obtaining copies of appeal leaflets, some may be sent to the library by the organisers who are aware of the need for such material to be preserved, but much of it is not sent. Again, the library, record office or museum staff may be of great assistance in bringing in material which they receive at home or find when they are out at lunch or shopping. However, it is necessary to educate the public in the usefulness to research of ensuring that such material is preserved in some form or other.

Application forms

Application forms may not, on the surface, appear to be part of an ephemera collection. However, their format is such that they may be regarded as ephemera and if they are examined closely they can provide useful information on the organisation for which membership is being sought or job which is being applied for. For instance, the application form for membership of the Southern Electric Group[40] gives details of the aims of the Society on one side, the various categories of membership and what the members receive for their subscription whilst on the reverse there is the application form as such, the address to which it is to be sent and the membership rates. The information on the Society may not be easily available in any other form so it is important that at least one example is retained. Often, such forms are to be found in periodicals which are of related interest around the time of formation of the society concerned so that it reaches those most likely to join.

Application forms for jobs are not usually obtained by libraries. Usually they form part of what might be called 'personal ephemera' in that someone might send for details and then decide not to apply. Such forms will give an indication of the personal information that is sought by employers for a particular job or the type of application form that is used by an organisation. In addition to the application form, there may also be a job specification attached as well (see job specifications). In the case of this type of application form, it is more by chance than by deliberate collection that examples are to be found in library collections although it should be possible to ensure that at least one copy of the library's own application form is in the files so that an example is available for future reference.

Bank notes and cheques

Although the only banknotes that are legal tender in England are those issued by the Bank of England, this has not always been the case. In the eighteenth and nineteenth centuries many banks issued their own notes, some of which were very attractive and are now much sought after by collectors. Irrespective of the attractiveness of the note, they also contain useful information which may not be found elsewhere. In addition to the name of the bank and the face value of the note, it may also contain the names of the directors, the address of the bank and an illustration either of the bank's premises or of a local landmark. For example, a £5 note issued by the Bristol Tolzey Bank in 1818 contains a drawing of Bristol High Cross. Often, banknotes will give a little extra information on the issuing bank which is not recorded elsewhere especially where the bank was a shortlived local one.

Cheques also form part of ephemera. Today, these will basically give the name and address of the bank, its sorting code and, for the graphic artist, the design of the cheque. A blank cheque will be of little use to the historian, but it will be of interest to the graphic artist and those engaged in producing period dramas or documentaries where authenticity is important. It is with used cheques that the historian may be able to extract information on the person who wrote

5

the cheque and to whom it was paid. Unfortunately, it does not give the reason why the cheque was drawn in the first instance and the cost of specific goods and services, unless the cheque has gained some fame in the past. For instance, the cheque used by the Manchester Ship Canal Company in 1887 to purchase the Bridgewater Canal has achieved a certain amount of distinction for it was said to have been the largest cheque written up to that time and as a result has been used as an illustration in books on the Manchester Ship Canal. Although on its own a cheque may provide only a very limited amount of information, if it relates to a firm whose accounts and records have survived, it may be possible to trace why the cheque was drawn or received. It will not, however, indicate the state of a person's or firm's account at the time the cheque was issued unless there is a statement to go with the cheque.

Beer mats

Although beer mats might not be regarded as items of ephemera, they do fit the definition and can provide useful information on the brewery whose products are being advertised as well as being of interest to the graphic artist. At one time most towns had their own local brewery but the numbers have declined with the advent of large combines which produce a standardised beer. More recently, however, there has been a trend away from a national type of beer, back to more local ones, which has resulted in the introduction of beer mats of more local interest. Although beer mats may have a standard form and appearance, the content may vary widely. For example, Wilson's brewery at Newton Heath, Manchester have produced one which shows the brewery whilst Whitegate Taverns have one which has a picture on one side and a list of its premises on the reverse.

It is not to be expected that a local studies library would collect all the beer mats in use in its area, but one would expect it to try to acquire examples of ones produced by local breweries and public houses, especially if they contain information that might not be available elsewhere. As for obtaining examples, the most satisfactory way is to write to the brewery concerned and explain why they are being sought or if it is one produced by a particular public house, to approach the landlord and explain to him. More often than not, assistance will be forthcoming. It is not recommended just to 'collect' them from the public house as this might cause ill will with the landlord, although it must be admitted that many private collections have probably been built up this way. If a useful personal contact is made, it may be that examples of new ones will be sent automatically in the future as many breweries are becoming increasingly aware of their history and the importance of ensuring that a record remains not only of the company's history and its products, but also of its public relations.

Bills, billheads, invoices and orders

Bills, invoices and orders are often only kept for a relatively short period of time, although collections can be found in the archives of firms, organisations and even individuals which have either been retained or deposited in a library, record office or museum. Occasionally individual ones appear, but many are disposed of without a second thought being given as to their usefuness in the future. However, a close examination of this type of material will reveal that, in addition to the usual information one would expect to find on a bill or invoice, there is often other useful information to be discovered. This particularly applies to firms using their own printed stationary before the Second World War when many had elaborate letter heads. The author of an article on billheads in *Lancashire Life* commented:

> Although never welcome, the bills of our fore fathers nevertheless had a style all of their own. With engravings proclaiming pride in their premises, the senders conveyed the impression that you were positively privileged to do business with them. Whereas today's bills sneak up on you, almost shame faced in their little buff envelopes, the Victorians' invoices greeted recipients with a fanfare of embelishments[41]

The article then goes on to give some illustrations of billheads from the north-west including one from Peace and Norquoy of the New Islington Steam Joinery Works, Union Street, Ancoats, Manchester which included an axonometric drawing of the works, reproductions of the various medals won by the company for its patent sliding and folding partitions as well as an illustration of the partition. In addition, there was information on the address of the firm, its telegraphic address and telephone number, date of establishment of the company and the note that the firm were 'contractors to his majesty's government and war office'[42] and details of when accounts were rendered to customers. Sometimes, the illustrations were allowed to provide the necessary information as did that on the billhead used by Henry Pearson, wholesale provision dealer at 1 and 3 Mount Pleasant, Liverpool. This billhead consisted of a drawing of the shop premises with all the information on the front of the shop, a simple, uncluttered design, but giving all the essential information. Others did not include an illustration of the premises, but the products of the company or the type of work they undertook. For example, the billhead of John Swift's of Seven Stars Bridge at Wigan has the information that he was a 'gas and hot-water fitter, plumber, painter etc.', a list of the type of work that could be done and around the sides drawings of some of the products he could fit, including chandeliers, gas lights, water closets, baths and cooking ranges.[43] This information can be very useful as it might be the only place where there is any information on the man and his firm as often accounts of the activities of small concerns are extremely rare.

A third type of billhead is the one which suggests to the recipient the type of work undertaken rather than showing the firm's premises or products. For example, that issued by the City Pantechnicon, Elizabeth Street, Liverpool in the 1890s shows a train hauling two wagons advertising the company's line of business, namely removals, using what is described as an 'improved system of removing furniture, pictures etc. without packing', in other words, by container or specially constructed vehicle. In addition, the billhead provided information about the storage space the company had and that it was heated, fire-proof and had hot-water.[44]

However, not all billheads were as elaborate as those illustrated in the article, yet without the illustration they are still very informative. The basic information that could be found in a heading includes the name and address of the firm, its telephone and telegraph numbers and, more recently, the VAT number. Some also give the date the firm was established and the names of the directors. However, it is not possible to establish the actual date of the item unless it has been used and is dated, but it is possible to get an approximate date by using directories to trace the firm's period of existence and addresses which they occupied and this might provide an approximate date for it.

The following example shows very clearly the type of information that can be found on the average billhead of the late nineteenth and early twentieth centuries:

Exceldas Limited 'Filtrex' cigarettes
Regd. office and factory: 21 Albion St., Manchester
Telegrams: Nicotine-Manchester
Telephone: City 6857
Directors – M. Bakirgian   British (Armenian origin)
          M. Yegwart   Armenian (Ottoman origin)[45]

In addition to the usual information found on a billhead, some firms included their trademarks. In the example quoted above, there is useful information on the nationalities of the directors, which might be of interest to someone working on businesses run by foriegn minorities in the city.

Even today, letter and bill heads will contain useful information for the future as well as for the recipient of the item. In the case of some old established firm, the letterhead might not have changed for many years, or if it has, only slightly to correct things like telephone numbers and add post-codes. For example, the paper used by William Plant in 1975, 'Maker of Wood Blocks and Frames for Ladies' and Men's Hats. Cap Blocks. Millinery and Stretching Blocks. Steaming Ovens. Brass Table Gauges and Size Measures. Frames for Men's Tweed Hats and Children's Shapes. Helmet and Service Blocks. Men's Aluminium Press Dishes'[46], was very similar to that used in the period between the wars, except that the telephone number has been altered to give all figures and a post-code added. Other modern ones might merely give the name of the firm and the addresses of the shop and its branches. For example, the form used by Prontaprint for quotations gives the addresses of the branches of the organisation in Manchester together with their telephone numbers[47].

The information contained in the heading of bills, invoices and so on can be supplemented if the item has been used. This might result in information on the prices charged for goods and services at a clearly defined point in time and will be extremely useful to those engaged in research as accurate and detailed information of this sort is difficult to come by.

Very often billheads and invoices are to be found in archival collections rather than as individual items and as such should remain with the rest of the documentation rather than be split off to form a separate collection. Not only will they be found in the records of the firm to which they relate, but they might also appear in the material which printers keep as samples. However, individual copies do appear from time to time, usually from individuals who have discovered them tucked away. Sometimes these are donated to the library and at other times sold to dealers who will sell them through flea-markets and so forth.

Booklists

Booklists can vary in length depending on the purpose for which they were compiled. Some are extremely lengthy and as such should be regarded as minor publications, but others are extremely short. Often booklists are compiled for a specific purpose, such as to draw the attention of the public to a particular type of book that has been published or the works of a specific author or a specialist subject. Booklists can be produced by both libraries as well as publishers and bookshops. For example, Kent County Library has produced a leaflet of the publications it has for sale[48] which not only lists the various titles and their price, but also indicates at which library they can be purchased. Lincolnshire Library Service has published a list of books on Lincolnshire which indicates which are the main works on the county generally together with books on customs and folklore, agriculture and the main towns[49] and a note that the local studies library has many other items on local topics.

Although libraries produce booklists, more often than not it is a bookshop or publishing house which produces such lists. For example, Hudson's Bookshop in Birmingham produce a weekly list of new titles which includes details of the publisher, author, price and ISB number. Those produced by publishers tend to cover a specific subject field and often include a brief note on the contents of the books and the date of publication. It is not expected that libraries would retain in their local collection all book lists which have been produced, although the acquisitions department might retain them for a period of time. What is important is to try to ensure that those produced either by local bookshops or publishing houses are kept as they form part of the history of commerce in the area.

Booklists are also produced by fringe publishers and institutions which do not have a regular publishing programme. These lists often include material which is allied to the interests of the publishing organisation. For example, the Library Association issues a list of new books which its publishing side is bringing out in a given period. Another example is afforded by the Centre for Contemporary Cultural Studies at Birmingham University which issues several different lists of publications which the department or its staff have been involved with. Some of these lists are duplicated and rarely find their way into libraries. As with other booklists some may be sent to libraries in order to encourage the acquisition of the publications listed in them. Every effort should be made to ensure that copies of locally produced lists of publications emanating from a small publishing body should be kept as not only will they provide a record of the organisation's publishing activities, but also throw some light on the organisation itself and its field of interest, which might not be found elsewhere.

Bookmarks

There are many types of bookmark, some of which are purely decorative, but others are produced with the specific intention of

Newspaper billboards outside Southwood's newsagents shop, High Street, Salford, c1920 (Salford Local History Library)

publicising an event, organisation or product. For example, a bookmark, presumably issued by Stockport Public Library,[50] has on one side 'Fiction list No. 2. Historical novels and tales' together with a list of authors of such works and on the reverse there is an advertisement for the Stockport and District Trustee Savings Bank, which also includes information about the rates of interest paid on deposits, the amount of deposits in the bank and the date it was established. Often bookmarks are left on library counters for the public to pick up and use so it should be possible for library staff to ensure that examples of ones of local interest are collected and preserved for the future.

Sometimes commercial organisations issue bookmarks, especially those connected with the book trade. For example, Geoffrey Clinton's bookshop in Manchester specialised in theatrical books and has produced a bookmark which on one side advertises the shop and on the reverse an advertisement for a production of the Contact Theatre Company and details of where tickets can be purchased[51]. Another type of bookmark produced by a bookshop in Manchester consisted of an advertisement on one side and a blotter on the reverse.

Booking forms

Where an event is being organised, it is necessary to obtain bookings from either members of the organisation or from the general public. To this end booking forms are prepared and circulated either within a restricted group or more generally. Sometimes booking forms accompany literature on the event itself whilst on other occasions, the details of the event may be on the same sheet as the booking form. Although a booking form that has not been used is blank, it may contain some useful information on the type of event which is being organised such as the dates it is taking place, the venue and the cost of attending. For example, the booking form prepared for the First World Ephemera Congress[52] gives the name and address to which it is to be returned, the date of the Congress, a list of the various workshops that were to be held as well as details of the cost and hotels which would be used by those attending the gathering. A different type of booking form is that which was issued for advance booking for the 1983 Lyme Park Festival which consisted of a sheet listing the events, the dates of the various events, the price of tickets and at the very bottom, a tear off slip which could be used for booking.[53]

Broadsheets, posters and playbills

Broadsheets, posters and playbills are generally accepted as being part of the stock of a library and that they require special treatment on account of their size. Taken together, this material probably constitutes the largest single type of ephemera found in a public library. Although there are several different types of ephemera included in this grouping, namely broadsheets, posters and playbills, they all have one characteristic in common, that they are printed only on one side so that they can be displayed on a wall, hoarding or notice board without the loss of information.

Broadsheets have existed since the invention of printing and were one of the main means of communicating with the vast majority of the population, who were illiterate, until Sunday schools and compulsory education increased the level of literacy within the population, until the taxes on newspapers were removed so that their price was such that nearly everyone could afford to purchase one and until government controls over the printing press were lifted. Alice Lynes in her book *How to organise a local collection* commented that broadsheets contain 'much valuable information on many aspects of local study . . . they have been used as the principal source for some outstanding work'[54]. Broadsheets were used to publicise a wide range of information as well as give warnings to people about their behaviour. They can range from advertisements for new books to confessions of convicted criminals about to die at the scaffold, political lampoons, ballads, notices about absconded apprentices and servants, stolen goods and elections. The following are the headings of a number of broadsheets which are to be found in Manchester's Local History library and give an indication of the wide range of subjects and topics dealt with in broadsheets:

'A full, true and particular account of most barbarous ROBBERY and MURDER, Committed on the body of James Frogat, On Thursday Morning, the 5th day of September 1791'[55]

'At MANCHESTER. According to the last Regulation 1721. The POST goes out'[56]

'An Account of a most dreadful RIOT which happened at SHEFFIELD, July 27th, 1791'[57]

'Glorious news for the London Faculty! AND THE Shrewsbury Mercurial Doctor! '[58]

'To the Inhabitants of the Town and Neighbourhood of Manchester'[59]

'TEN GUINEAS BOUNTY, And a Crown to Drink his Majesty's Health'[60]

'Fifty-seven Men are Wanted to compleat the 72nd REGIMENT of FOOT or Royal Manchester Volunteers'[61]

'EXECUTION Of J. Worthington; T. Pennycuick and A.

Knight: and T. Kelly and O'Neil, lately executed for Highway Robberies'[62]

Although broadsheets as such are not produced today, they have been succeeded by the public notice, often to be seen outside local authority offices in libraries and on other public notice boards. The range of subjects covered has narrowed considerably, dealing with official matters rather than matters both official and general. Such subjects as smoke control areas, election notices, agendas for council committees and meetings and applications for planning permission in certain areas and for listed building consent, these latter are often to be found on the building affected rather than on an official notice board.

If broadsheets and official notices are taken as a general group, they can be divided into two basic groups: historic ones and contemporary ones. As the distinction implies, different methods will be required to collect the different types of broadsheet. Historic ones are either purchased, discovered or donated to the library whereas contemporary ones can be collected either as soon as they are finished with or a copy acquired at the time of issue. Most people realise the importance and value of historic broadsheets, especially the older ones, and may inform the library or record office that they have some to dispose of either by way of sale or donation. However, it is more difficult to convince the general public, as well as local authority officers and others in official positions, of the importance of ensuring that at least one copy of contemporary material is preserved, preferably in the library's files as well as in the files of the department from which the notice originated.

When historic broadsheets do appear on the market, which is not very frequently, they tend to be acquired either by collectors or by those who want to frame them and exhibit them on their walls or, if they are important enough, to be acquired by other dealers with a view to export. Such competition for this material tends to push the price up to a point where it is not possible for the librarian or archivist to afford it when acquisition budgets are restricted. However, it should not be imagined that broadsheets only turn up as individual items. Sometimes, they are to be found in scrapbooks compiled by individuals on a particular subject or area. Likewise, they may also be found amongst the specimens which jobbing printers have retained in their files or they can turn up in archive collections such as those of estates or estate agents. They can even be discovered when someone dies or when an individual, firm or organisation moves premises after a lengthy period in one place.

Historic broadsheets are not always to be found in a situation where they can be added to the stock of a library or record office without much extra work being involved or a copy having to be made. Problems are encountered with those broadsheets which have been folded and mounted in scrapbooks. When opened up, they can break into several pieces along the line of the fold. More of a problem are those which are to be found still *in situ* either on notice boards or gable ends. When the notice board is no longer in use, it might be possible to acquire it for the library or have a copy made for the library and the notice board sent to the local museum. For example, a small notice board from one of Manchester's workhouses was found during a clear out and passed on to the Local History Library. On both sides were notices relating to visiting times at the workhouse during the New Year period[63]. Fortunately, this board was small enough to be accomodated within the library, but if it had been a large one, there would have been problems of storage.

In the case of those broadsheets, and posters, which have been pasted or painted directly on brickwork, the matter is entirely different. It is not possible to take down a brick wall, brick by brick and reassemble it either in a library, record office and museum. It is, therefore, necessary for the library to resort to photography to get a copy and ensure that it is preserved for the future. Where it is not possible to get a good photographic copy, then the text and other relevant information should be copied, although the information obtained from the type of lettering used will be lost if this type of copy is made. Such notices and posters often appear when a building is being demolished and a gable wall exposed for the first time for many years.

Another source of historic broadsheets is from old photographs. A careful examination of photographs can sometimes result in the discovery of an unknown broadsheet or poster which might be a means of dating a photograph accurately. To fully exploit this source, it is often necesssary to spend a great deal of time and effort to achieve a satisfactory result. For example, there is a photograph of Smithy Door, Manchester, in the course of demolition in 1875. At the side of the building there are a number of posters which have been carefully enlarged by the library's photographer so that the majority of the text can be read. This could be said to be an extreme case, but as the photographer was interested in trying to date the photograph and its accompanying negative accurately, the detail from the broadsheets was an added bonus, but it does show what can be done with photographs in order to obtain useful information and when it is successful it can be very rewarding.

Broadsheets tend to deal with a wide range of subjects, but there are some which, because of their association with the organisation issuing them, have tended to be regarded as something slightly different. These are playbills which were displayed outside theatres and music halls to advertise the shows which were being presented at the time. Playbills, and their parallel ones for music halls and concerts, contain a great deal of information. Those relating to theatrical performances will not only give the name of the theatre and the production, but also the names of the actors and actresses and the roles they are playing, the times of performances and price of seats.

Theatre playbills will often survive where broadsheets and posters do not as they have for a long time been regarded as collector's items and consequently private collectors have built up extensive collections. Some of these collections will relate to a specific theatre or theatres in a particular town whilst others will be more general in the coverage relating to a particular actor or actress. Not only are playbills to be found in private collections, but they may also be discovered hidden away in little used rooms in theatres and cinemas when the building is either refurbished, sold or demolished. In addition, libraries have also been able to build up collections of playbills often relating to theatres in their own areas.

Playbills have changed over the years. Originally, they tended to be plain, giving the information only, but in the nineteenth century, they became more elaborate. A writer in *City Jackdaw* commented in 1879:

Playbill has hit the right nail on the head in complaining of the hideousness of our present playbills. Many persons have great pleasure in keeping their playbills, as a white stone amidst the monotony and disappointment of life. When the flimsy, yard-long lamp black playbills, which were doubtless necessary during the candle and oil lamp lighted playhouses of our forefathers, came to an end some few years back and were replaced by a neat printed, good paper one in lieu thereof, every true lover of the theatre was pleased, as they were pleasanter to look at, cleaner to handle, easier to refer to and better to keep . . . . At first, there were facts relative to actors and theatres, next came the intruding advertisements, wherein the case of the piece is of second or third rate consideration. If it be necessary to make the bill pay, at 1d each, and there must be advertisments, let a neat bill, note paper size, say about 9 inches by 6 inches, so as to be easy for reference and to keep, the cast of the plays on the first pages, the advertisements afterwards, and not as at present a monstrosity of about a foot square, and the cast in the centre, surrounded by corn solvents and surgical instrument advertisements . . . . [64]

The author goes on to complain that there is no reference to the date or the theatre on many of the playbills and says that although this information could be found in libraries, people do not have time to go and search it out.

Modern theatre playbills tend to be printed in several colours and to be eyecatching. They give the name of the theatre and the productions, the dates of the run, booking arrangements and the names of the leading actors and actresses. Not only are they to be seen outside the theatre, but in other prominent places throughout the town. To obtain copies of modern theatrical playbills, it is often possible to arrange with the theatre to keep one for the library as the theatre appears to be aware of its history and the importance of preserving information for the future.

As with broadsheets, it is sometimes possible to use photographs to obtain copies of playbills which have not survived. For example, there is a photograph[65] of the demolition of the Gentlemen's Concert Hall in Manchester in front of which there are hoardings on which are several posters including one for a production of 'New East Lynne', which is legible without the need for magnification, but if it is magnified, it is possible to discover the theatre at which the performance was taking place and the dates of performances. Unlike some playbills this one is also highly illustrated.

Posters can also be said to be a more recent form of broadsheet in that they impart information, although not official information, except in wartime. Also, it could be argued that posters are also a form of advertising as most posters are aimed at trying to persuade the public to purchase a particular product, although there are those posters which aim to put over a particular point of view, such as those which appear around election times or those pointing out the dangers of drink and driving or for a particular charity at the time of its annual appeal.

In the nineteenth century, it was often the habit to paint posters on the gable ends of walls where they could be seen by passers by and users of public transport. Consequently, some of them are high up on the building and despite their exposed position have survived remarkably well. For example, one swimwear manufacturer had a poster painted high on a gable wall which was clearly visible from the approach to Piccadilly Station, Manchester, until the building was demolished. Another one, for Zebra grate polish, was painted on the gable of a house overlooking Slade Lane Railway Junction where it could be seen by travellers. In the case of these painted posters, it is impossible to obtain the original for the library so it is necessary to obtain a photographic record of them before they disappear.

When compared with broadsheets and playbills, posters are less likely to survive either in private collections or in the collections maintained by public organisations as they do not have the appeal of the other types of material, although there is an increasing tendency for certain types to be collected. Added to this, there is also the fact that many posters are either torn down when they are replaced or pasted over with new ones, especially those which have been put up illegally on walls, fences and boarded up windows. Sometimes the art work or a photograph might survive, but with the very large ones, unless the printer or the agency keep copies, few will survive. Photography can assist in this as it is possible to photograph a wall of posters and so preserve their form. For instance, there is an excellent photograph of the Lower Mosley Street wall of the Gentlemen's Concert Hall in Manchester taken in 1896[66] which shows the wall covered in posters for such products as Chiver's jellies, Zebra grate polish, Singer sewing machines, Hartley's jams, Nestle's milk and suits at Lewis's shop. This photograph, with its many advertisements and posters of products of the 1890s has much useful information for the social historian, the graphic artist and the designer.

Some posters are highly ornate and decorative. For example, some of those produced by London Transport between 1900 and 1939 are not only highly coloured, but also very informative. One which was published advertised Golders Green and showed a new semi-detached house set in pleasant surroundings and the caption 'The soonest reached at any time. GOLDERS GREEN (Hendon and Finchley). A place of delightful prospects.'[67] Another issued in 1907 advertised the Hampstead Railway with a non-stop service from Golders Green to Charing Cross in 16 minutes.[68] The illustration was of a speeding tube train and also included the timetable for services on the line. A more recent one issued by London Transport comes from 1939 and showed a barrage balloon over London with the caption 'Cheap tickets to town. Shop between 10 and 4.'[69] In addition to information about services and where to live, some posters also gave useful information on new stations. For instance, one issued in 1913 announced the opening of a new underground station at Paddington and points out that there was a moving staircase and subway connections as well as the fact that the station would open on 1 December.[70] Many of these posters have survived because London Transport has taken a pride in them and retained examples in their archives, some of which are now on display in the London Transport Museum at Covent Garden to be admired by generations who have never seen the originals. Unfortunately too few businesses and other types of undertaking think in such terms and once an advertising poster is finished with they discard it.

Modern posters can advertise a wide range of products and events, from concerts to foods and cars. Although many appear on officially permitted hoardings, there are a great many which are fly-posted on walls and so on. Often, these relate to pop concerts and other fringe activities where cheap publicity is required. It is these miscellaneous types of poster which the library should try to get either as originals or as photographic copies as they do contain information on where tickets can be obtained from, prices charged and who is appearing as well as where the event is taking place. Often, the organisers of such events are reluctant to let an official body like a library have copies, fearing that they may be reported and prosecuted for fly-posting, but the camera can help in ensuring that at least a copy survives. One record photographer in Manchester once took one particular area and recorded not only all the fly posters, but also all the graffiti, a unique record.

Photographs of posters and notices can also be used to ensure that notices and posters in shop windows are recorded. For example, during the period when decimalisation was being introduced, many shops displayed posters in the windows which gave both decimal and pre-decimal prices. As far as many of the shops were concerned, these were one-off posters relating purely to the shop concerned. The librarian of Manchester's Local History Library decided that it would be useful if a record could be made of some of these to complement the other material on decimalisation which had been collected. As a result a photographer was commissioned to photograph shop windows showing the dual prices.

One of the easiest ways to obtain copies of posters, and other official notices, is from within the library itself. Very often, there are notices boards where posters and advertisements are displayed for public information. An arrangement for them to be passed to the local studies collection once they are no longer required can result in a substantial collection of contemporary posters and notices being acquired.

When the local authority or some other official body issues posters, it might be possible to obtain copies direct, through official channels. However, this is often more difficult than it might appear as although senior members of the staff may be agreeable for this to happen, the actual task of ensuring copies are collected together and forwarded will be passed to a junior member of staff who may not be interested in it and soon forgets to do it or is moved or leaves and no-one else is briefed to carry this on. For example, in the early 1970s, Manchester Local History Library tried to arrange with British Rail's regional office in Manchester for copies of relevant leaflets and posters to be passed to the library to ensure that the library's collection of local material on railways was as complete as possible. Initially, some material was received, but it was not long before personnel changed at

Shop ephemera, Hulme, 1939 (Daily Mail)

British Rail and no further material was received, although attempts were made to revive the arrangement. This shows the problem of trying to get this and other types of advertising material deposited in a library – the will might be there, but the effort is too much for someone who is not interested in the preservation of material.

Calendars

Although many calendars are commercially produced, there are also a great many produced to which firms add their own names as advertisement. Sometimes, the illustrations will be of local interest, but more often than not it is the additional information that is useful. In addition to the name of the firm, the calendar will often include the telephone number of the firm and an indication of the type of work that they do. Although large firms may give calendars, it is not restricted to such firms. For instance, a local decorating firm may give ones away to favoured customers and if these survive, it may be the only indication of their existence and type of work they carry out as is the case with Moran's, who are decorators in Disley and whose calendar for 1983 included information on the type of work the firm did and the telephone number of the firm. Tradesmen also give calendars to customers so that they have an easy reminder of telephone numbers and important dates. For instance, the local milkman may give his customers a calendar each year with his name, address and telephone number as well as information as to when it is necessary to order additional pints of milk.

As with many other types of ephemera, it is often the personal contact which results in the library acquiring copies for its files. Sometimes, they will be sent to the library, but on other occasions members of staff may be encouraged to bring them in once the old year has ended.

Cards

Greetings cards are not normally to be found in local collections, although a department specialising in the fine arts and art in general might build up a collection to show the various types of design or type of card which was popular at a given time. Usually, arts departments are interested in the design and the illustration rather than any details of who sent the card and why. However, a local collection may include material which has a local significance. For instance, it may keep copies of cards issued by the local authority at Christmas or those sent by local firms and organisations which contain information about the activities of the sender or those which have a local illustration on them, some of which might be commercially produced. For example, in 1980, the Christmas card issued by the Greater Manchester Museum of Science and Industry showed Olive Mount cutting on the Liverpool and Manchester Railway. Another example comes from a firm of Manchester architects which for a number of years used reproductions of drawings of prominent buildings done by the firm's founder in the nineteenth century whilst another firm of architects in 1980 used an illustration of some eighteenth century stained glass which the firm had been responsible for getting reinstated after the church in which it was housed became redundant. In both cases, the firm's name and address were in prominent places. In all examples given, Manchester Local History Library was not aware that these cards had been produced as they were privately printed for circulation to friends and clients.

Christmas and birthday cards are not the only type of card to be produced, although they are the ones which most people are familar with and which form the bulk of any card collection. There are many other types of card the most important of which for the library are those issued expressing sympathy on the death of someone. These were common in the nineteenth century and if they relate to a local dignitary, they might give a clue as to when to start looking for an obituary notice in the paper. Even ones issued for the death of ordinary people can be of assistance to the family historian.

Probably the easiest way for a collection of cards of a general nature to be built up is to ask for members of staff to bring ones in when they have finished with them. In this way, a representative collection would be built up. One would not expect a library to build up a collection of every card produced except where they are of local interest. Even with cards, it is sometimes possible to find them in unusual places. For instance, amongst rubbish in a derelict building one from the Greater Manchester Spastics Society Ltd[71] was discovered. This card not only conveyed seasonal greetings to the recipient, but was also an appeal for more funds to enable the work to be continued.

Catalogues

Most catalogues come in what can be loosely described as 'bookform' and as such do not form part of ephemera. For example, those issued by the mail order companies are substantial volumes

Election poster, 1874 (Manchester Local History Library)

which can be treated as books in their own right. However, these are rarely acquired by libraries as they do not form part of 'main stream' publishing and the companies on the whole appear reluctant to send a copy of a new catalogue to the library, as Manchester Social Sciences Library discovered when they tried to start a collection. However, some of the early twentieth century catalogues have now acquired what might be described as respectability in that they have been reprinted as has the Gamages Christmas Bazaar catalogue for 1913.[72] A collection of mail order catalogues can be extremely useful to social historians in the future as they will give an indication of the prices charged for a wide range of goods which might not be available elsewhere.

In addition to mail order catalogues, there are also those issued by the various auction rooms. Again, these tend to be in book form rather than single sheets and consequently can be treated as books rather than as ephemera. The same also applies to catalogues issued in connection with major exhibitions at art galleries and museums. For example, the catalogues issued for the Lowry exhibition in 1977[73] and the El Dorado exhibition in 1978[74] are substantial publications containing a great deal of other information in addition to the catalogue of exhibits.

Despite the existence of catalogues which can be treated as books, there are a great many other catalogues issued which can be described as ephemera. These fall into three main groupings: auction catalogues, trade catalogues and exhibition catalogues. As with other forms of ephemera, some may be printed, some may be duplicated and others merely handwritten and duplicated. Often, these catalogues are given away free to those visiting the exhibition whereas those for major exhibitions are usually sold.

Sale or auction catalogues can be divided into two groups. There are those which are prepared and issued in relation to sales at auction rooms which will list the lots that are to be sold, a brief description of the object and a note on its provenance, if it is an antique. Sometimes, there will be a rough guide to the price which the auctioneer expects the lot to fetch. (This sheet is often also to be found in the larger catalogues issued for major sales.)

The second group of sale catalogues relates to property sales. When a house is placed in the hands of an estate agent, a leaflet is prepared giving details of the property, including the size of rooms, gardens and so forth and any specific features considered worthy of note and the price. Sometimes, houses are auctioned and again, similar information is given to enable those making bids to assess the price they should bid up to.

Trade catalogues cover a wide range of material. Usually, trade catalogues are issued by wholesalers or manufacturers. Some, like mail order catalogues are large volumes, but others are simply sheets of paper relating to a particular product such as the types of locks supplied by a particular company or wholesale firm. Trade catalogues can be difficult for a library to obtain as they tend to be sent or given to those who are directly involved in the use of the product. However, it is surprising how many of these catalogues find their way into second-hand book lists. An example of such a leaflet is that produced by Hunter Penrose Ltd, 109 Farrington Road, London EC1[75] for stereotyping machinery they manufactured. Not only does the catalogue, which consists of several sheets stapled together, indicate the type of machine the firm made, but also their cost, size and the cost of packaging and despatch from London. Often, those which relate to historic periods are to be found in archival collections relating to a particular firm rather than to individual items.

Exhibition catalogues vary in size enormously. Mention has already been made of the substantial ones issued in connection with major exhibitions, but there are many more issued for smaller exhibitions in local art galleries and museums. Often, these will be duplicated sheets and may include some biographical material on the person whose work is being displayed, the titles given to the works on display and the price, if they are for sale. Of this information, it is the biographical material which is the most useful as it may be the only information about this available. For example, an exhibition at the Ginnel Gallery in Manchester of work by Elizabeth Shackleton resulted in the production of two items of ephemera. One was a printed sheet giving details of the life and work of the artist and the other was a list of the paintings together with lines written on each one by the artist herself.[76] Often this material can be picked up when an exhibition is visited. It may be that if there is a department of the library specialising in art, they will collect this type of material as well. In order to prevent duplication, it might be necessary to come to an arrangement between departments to ensure that one department has a complete collection whilst the other has an entry in the relevent index or catalogue and access to them if required by readers.

Certificates

Certificates are issued for a variety of purposes, for example, examinations, motor vehicle test certificates, stock and share certificates. In many cases, libraries may only have a few examples of such certificates although in record offices, there may be many more to be found in business or personal archive collections. There are also certificates issued in relation to shows and exhibitions, especially those held in the nineteenth century. Many companies took great pride in displaying the certificates they had been awarded at exhibitions, especially international ones. However, it is more common to come across those issued at local exhibitions and shows such as those organised by the local horticultural society. These certificates will show the name of the organising body, the name of the winner and what class it was won for and the date. It may also give the name of the secretary of the society and more rarely the date the society was founded.

Certificates awarded to individuals usually signify an achievement in some field or other, for example, certificates issued to prove how many 'O' and 'A' level examinations have been passed. The amount of information on these personal types of certificates will vary very widely. Some contain the barest information only whereas others will be very detailed. For instance, one issued by the Manchester School of Music in 1909 gives the date the school was founded and enlarged, its address, the patrons and former patrons, the principal's name as well as the subject for which the certificate was awarded, the name of the recipient, the level of pass and the date[77]. Often, this type of certificate reaches the library when someone dies and papers are being sorted out and disposed of, although individual ones may be given when people are clearing out things they no longer require.

Circulars

Many circulars take the form of advertising literature or appeal leaflets, but there are others which do not fit into either category, except by stretching definitions to their widest extent. Such items could include notices circulating in an area advising the general public of special services at the local church or by political parties wanting to keep the public informed of what they are doing or their views on a particular subject.

More often than not circulars are prepared for a specific purpose to inform the public within a limited area of a particular issue or event on which comments might be required or attendance requested. For example, a local planning department might circulate residents in a clearly defined area about a development which is felt could affect the amenities of the area or they might be circulated by an action group against a specific planning application. Sometimes, such circulars are accompanied by petitions. The main importance of such material is that it sets out the views of one side and seeks to obtain either support for that view or awareness of that view. However, it must be remembered that all issues have two sides, although only one side's view might survive. It is, therefore, important for the library to attempt to obtain copies of circulars issued by both sides so that those engaged in research in the future can make their own judgement on the rights and wrongs of an issue.

It can be difficult for libraries to obtain copies of circulars when they cover a limited area and apply to specific issues. It might be possible to encourage those involved to let the library have copies for their files by pointing out that copies of the opposing case may be found in the library's files and that in the future, there may be no record of their opposition. It is also possible to encourage members of staff to collect and bring in circulars which they receive at home.

Clippings

Newspaper clippings can be regarded as a form of ephemera although they may come from a complete work or publication, namely a newspaper or a periodical. Most libraries clip newspapers for items which are of relevance to the subject field of the library. For example, a commercial department may well clip material relating to trade, commerce and industry whilst a music department might clip reviews of concerts and other items of related interest. Likewise, in special libraries, the library or information dissemination section may clip relevant material from newspapers and circulate it to a number of people. It could be said that clipping newspapers is a form of indexing them in a more convenient form than making entries on cards and the reader having to consult the relevant volume. Additionally, clippings are more easily arranged in an order which suits the needs of the library or organisation and it is much easier to make additional copies if the demand arises.

Libraries are, however, not the only organisations to be involved in the clipping of newspapers. Individuals also do so, often concentrating on material which is of direct interest to their own personal activities. Such clippings can be found in a variety of places and can turn up in the most unlikely of places. Sometimes a person is well organised and mounts them in a scrapbook, but usually they are found in drawers, put inside programmes and even used as bookmarks or left to pile up, unsorted for many years.

Although the actual clipped article can be found in the newspaper, the full value and importance of this type of ephemera should not be underestimated. Often, clippings can provide leads to further information on the subject, particularly in the nineteenth century where newspaper indexes do not exist or have not been compiled. Newspaper clippings acquired by a library will probably be absorbed into the library's own clippings files as it makes for easier use and greater convenience.

Mention should also be made of scrapbooks of newspaper clippings which have been compiled either by previous generations of librarians or by individuals. Although they may be treated as books from the point of view of classification, cataloguing and shelving, it must be remembered that the contents are in effect ephemera. If such collections of clippings exist, the only way to fully exploit them is to index them in depth.

Commemorative items

For many years, it has been the practice to produce commemorative items for specific events, such as jubilees, centenaries, the opening of major public buildings and royal visits. Many of these items are produced in a three dimensional format such as mugs, coins, keyrings, but there are others which are on other material, for example paper and fabric. Although it could be argued that these items are the province of the museum or art gallery, some do find their way into libraries. It is important that there should be close co-operation between the various collecting agencies as those which are on fabric will require different techniques of conservation from those on paper. There should be a policy of each organisation passing on material which is more suitably housed and looked after by the other, but it is important to ensure that accurate records are kept of who has what.

Many commemorative items which have been published are available commercially and it is important to be aware of their publication. Usually, events to which they relate are well publicised and information on what is being produced is to be found either in official programmes or in the press. Some will even have the appearance of books or pamphlets, yet when fully investigated are really items of ephemera. For example, Manchester City Planning Department produced a leaflet[78] to commemorate the centenary of the opening of the Town Hall in 1877. This appears to be a booklet, but when opened up, it is a single sheet printed on both sides with a number of folds, each fold delineating a section on the building.

Compliment slips

Although the usefulness of compliment slips may appear to be

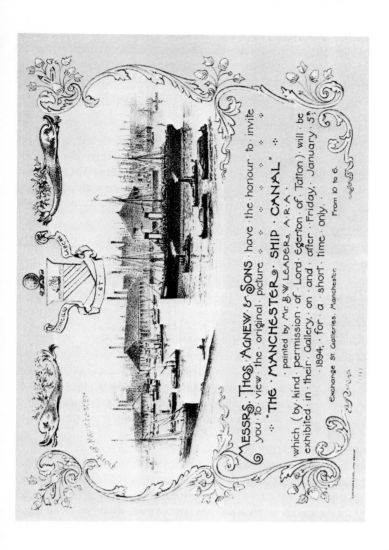

Invitation to an exhibition, 1894 (Manchester Local History Library)

limited, they are able to provide information such as the name and address of the company or organisation who sent it out. It will also contain the telephone number and possibly the department where it originated. Some of the more elaborate ones contain an illustration of the building, as that used by Manchester Central Library does, whilst others may contain the coat of arms or crest of the organisation, like that used by the Polytechnic of the South Bank.

The information contained on individual slips may be limited but if a series is held by the library and they are properly dated, it may be possible to trace changes of address, telephone number and sometimes even products from them. Individual ones may also have an interest to the graphic artist who is interested in the different styles used. It is always useful to check ones which are received in a department to ensure that local ones are kept and it might be possible to keep a set of those received which can then be passed to libraries in whose area the organisation or firm is based.

Competition entry forms

At first sight competition entry forms may not appear to be obvious items to collect, yet they do form part of the record of a company's activities and show one particular method adopted to try to promote sales or encourage the use of a particular product. Few libraries, however, collect such items, even when the company is a local one as it tends to be forgotten that they are part of the activities of that company. Sometimes, competition entry forms are to be found in the more popular type of journal which is not taken by libraries or given out in shops when a particular product is purchased or even pushed through letter boxes as part of a mass circulation programme. For example, newspaper bingo cards could fit into this latter category. The information obtained from such items includes the name of the promoting company or organisation, the prizes, what has to be done to win and the product being promoted. For example, one competition which was organised in 1983 related to sausages and the leaflet was a highly coloured one with the prizes listed on one side and what had to be done on the other.[79]

In addition to competitions organised on a national or regional scale with very attractive prizes, there are a great many local competitions, such as local rose and beauty queens. Where the competition is a local one and where there are entry forms, these should be collected as they are part of an area's history. Such forms may also give the qualifications that have to be met by entrants as well as the names of the judges and the prize for the winner. The information that is obtained from such forms may supplement the information on the actual competition in the local newspaper.

Constitutions

Constitutions are an important part of any society in that they lay down details of how the society is to be run. Although some are very lengthy, many are relatively short, taking up one page or less. Sometimes they are printed and circulated to members, but on other occasions, they are either handwritten into the minute book or a single copy exists which is available on application. If a library subscribes to a society, or a society donates material to a library the society should be persuaded to let the library have a copy of its constitution so that the records held by the library are as complete as possible.

Election literature

After broadsheets, playbills and posters, election literature is probably the most common form of ephemera that is found in libraries, particularly in local collections. Like many other types of ephemera, it can be divided into historic material and material which relates to a current election campaign. However, a further division can be made, namely into local and national elections. Irrespective of whether they are local or not, the type of material which emanates from the various political parties at election time is the same, namely posters, election addresses, handbills and poll cards. In addition, material which relates to earlier elections, particularly those of the nineteenth century, may also include political cartoons.

Although the type of material constituting election literature is very similar, the content varies from period to period. In the case of the nineteenth and early twentieth century general election campaigns, the material put out by each candidate would vary from area to area and in some cases, local issues would be stressed. However, since about 1919, there has been an increasing tendency for the same material to be issued by candidates in different parts of the country, prepared by the party's head office. The only difference will be in the candidate's name, photograph, biographical details and possibly a personal message from him. It is with local election material that some variation will exist in the information contained in the leaflet as candidates will concentrate on local issues. For example, in one area it might be the threat posed to the green belt whilst in a neighbouring ward, it might be the lack of nursery facilities or speeding traffic. The only way these local differences can be discovered is by collecting all the election literature that has been produced.

Ensuring that the library has complete coverage of all the literature produced at a modern election calls for organisation. The most obvious way is to write to the agents of each candidate explaining why the library wants copies of the candidate's election address and other material that may be issued. In many cases, this proves to be successful and can result in an extremely good coverage of the main political parties. However, experience has shown that this is not necessarily the case with the smaller parties and fringe candidates. In Manchester, writing to agents has proved to be very successful and has resulted in the acquisition not only of literature produced in English, but also in other languages where there is a large ethnic minority. Sometimes, it has been found that the local party headquarters will co-ordinate the collection of material and send it altogether.

The most difficult material to collect is that issued by the various fringe parties as they often do not have a central office and may stand in only one ward or constituency. The only way to check that there are none standing in a particular area is to check with the list of candidates posted outside the local authority offices after all nominations have been handed in and then to write either to the agent or the candidate. Frequently, such candidates will not respond to requests from libraries. In order to ensure that these fringe election leaflets are obtained, it is useful to enlist the help of the library department staff, asking them to bring in all the material they receive, for it is better to have too many copies of an item than not to have any at all. To remind staff, it is useful to send a memo round just before an election or by-election to remind people of the need to send the material in. Responses will vary from library to library, but there is usually some material which is obtained which is not acquired by any other means.

Envelopes

Many envelopes are not worth collecting as they do not contain any information other than the person to whom they are addressed, the postmark and possibly the address to return it to if undelivered. There are, however, an increasing number, produced for special occasions, which do convey additional information which may add to that already available on a particular subject or which may increase the range of material produced to commemorate some event or other. For example, when the celebrations were held for the 150th anniversary of the opening of the Liverpool and Manchester Railway, an exhibition was held at the original Manchester terminus for which special envelopes were produced bearing the ornate legend 'The Great Railway Exposition 1830–1980'. Unfortunately, there is no indication of where the exposition was being held and its exact dates, this information is a result of local knowledge and should be added either to the card used for indexing the item or on a sheet attached to it. Much more simple is one which the Townswomen's Guilds produced to make the public aware of their golden jubilee which merely states 'Townswomen's Guilds Golden Jubilee 1929–1979' in a green and red band across one corner of the envelope. Libraries should be on the look out for these special envelopes and where they are of local significance, ensure that an example is in the collection. Some may be received through the post, but it may be necessary to go out and buy others to ensure that a copy is in the collection. This particularly applies to those prepared for local events where a special cover has been prepared.

Excursion and holiday leaflets

Leaflets announcing excursions by rail, coach and air and holiday leaflets are important sources of information. Although they may be regarded as advance advertising, they can also be treated as a type of ephemera in their own right as they are very specialist in their approach and are available from clearly defined places. Such material is often to be found in railway and coach stations, bus stations and airports. It gives an indication of the places which members of the public are being encouraged to visit either for a holiday or for a day out. Some will give the time of departure, the time of arrival, return times and the cost, whereas others, where public transport is used, will give the service to use and its frequency. Where overnight accommodation is required, details of this will also be given on the leaflet.

Leaflets used for this kind of advertising tend to vary widely in size, appearance and format. Some, like those produced by British Rail in the Manchester area for their Merrymaker day excursions are single sheets with the destination and date of the trip, times of departure and return to the various stations which the train calls at, the fare and when booking opens. Others are much more elaborate like the one for the Cumbrian Mountain Express, the Cumbrian Coast Express and the White Rose in 1982 which was printed and included timetables for the journey as well as times of connecting trains and the fares and booking conditions. It also gives details of the route to be travelled and the steam locomotives to be used[80]. Those leaflets produced by bus and coach companies can be more elaborate than some of the railway ones and may often include several excursions or trips on the same

MANCHESTER SHIP CANAL.

STAND A.

TRAFFORD WHARF.

No. 133

This portion to be given up on entering the Stand.

No. 133 OFFICIAL OPENING OF THE MANCHESTER SHIP CANAL BY HER MAJESTY THE QUEEN.

MONDAY, 21ST MAY 1894.

ADMIT ONE PERSON TO STAND A, TRAFFORD WHARF

(Entrance in Trafford Road, opposite the Dock Office).

COMPLIMENTARY.

Invitations to the opening of the Manchester Ship Canal, 1894
(Manchester Local History Library)

leaflet. For example, the one produced by Cheshire County Council dealing with trips into Cheshire from Manchester using public transport names thirteen places that can be visited, gives brief details of what can be seen and how to get there either by rail or bus and the frequency of the service.[81] As with other items of ephemera, care has to be taken to ensure that new editions are acquired when they are issued. For example, the leaflet produced by Cheshire referred to above was undated originally, but a new edition issued in 1983 looked in all respects exactly the same as the previous edition except that the date 1983 was added in a corner, although it was not particularly obvious.

The most successful way to ensure that the library has a comprehensive collection of this type of material, or a representative sample at the very least, is to visit the places where this material is on display regularly and pick up a copy for the library. It might be that a member of staff travels into work regularly by train or bus and passes through the station or bus terminus and is able to pick up material on the way to or from work.

Holiday brochures and leaflets also form part of ephemera although the main brochures issued by the travel companies are minor publications. However, there are also many smaller leaflets produced by travel companies and even by local travel agents which fit the definition of ephemera. Often, this material relates to holidays of two or three days or for weekends. For example, one of the Cook's offices in Manchester arranged a five days visit to Amsterdam in conjunction with North Sea Ferries. The brochure was a single sheet folded several times giving details of date of departure, travel arrangements, accommodation and a brief note about Amsterdam itself[82].

It can be difficult to build up a collection of holiday brochures although some departments may do so as a special collection of material relating to either travel or social history. However, where the tour is organised by a local firm or there is an important local departure point, such as the local airport, attempts should be made to collect the material. Sometimes this can be achieved by visiting travel agents and collecting the material from that which they have on display.

Fixture lists

Many sports clubs publish fixture lists in a form which is easily carried about by members and other people who are interested in watching the various matches. These lists show the matches which are to be played at home and away as well as the starting time of the matches and sometimes space is left for the result to be written in. To obtain copies of such lists, it is often necessary to write to the club concerned and ask for a copy although a member of staff who is also a supporter may be prepared to give it to the library at the end of the season, which may mean that the results are also included.

On the surface, the preservation of a fixture list may appear to add little to the information which can be obtained from the local paper. However, with small local clubs, it may be the only information available without much time-consuming research. They can be extremely useful when a club is trying to establish when it was founded and no proper records remain. For instance, High Lane Cricket Club, near Stockport, has very incomplete records and there is a doubt as to whether the club was founded in 1885 or 1886. If fixture lists had been prepared and a single copy kept for each year, this problem would not have arisen. In addition to the information on the club's fixtures, there may also be advertisements for local firms, which can prove useful on their own account.

Sometimes, fixture lists appear in poster form. The aim of this format is to encourage local shops and business premises to display them so that members of the public can see when fixtures are taking place. Sometimes, local firms are encouraged to sponsor matches and for this they advertise around the list. High Lane Cricket Club is an example of one club which has done this and the additional information on the local businesses which it contains can be useful for researchers in the future, not only on the history of the club, but also on the village itself.

Gift vouchers

Many people think of gift vouchers as being issued by shops in return for a payment and then sent as presents, but there are other types of gift voucher which do have a local interest. These are those which are issued by places like garages when a certain quantity of petrol or oil has been purchased and which can be exchanged for a free gift when the requisite number of vouchers have been collected. These vouchers will give the name of the place issuing them and what they can be exchanged for. For example, one issued in 1983 by a Levenshulme garage also lists a second garage owned by the company as well as the details of when a voucher is issued[84]. The main value of this type of material lies in the fact that it shows the extent to which some companies will go to attract additional custom in a highly competitive market. As with other ephemera, probably the easiest way to obtain examples is to encourage members of staff to bring in ones which they do not want.

Guarantees and instruction sheets

It is not until the full extent of ephemera is considered is it realised that many everyday items of life do fit the definition. For instance, around every home there are guarantees for things which have been purchased as well as sheets containing either assembly or operating instructions. Although their usefulness is limited in the library context, the museum curator might find such material very useful. Not only can guarantees be displayed next to objects showing the conditions which appertained to its use, but the instruction sheet may enable him to use a machine which has long been obsolete and everyone has forgotten about its use and how to operate it.

From the researcher's point of view, this material will indicate the type of equipment found in a home and the conditions which applied to its repair free of charge within a given period of time. If libraries are given copies of this type of material which relate to local firms or products, they should be kept as there may be a demand for them in the future, especially if a local museum obtains an item and wants to work it, but is uncertain how to do so. Again it is a question of co-operation between various organisations in making the fullest use of the information that has survived.

Guides and trails

As with many items, guides and trails can vary in size. It is not the guide book that is of concern in this section, but the short items, often little more than a single sheet or a folded sheet that are produced by local churches or societies. For example, that produced by Christ Church, Moss Side[85] is a duplicated sheet giving brief details of the building whilst that to the Castlefield Visitor's Centre in Manchester is printed[86]. Some guides are published to assist people to find their way around buildings such as the one issued by Manchester Public Libraries entitled *A floor by floor guide to Manchester Central Library*[87], which lists the various departments, their fields of interest and opening hours of the departments.

Some guides, however, are more elaborate although ephemera in their format. Those produced by the Black Country Museum[88], Abbeydale Industrial Hamlet[89] and the English Tourist Board for Manchester[90] come into this catagory. Often such items are either given away free of charge or only a nominal charge is made for them. It can be difficult to discover what has been issued and what has not. It is, therefore, a question of keeping one's eyes open, not necessarily in the local area for this type of material as it is frequently available outside the area, intended for would-be visitors.

⇥✳ MENU. ✳⇤

Vins	
PUNCH	**POTAGES** Tortue Clair à la Royale
SHERRY AMONTILLADO	**POISSONS** Saumon à la Persil et Concombres Filets de Soles Frire à la Tartare
HOCK	**ENTRÉES** Vol au Vent de Ris de Veau à la Financière Chaudfroid de Cailles à la Victoria Asperges en Branche au Beurre
CHAMPAGNE BOLLINGER'S MAGNUMS AND BOTTLES, 1887 LOUISROEDERER'S CARTE BLANCHE 1884	**RELEVÉS** Quartiers d'Agneau et Salade Chapon à la Toulouse Aloyau à l'Anglaise
CLARET SMITH HAUT LAFITE	Haricots Verts aux Pommes de Terre Tomatoes Farcies Jambon d'York
—	**RÔTS** Poulet Printanier au Cresson Canetons Petits Pois à la Française
	Prawns en Pyramides
PORT DAN LEE'S	**ENTREMETS SUCRES** Gelée Madeira et Marischino Gateau de Compôte d'Abricot Crême à l'Italienne Gelée d'Oranges et Groseilles Charlotte Russe
LIQUEURS **COFFEE, &c.**	Ices
	DESSERT.

Menu for state banquet after the official opening of the Manchester Ship Canal, 1894 (Manchester Local History Library)

Trails, on the other hand, tend to be available in the locality and these are usually very simply produced so that they are easy to handle when following the route. Although many are produced by societies, a great many are published by local authorities and can be extremely difficult to trace. No-one thinks to pass a copy to the local library with the result that the library finds its has not got a copy when it needs one. For example the *Mersey Valley Walking Guide No. 1*[91] was issued by the Mersey Valley Joint Committee on which Manchester City Council is represented, but there is no copy of the guide in the library, yet it is a very useful local item and also contains information on other publications issued on the valley. Likewise, several trails produced by the Education Service of the North Western Museum of Science and Industry did not find their way into the library although some of the information was not to be found anywhere else.[92] More recently, a trail around Manchester's pillar boxes was published by the Post Office[93], but the library only discovered it from an article in the local newspaper, whilst an important one on the Ashworth and Cheesden Valleys was discovered in Wigan[94] at the railway station and appears to be one of a series on 'wayfarer walks'. In order to trace what has been produced, it is a case of educating other departments of the local authority and public corporations so that they are aware of the need to send a copy to the library. In the case of those produced by societies, this is not so much the case as often they undertake much of their research in the library and are only too keen to ensure that the library has a copy as it will mean publicity for them. Some of those produced by societies are not only useful in that they contain information about places to be seen on the walk, but may also contain information on the society itself as that produced by the Warwick Society on Warwick does.[95]

Household ephemera

Household ephemera is a very general description for the many little pieces of paper which accumulate in any household. Many form part of a person's private archive such as bank statements and bills, but there are items which are of a more general nature such as the leaflets included in gas, electricity and telephone bills encouraging people to install certain appliances or informing consumers of a change in the tariff rates. Often, this material is disposed of as soon as it arrives, but it may be of use in the future when someone is researching into the subject of, say, electricity supply and electrical appliances in the house. For example, in 1983, Norweb included a leaflet on customer care[96] whilst the Gas Board had one on the servicing of central heating systems[97]. Although the information may be limited, if it is collected and used in conjuction with other material which has been preserved, it will all help to provide a more complete picture.

Information leaflets

Leaflets are not only used for advertising purposes, but they can also be used to give information to the public. Usually, it is information of a general kind which an organisation wishes to tell the public and which they may wish to refer to at some later date. For example, on the reorganisation of local government in 1794, Tameside in Greater Manchester produced a leaflet which gave details of local government services, which authority was responsible for them, the addresses of the various district departments and their telephone numbers.[98] The aim of this leaflet was to provide residents with information on the new authority and to try and weld several small local authorities into a single unit.

Sometimes, information leaflets are produced to provide details of a specific service or activity in an area. For example in September 1983, a leaflet was produced on parking in central Manchester[99] which gave details of the various car parks, their locations and charges. These were widely distributed throughout the town so that it was easy to acquire copies for the files. Many towns produce leaflets on their attractions so that visitors have something easy to read and yet give the important information that is required. For instance, one produced for the Torbay area lists places of interest and how to get there[100] as does one produced by the Devon Association of Tourist Attractions[101].

It is, however, not only local authorities and those engaged in the tourist trade who produce such leaflets. The British Library Lending Division for example, produces a leaflet on the international photocopying services it offers and another on its services generally[102]. Others include technical information of a product for the user such as that produced by Phostrogen Ltd on chemiculture for garden use[103], which also lists other leaflets which they publish. Not all these items would be collected by a local library. For instance one would not expect a local collection to have the Phostrogen leaflet, but it may be found in a technical library or one which specialises in horticulture or agriculture.

Sometimes these public information type leaflets are in the form of a broadsheet or poster which can be displayed in a prominent location.

Where this is the case, they should be treated as posters rather than leaflets, although they are still part of ephemera.

Other leaflets containing information that may be useful to the public are produced by commercial organisations and societies. For example, there is a list of eating places in Stamford which includes information on seating capacity, opening hours, whether licensed or not, the type of meals served and includes public houses, restaurants and cafés as well as fish cafés.[104]

Organisations also produce leaflets which give advice to the public and which advise them of problems. For example, the Ashton and District Bridlepath Association has published a leaflet drawing attention to the problem of cars passing horses.[105] One produced by RoSPA relates to training for motorcycle riders and has been overstamped with the name and address of the local person responsible for organising training.[106]

Insurance certificates and policies

Although insurance policies and certificates are mainly part of a person's private collection of material, they are of some value to the local historian for they will give details of the person, property or vehicle insurance and may also give information of exclusions and the various categories of insurance. However, there are also much older policies and certificates which deal with more general matters like the one issued by the Sun Fire Office relating to insuring houses, goods, wares and merchandise from loss and damage by fire in 1752.[107] This is a document giving details of what can be insured and what cannot as well as the categories of insurance. For example 'Common insurances are buildings covered with slate, tile or lead, and built on all sides with brick or stone, and the Goods and merchandize therein, not hazardous, and where no hazardous Trades are carry'd on. Hazardous insurances are timber or plaster buildings . . . . Doubly hazardous insurances are thatch'd buildings . . . '.

Invitations

There are many types of invitation ranging from those issued for civic occasions to ones issued for parties or private views of exhibitions. Their survival and preservation is, to some extent, a matter of chance as many are thrown away once the event to which they relate has taken place. The usefulness to historians in the future will vary according to the type of invitation and the information contained on it.

Probably the least useful invitations are those which form part of household or personal ephemera, such as invitations to parties, weddings and so on. They often give little information as to the people concerned and why the party is being held except the name and address of the host, the venue of the party and its time and date. Wedding invitations contain a little more information as they will give the name of the bride and groom, the name of the bride's parents, where the ceremony is to take place and the reception afterwards. They will probably be of more use and interest to the genealogist and family historian than to the historian, although the social historian might be able to find some interesting information in the study of a large number of such invitations. Often, this type of invitation will arrive in the library as a result of a collection of personal papers being donated to the library.

Invitation to previews of exhibitions are usually a little more informative. They will give the date and time of the preview, where it is being held, the title of the exhibition, the name of the artist and the dates of the exhibition. Although the information may be minimal, particularly in the case of small commercially run galleries, it may be the only information available on an exhibition. For example, the invitation to the preview of the Shackleton exhibition at the Ginnel Gallery in Manchester also included a plan showing the location of the gallery in addition to the usual information. Other invitations to previews can take an unusual form like that for the preview of the work done in 1983 for an MA Graphic Design at Manchester Polytechnic which looked like a label from a gramophone record and was aimed at being eye-catching. In some cases, the invitation will supplement items on the exhibition like the catalogue of exhibits and biographical information on the artist.

Other invitations may be for the opening or reopening of buildings. Sometimes these are accompanied by details of the work that has been carried out and the reason for the ceremony taking place. For example, the invitation to the reopening of the former Moravian Theological College at Fairfield, Droylsden after its conversion into a Sunday school and hall in 1983 not only included tickets for the service and concert in the evening, but also for the buffet which followed and a sheet giving details of the work, amplification of the details of the afternoon's events and details of who was to open the building. Although some of this information was available elsewhere, it was the first time that the full picture had been put together in a single place.

Invitations to civic functions are important as they show the social side of local government. There are many reasons why such invitations are issued: the welcome home of a successful sports team, to provide hospitality to a visiting dignitary, to a local society celebrating a milestone in its history or the mayor's annual reception. Often, the head of the library service is invited to such functions, so it should be part of an automatic process for the invitation to be passed to the local collection after the event is over. Such invitations will often give the reason for the event being held, the name of the mayor and the date of the event. For example the invitation to the reopening of the Roman fort at Castlefield, Manchester gave the date of the event, but no time or who was performing the ceremony, whereas one issued for Founder's Day at Manchester University gave details of the venue, time and the names of those receiving honorary degrees at the ceremony.

Another sort of invitation is that issued for trade exhibitions. Often, these are not received by the library but when they are it is worth attending as there may be local material from firms which can be collected and added to the library's local collection. Usually, however, such invitations tend to go to specialist departments within a local authority, such as the architects or engineers, but it may be possible to encourage someone from that department to pick up and pass on local material. Such invitations will provide the date of the exhibition, the times it is open, who is organising it and the types of product on display. Sometimes, commercial concerns issue invitations to public lectures such as that organised by Crown Paints and entitled the Manchester Colour Lecture. The invitation to this event not only gives the necessary information to enable someone to attend, but also biographical details of the person giving the lecture, which may be more up to date than those contained in the various reference books.

In many cases, invitations can only be acquired by the library from someone who has received one. Wherever possible, an attempt should be made to collect invitations, especially civic ones, and to persuade those who attend and who are known to the library staff, to pass them on once the event is over. Although they may supply only a small amount of information, that information will be helpful in building up a picture of local life and activities.

Job specifications

As with many other items of ephemera, this type of material tends only to be acquired by chance, although firms may keep copies amongst their archives. The main value of this type of material is that it will describe the various duties assigned to a post or a job. This

PRESTWICH, *December* 8*th,* 1795.

STOLEN,

LAST NIGHT, or early THIS MORNING,

Out of a BLEACHING CROFT,

Belonging to THOMAS BRADSHAW, of PRESTWICH,

Near KERSAL MOOR,

One PIECE of

Half-ell Thickfet,

Printed and dyed Red,

Being in an unfinifhed State, about Half White,

Marked JM DT │J.B│ 2533
CR   33.

Whoever can give any Information, fo that the Offender or Offenders may be brought to Juftice, fhall, on Conviction, receive a Reward of FIVE GUINEAS, from the Society for the Profecution of Felons and Receivers of Stolen Goods, at the *Golden Lion, Deanfgate.*

All Pawnbrokers, Dyers, &c. are defired to ftop the fame, if offered to Finifh, Sell, Pawn, or otherwife.

MANCHESTER, HARROP, PRINTER.

Broadsheet, 1795 (Manchester Local History Library)

information may not be available elsewhere and will be of interest to historians in the future. It might also give the salary range and position in the structure of the firm or organisation.

Labels and wrappers

Labels and wrappers are often of more interest to the graphic artist and the museum curator as they can be visually very attractive. The graphic artist will use them to get an idea of what was done in the past whilst the museum curator may use them to liven up a display. However, they will also have an interest to the local studies librarian, especially those of a local nature. Labels and wrappers will not only give details of the contents of the packet, jar or bottle, but also the name and address of the producer, packer and the weight of the contents as well as what the contents are. In cases where the product has to be made up, instructions may also be found on the packaging. Although most will contain illustrations of the contents, some may include an illustration of the firm's premises. For example, in 1974 *The Sunday Times* published some examples of ephemera in connection with the Ephemera Society's exhibition 'Here today, gone tomorrow'[108] amongst which was a baker's wrapper from St Leonard's dating from about 1890. Not only did the wrapper give the name and address of the baker, but also details of the firm's specialities and a bird's-eye view of the pier and promenade. Sometimes, the paper used is not very substantial as witnessed by the wrapper produced for Lazzaroni's macaroons, which is like tissue paper. Even so, this contains a great deal of information on the firm, claims for the product and reproductions of medals the firm has won, which enables a small picture of the firm to be built up.

The collection of labels and wrappers is not one in which many libraries engage, not even those of local firms, yet such items may provide information which cannot be found elsewhere. Admittedly, it is not easy to collect this type of material unless the product has actually been purchased. However, it is possible that those using such labels will ensure that at least one copy remains in the company's archives for reference in the future. If no such policy exists, it is important that firms and business premises are encouraged to do so as they are part of a company's history.

Lapel flags and badges

Some lapel flags issued to those making a contribution to a street collection do contain information on the collecting organisation whereas others merely give the name of the collecting body. Increasingly, however, such labels and flags are being issued for other purposes, usually by bodies objecting to something. For example, during the Common Market referendum, the Keep Britain in Europe movement issued lapel stickers[83] whilst Nalgo has issued several relating to the threat to abolish the metropolitan county councils.

Lottery tickets, bingo cards and pools coupons

These are not the most obvious items to add to an ephemera collection and it is not envisaged that a large number would be collected. However, it is important that a sample is retained where there is a local connection. For example, those issued by the local authority or a local football club or theatre to augment their income from ticket sales or to finance a particular type of development. Sometimes, posters and notices are issued drawing the public's attention to a lottery such as that issued in 1805 for the State Lottery[109], which gives details of where the tickets could be purchased and the date of the draw. One can also include in this section promotions by petrol companies and shops where two halves of a coupon have to be matched to win.

Licences

Licences are necessary for a number of activities – driving a motorised vehicle, the right to watch television, to broadcast over citizen's band radio, to own a dog, hawk goods and so on. It is not suggested that every licence issued should ultimately find its way into the library, but a representative sample should, particularly where the fee is given. In these cases, it is useful to try to get another one whenever the fee is raised so that its rise can be traced. Although it is useful to have copies of licences issued by national bodies, such as those issued for televisions, some of the more interesting types are those issued by local authorities under powers vested in them by local byelaws, as they may contain information on the restrictions of use or give reasons why they can be rescinded. Most licences will give the name and address of the holder as well as the reason for its issue and the fee paid for it.

Membership lists

These are often compiled by societies and will give the names and addresses of members. Sometimes the list will also include the date the person joined the society. Although some lists may be published separately, they can often be found bound in with publications or printed at the back of annual reports.

Menus

Basically, there are two distinct types of menu: those produced for a special occasion and those produced by a hotel, restaurant or café for general use. Menus which are produced for special occasions often give details of why the meal is being held, where it is being held and the date of it. It may also include, additional to the details about the meal and wines to be served, information about the toasts to be drunk and who is to propose the toast and reply to it. However, some do provide additional information about the organisation arranging the dinner. For example, the menu card for the Oldham, Rochdale and District Building Trades Employers' Association Annual Dinner in 1980 also included a list of past presidents and the years they served as well as the date the body was founded. This information might be very helpful to someone working on the construction industry or trade associations as it gives a series of names which can be followed up. It can be difficult to obtain copies of menus from these functions unless the library is represented or someone who attends donates their copy to the library. Hopefully, the organisation itself will keep a copy in its archives.

On a more mundane level, it is always useful to try to obtain copies of menus from local restaurants and hotels. Such items can provide information on the choice available to those eating in the establishment as well as the price they had to pay. In some cases the owner can be persuaded to let the library have copies once they have been replaced, but in some places copies are available for people to take away with them. For example, Smithills Coaching House at Bolton had at least four different menu sheets available in July 1981, three of which gave details of the food served for each course and the price charged. There was also information on the size of the rooms available for hire and the type of special function they were prepared to hire the rooms for.[110]

Newsletters

Although some newsletters are substantial publications, there are many which are little more than two or three sheets stapled together and circulated to members to keep them informed of what is going on. For example, the newsletter issued by the Lancashire and Cheshire Antiquarian Society comes out about three times a year and is a single duplicated sheet, although on occasions it is slightly longer. As these items often build into a volume after a period of time, it may be that libraries regard them as a periodical or a serial and when there are sufficient, bind them and treat them as books. It is important that newsletters are retained, although the information contained in them may be limited, as they will show the extent of a society's activities. In many cases, where a library subscribes to a society or to its main publication, copies of the newsletter will be regularly received, but where there is no subscription paid, it may be a matter of arranging for copies to be given to the library or of offering to make a small donation in return for their receipt so that a full picture of society activity in an area can be built up.

Newspapers

Strictly speaking, newspapers do not form part of the study of ephemera as they are often much longer than three or four pages and are available from recognised sources, but there are an increasing number of free or community newspapers, some of which are only two or three pages in length and circulate in a particular locality. Every effort should be made to try to obtain copies of these free papers as they will often contain detailed information on the area where they circulate, information which might not be available in other more general papers. It can be extremely difficult to discover what is being published and its distribution pattern. It is often up to the branches to draw the attention of the local collection to such papers and try to establish a link so that copies do reach the main collection.

The established press also issue special editions of their papers, often to commemorate a particular event or the opening of the football season. Sometimes, however, special issues are produced on a subject which will attract readers and increase sales. For example, both the *Manchester Evening News* and the *Stockport Advertiser* have published supplements of photographs of their respective towns in the Victorian and Edwardian eras. Although it could be argued that this type of newspaper publication should be treated as part of the main newspaper publishing programme, they are often overlooked as they

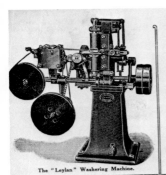

The "Leylan" Washering Machine.

LEYLAN WORKS,
PALEY PLACE,
WAKEFIELD ROAD,

TELEGRAMS:
"LEYLAN," BRADFORD.

Bradford, March 30th 1931.

FROM

Boylan & Keighley, PROPRIETOR:
W. KEIGHLEY.

ENGINEERS. ETC.

SOLE MAKERS OF

THE "LEYLAN" PATENT COMBINED
TUBE ROLLING & CUTTING MACHINE.

Your Reference JF/EL.

ER

To Messrs.John Hamilton & Sons,Ltd.Pollard Street,MANCHEST

Specialities.

"The Repeater"
Combined
Punching and
Eyeletting
Machine.

—

Boylan's Patent
Cloth Serrating
Machine
for Cutting Cloth
Patterns.

—

The "Leylan" Tag
Washering
Machine
(Power and Treadle).

—

Single and Multiple
Spindle
Ticket Drills,
for power.

—

Tube Cutting
Machines.
All Lengths and for any
Diameter.

—

Automatic
Tube Winding
Machines.

Gentm.
In reply to your favour of the 28th inst,we have
pleasure in handing you leaflet with particulars and
illustrations of our Ticket Drilling Machines.
The present price of the Single Spindle Machine is
£24/10/0.TWENTY FOUR POUNDS TEN SHILLINGS.
Less 15% for re-sale,cash at one month.
Delivery on rail Bradford.
This machine we can deliver in seven days after receipt
of order.
With respect to the Double Spindle Machine to work up to
12" centers,this would have to be of the Bridge Type,as
our standard Double Spindle Machine will only go up to
8½" centers.
The price of the Bridge Type Machine with Two Spindles
would be £37/0/0.THIRTY SEVEN POUNDS,terms and delivery
as above.
This machine would be to build and we could give delivry
in about 21 days after receipt of order.
Trusting that we may be favoured with your instructions,
we remain.
Yours faithfully.
BOYLAN & KEIGHLEY.
W.Keighley

EMPTY CASES TO BE RETURNED CARRIAGE PAID.

Letter heading, 1931 (author)

101

will not be delivered as part of the subscription paid by the library. Thus, it is necessary for someone to go out and purchase a copy or copies for the files. Fortunately, it is often very easy to know when such a publication is due as it is well advertised beforehand.

Newspaper billboards

These are the sheets of paper on which the headlines are printed and can be seen outside newspaper shops and in front of newsvendors stands. They are intended to be eye-catching to encourage the public to buy. Often they are destroyed before they can be saved although they will appear on photographs. They are interesting because they show what was considered the main story of the day. They could be used in museums to enliven displays of street scenes.

Order forms

These items are often produced in association with things that are for sale either only by post, where there is a reduced price if paid for by a certain date or where they are not easily available within shops. For example, when the Manchester Branch of the Historical Association published their teaching unit *Orphan Annie*[111] they also issued an order form on which there were details of the contents of the teaching pack, the market it was aimed at and the price to members and non-members and likewise when Manchester Education Committee published *Manchester Ballads*[112], they too issued an order form and gave details of the price, the origins of the project and where copies could be obtained from.

Order forms are not, however, restricted to publications. There are many other goods which can only be purchased by post because they are special offers. For example, during the summer of 1983, Boots were offering a furry bunny, details of which were available on a leaflet given away within the shop[113]. The main interest in this type of leaflet lies for the social historian in the future when researching into such subjects as children's toys and possibly the economic historian investigating methods of selling to the public and advertising methods.

Personal cards

Visiting cards, identity cards and business cards are another form of ephemera which might find its way into library collections. Many people have their own personal cards on which there is printed their name, address, telephone number and possibly their occupation or profession. This information might be of interest to those engaged in genealogical research as it might be information that is not available elsewhere.

Identity cards were used on a large scale during war time, but gradually disappeared with the advent of peace. However, with the need for increased security in public buildings and work in sensitive areas, they have gradually been reintroduced. Modern ones often carry a photograph of the holder, where they work and a signature whereas the older ones, issued in the Second World War carried name, address and registration number. It is difficult to collect modern ones as they are normally taken back by the organisation when a person leaves and destroyed to prevent misuse.

The third form of personal card are those used on business. Not only do they contain the name of the person who presented it, but also details of the firm represented such as address, telephone number and a brief description of its area of activity. For example: 'Period Binders. Fine and General Bookbinders Lower Bristol Road, Twerton, Bath, BA2 9ES. Tel.: (0225) 20698. Antiquarian and Secondhand Booksellers'. This card gives some information on the company and taken with other information produced, would help to build up a picture of the firm's activities. Even the card on its own informs the person looking at it that the firm is not only in the bookbinding business.

Postcards

Although most postcards are of the picture variety and as such fall outside the scope of this work, there are some which might be described as ephemera, although they may find their way into an illustrations collection. For example, the admission ticket for the Greg Mill at Styal is in the form of a postcard. One side bears a sectional drawing of the mill and validating stamp whilst the other provides space for an address and details of Styal Mill and Country Park. A similar type of thing is a postcard produced by the Gladstone Pottery Museum of a poster of John Locketts for his products in the nineteenth century. Again, it might be regarded as fitting another type of ephemera, but in the form that it is generally available, it is a postcard.

Printer's specimens

One of the most fruitful sources of ephemera is the workshops of jobbing printers. Often, such printers will keep samples of the work that they have undertaken so that potential customers can gain some idea of the standard of workmanship. The type of material that is found in such places will vary enormously, depending on what the printer has decided to keep. Whatever material is found, there will be some which is new to the library and will be worth adding to the collection although it may be the only information on the subject or firm in the collection.

Probably the easiest way to obtain such material is to visit the printer and ask if he has any samples he does not want, or if he is seeking extra space, to offer him safe storage at the library.

Alternatively, if a small printer closes down, his records may be sent to a record office or library and this can result in acquisition of the various specimens that he has retained. In some cases, the sorting of the material may be a vast, but very rewarding, task. However, when many jobbing printers close down, the material is left to gather dust and be vandalised. It may be possible to rescue some for the library, but much will probably be damaged and lost. It is advisable to seek permission before entering a building which is derelict or empty to look for material, but sometimes it is necessary to mount a rescue operation to prevent the material being sent to the local tip or incinerator.

Proclamations

In many cases, copies of proclamations are to be found in official records. Usually, this type of ephemera relates to national occasions and are issued by the monarch. Events such as the death of a member of the royal family, declarations of states of emergency, the declaration of war and accessions to the throne are dealt with in this way. With the advent of modern forms of media and increased literacy, the original objective behind proclamations has disappeared, namely that they were read at certain points throughout the town before being posted in a prominent position. It is often the posted version which has survived in libraries and other records. For example, Manchester Local History Library has a printed version of a proclamation of 1690 relating to an attempted rebellion in the area against William and Mary.[114]

Programmes

To many people, a programme is a booklet or pamphlet which

contains information on the event or activity which is being attended. Usually they are purchased in relation to theatrical performances, concerts or sporting events although in the late nineteenth century and early twentieth century, they were also issued in connection with bazaars and fêtes. Programmes can vary widely in size from a few sheets stapled together to substantial volumes containing far more information on the production or event featured. Most programmes relating to theatrical performances and concerts will give the title of the play or opera or a list of the works to be performed, the number of intervals, the venues and times of the performances, the names of the performers and background notes. In addition, there may also be advertisements for local firms, although these are usually only found in those programmes which are of more than three or four pages. Programmes issued for sports events will include the names of the teams taking part, messages from various people as well as a large number of advertisements.

The other type of programme which tends to be like a booklet is that issued in relation to bazaars and fêtes. Some can be very substantial works like that issued in November 1900 by St Gabriel's Church, Hulme, Manchester to raise funds for a new church school building and called a Grand Naval Bazaar[115]. This programme not only listed the stalls and the people who were looking after them on each day, but there were notes on which event each stall was meant to depict, the person opening the bazaar each day, a brief history of the church and school as well as many local advertisements. Copies of programmes like this are not always easy to discover as they were often discarded when finished with, although one might survive with the records of the organisation which held the event. Today, if a programme is issued for a bazaar or fête, it tends to be very much slimmer, often a printed or duplicated sheet giving a brief outline of proceedings, the name of the opener and the venue and time of opening as well as an indication of what the funds raised are to be used for. Often, such items will be on sale within local shops and it is, therefore, important to keep an eye open in local newsagents for these items.

Obtaining copies of theatrical and concert programmes can cause problems. Sometimes, managements are not keen to supply libraries with copies, but will be prepared to allow them to purchase copies. On other occasions, they are very co-operative in providing copies for the library. However, many programmes issued by professional companies and concert promoters are of the minor publication size and not ephemera. It is with the programmes produced by amateur societies that the problems arise as it is difficult to know what is being performed and where, yet what they produce is important as it throws light on the activities of people in their spare time and provides an insight into the cultural activities of an area. Such programmes are often very much smaller and flimsier than those produced by professional performances and although they contain the basic information, will contain little more. For example, the programme, which doubles as a ticket, issued for a performance of Haydn's 'The Creation' in Aylesbury in 1969 consists of a cover with an insert containing the names of the soloists, the name of the orchestra and conductor, a programme note, brief biographical notes on the soloists and future concerts. Full use is made of all the space available, including the inside cover and the end cover to get the information in[116]. To get copies of programmes issued for local events it is necessary to watch the local press carefully as they are often mentioned there and to write to the organiser asking for a copy or to encourage a member of staff who is a member of the society to bring a copy in or to purchase an additional copy if they are attending and refund the cost of that copy.

Complete runs of programmes, for both professional and amateur productions, can be an important source of information. For example, those relating to a particular theatre or dramatic society will show the changing type of play performed over a period of time. Similarly, concert programmes will show changing tastes in music over a period.

Programme cards

Societies also produce programmes of meetings and often these are published on membership cards so that the members will have a permanent reminder as to what is being held, when and where. Sometimes, such cards will also contain the names and addresses of the society's officers. For example, the programme card for the Manchester Region Industrial Archaeological Society has its programme on the inside whilst on the back there are the officers' names. Some of the more active societies produce programme cards which are more substantial and could be bound together when several years' have been received. For instance, that produced by the Manchester Literary and Philosophical Society runs to 16 pages and has stiffish covers. The Society, however, also produces a sheet listing the various meetings, their venues and dates and the members of the Council.

Sometimes, programme leaflets or cards are issued on a more general basis, especially if the organisation is a national one and is interested in attracting non-members to its meetings. For example, the Centenary of Electric Railways Committee issued its programme of meetings through various railway journals in 1979[117], which also included a list of the various societies which had joined together to form the committee.

To obtain copies of programme cards, unless the library subscribes to a particular society, it is necessary to write and ask for copies for the files, but sometimes societies anxious for publicity will send copies to be displayed within the library, so that when the session is over they can be added to stock. For example, Manchester Local History Library has about six such cards on display which are added to the library's miscellaneous collection when their currency is over. If the library subscribes to a society, it is more than likely that copies will be sent automatically.

Programmes of events

These tend to be issued for what might be described as 'one-off' occasions such as conferences or festivals. They may circulate only to those who are attending or who might attend or they may be on general distribution for the public to pick up. For instance, the programme for the British Records Association Conference in Liverpool in 1980 on 'Archives in the North West' had a restricted circulation and as well as including details of the speakers and the timetable, also included a booking form, an example of where a document is designed to serve two purposes. Not all programmes of events are brief items on one or two sheets, sometimes they are able to be classed as minor publications as is the case with the provisional programme issued for *Ephemera 80*[118] which ran to twelve pages and not only gave details of the speakers, but also elaborated on the programme and the reason why the exhibition was being held.

The more general programmes of events are those intended for the public and are often produced in association with festivals or a programme at an art gallery or museum. For instance, the programme for the Buxton Festival in 1981 consisted of a single folded sheet containing details of all the events and a few explanatory notes on one side and on the other a diary of events and booking details.[119] However, not all such items contain booking forms, many will merely give details of the events and, where booking is necessary, where it can be done. For example, the programme of events for the summer at Stamford Arts Centre[120] gives a list of events in the town and where booking can be made, as well as dates when exhibitions are being held and where.

Programme of events information can appear in many forms. Some are in booklet form, others are folded sheets whilst some are in card or

Some material on display in Kirkcaldy Museum, 1984 (Author)

postcard format. For example, one produced by Rochdale Libraries and Arts Service in November 1973, dealing with what was on in the town during the month, has a photograph of a children's procession in the town on the front with details inside of the events. It is, therefore, necessary to look for this material in a variety of formats and not expect it to be in just one or possibly two types.

Propaganda material

Although there is a great deal of propaganda material published in book form, there is also a vast amount published in leaflet form, much of it in the form of handbills which are handed out in the street or pushed through letter-boxes of homes. Some of it will be of national interest whilst other material may be of local significance. The problem is deciding what should be collected and what should not. Certainly, a representative sample of items given out in the street should be collected by every local library even if it is not of local significance to show the type of material that is being distributed in an area and the areas of concern to certain sections of the population. For instance, in 1976, leaflets were being handed out in central Manchester on the Cyprus issue. Whether any of these have survived is uncertain, but it does show that some people in Manchester were concerned about the Greek Cypriots in a partitioned Cyprus.

Sometimes, propaganda material is issued on a national scale. For instance the Friends of the Earth issued a leaflet on the threat to whales[121]. This material was supplemented by locally produced material as was the case in Birmingham where the local branch produced two duplicated leaflets on the subject[122]. These latter leaflets, although part of a national campaign, are in effect local items which should find their way into a local collection as they have been produced by a local branch of an organisation. Similarly, when CND produced a leaflet on 'The day after' and distributed it in the Foleshill area of Coventry, on the reverse side there were details of a local meeting to discuss it and information on how to join the local branch of CND.

The problem with collecting propaganda material is that some of it may run counter to the policies or beliefs of those responsible for the library. This should not, however, be allowed to prevent a local collection including material like this as it is essential if a complete picture of life in the community is to be preserved. To get this material, it is often necessary to go out of one's way to ensure that a copy is given to you in the street or, if it is delivered to one's home, to take it into the library.

Prospectuses

Usually this type of material is produced for educational establishments and courses. Many prospectuses are substantial booklets giving details of many courses, but there are also ones which relate to specific courses such as that issued by Liverpool University Institute of Extension Studies for its Diploma in Local History in which details of the course are given and its cost. In many respects, this type of material is similar to advance publicity material.

Questionnaires

Public participation in decision making, especially in the planning field, has been a feature of the 1970s and early 1980s. Numerous questionnaires have been produced and distributed within defined areas on a wide variety of subjects. When those which have been returned have been analysed, they may be destroyed and it may be that a copy of the original is not retained. The result is that when the results are published, there is no record of the questions which have been asked. It is fortunate that sometimes the report containing the results also includes a copy of the questionnaire.

It is not only local authorities which issue questionnaires. Commercial undertakings often do so in connection with market research. Sometimes these are completed in the street by someone stopping a passer-by and asking the questions. Others, however, may be sent through the post to selected people, who may or may not respond to them. Whichever method is used it can be difficult for the library to obtain a copy for its files, especially if it is being carried out on behalf of a local firm. In these cases, it is useful to try to obtain a copy as it may throw a little more light on the company's activities and be of use in the future when its history comes to be written.

The other possible method of distribution of questionnaires is to leave them for people to fill in and return. This method is used by North Sea Ferries where a questionnaire is left in each cabin for passengers to complete and return either by leaving it in the cabin or by post. One wonders whether a copy is to be found in the company's own archives or in Hull's local collection. Again, it is difficult to establish what has been produced and what has not and it is more a question of chance whether one actually reaches the library for its collection.

Ration books

Ration books are a reminder of times when there were shortages of particular commodities. In the United Kingdom, ration books are often associated with war time, although in other countries, they are issued in order to try to achieve a fair distribution of scarce commodities, usually food. The most usual type of ration book to survive are those issued during and immediately after the Second World War. Usually these turn up when someone is clearing out a house, but many were thrown away when rationing ended. More recently, in 1973 petrol rationing was contemplated during troubles in the Middle East and ration books actually issued. Even these are now beginning to appear on the market as collectable items.

The usefulness of ration books lies in the fact that they illustrate the type of goods which were rationed and how much people were entitled to each week, although the actual physical quantities were not often given. For example, a ration book issued in 1953–4 covered such commodities as sugar, bacon, cheese, fats, eggs, meat and sweets, although not all were in use at this time. It will also indicate which retailer the person used, the retailer's address and instructions for use as well as the name and address of the person to whom the ration book belonged.

Recipes

Recipes, particularly local ones, tend to be published in book form, but some do appear on broadsheets or packets and wrappers. For instance, Manchester Local History Library has a broadsheet dating from 1812 which lists six different rice dishes. The main value is to show the type of diet which people were being recommended or suggested. Sometimes, these items will give an interesting side-light on the type of person the recipe is intended for. The rice broadsheet in Manchester says that it is recommended 'to the cottager; who is desired to consider, whether FOUR POUNDS OF DRESSED RICE, which will cost him less than ONE POUND OF BREAD, will not fill his children's bellies better, and do them more good'.[123]

Reports

Although many reports are lengthy documents, there are others which are much shorter in format. For example, ADCEMP's interim report is only four pages long and is really an item of ephemera in its own right. It is often the shorter reports which get overlooked as they do not receive the same amount of publicity as the larger ones. Some companies also produce their annual report and statement of accounts in a form which is similar to an item of ephemera. For example, the Rochdale Canal Company in the 1930s produced its annual report and accounts in this format. Basically, it was a folded foolscap sheet on one side of which there were details of when the annual meeting was to be held and where, the list of directors and any alterations to the board and inside, the year's accounts. Usually such items are to be found with the company's official records, but sometimes, individual shareholders might receive them and retain them. If individual copies do reach the library, they should be placed with any other material on the company, especially if the library or record office have the company's records.

Rent books

Although rent books may be regarded as items of personal ephemera, they can also be found as individual items within a library or record office. Usually those which are found in such places have been completed and are no longer valid and as such will give a little information on the rent which was payable for a certain property at a given point in time. If there is a run of them for a number of years, it is possible to trace the rise of the rent over that period. They may also contain information on the conditions appertaining to the lease and the amount of notice required to terminate it.

Rules and rule books

Rules are essential for the smooth running of all aspects of life, whether of a factory, railway or park. Rules and rule books appear in many formats and in many sizes. Some, like those for railways will run into several hundred pages and as such are minor publications. There are, however, others which are less complex and may appear either as duplicated sheets or extracts from them are issued in a form that enables them to be displayed. For example, in many cotton mills it was common to see extracts from the 'Cotton cloth factory regulations, 1929' displayed in a prominent position. In addition to the various regulations that were given, there were also humidity tables, which theoretically enabled both employer and employee to know what conditions were regarded as unhealthy to work in.

Local authorities will tend to issue extracts from the byelaws as notices and posters. For example, it is common to see the relevant extracts relating to parks posted up at the entrance together with the level of fine imposed for infringing the byelaws. These are updated from time to time and if a set covering a period is obtained, it will show the changing value of money as the level of fine increases. They will also indicate changing social habits. For example, in the 1970s when skate-boarding was a craze sweeping the country, many authorities issued new byelaws banning such activities in public places.

It can be difficult to obtain copies of rules as they tend to have a restricted circulation. Sometimes, organisations will donate copies of current rules and superseded ones to the library, but they also appear in second-hand bookshops and even junk shops where people specialise in house clearance and realise that such material will have a small value.

Score cards

Score cards are usually issued to people playing a game either on their own or with someone else. Although the actual score might not be of interest to anyone other than those playing, the cards often contain the rules of the game and may even contain advertisements for local firms. For example, one issued by the Park House Putting Course in Weston-super-Mare in 1982 included the rules on one side and an advertisement for road runners on the other[124].

Service sheets

Religious institutions are the producers of many different types of ephemera. In addition to parish magazines, which could be called minor publications, there are notices listing the week's services, notices for meetings and social events, and special service sheets produced for a specific service when there will be a large congregation or when the congregation is not familiar with the hymn and prayerbook used. The type of special service sheet most people come into contact with are those for christenings, weddings and funerals. Of these, only the one for the wedding may be specially prepared and printed, usually by the couple getting married, and will include the name of the couple, the name of the church and time of the ceremony and the hymns to be sung. The others tend to be printed by the church for the convenience of those attending.

Other special service sheets do exist which have a more general application. For example, the dedication of a new window or piece of furniture or Remembrance Sunday may require a special service sheet to be produced. Usually such sheets will include the date of the service and the reason why it is being held, the hymns to be sung, the lessons to be read, prayers and order of events. A good example of this type of special service sheet is the one produced for the thanksgiving service at St Philip with St Stephen, Salford after its restoration. This sheet contained all the aforementioned, but also gave the cost of the work, the name of the architect, the contractors and grant-giving bodies. Sometimes, details of the work are included as they were in the sheet produced for the installation of the Peckett window in St Ann's Church, Manchester where the history of the glass was given.

It can be difficult to obtain copies of such sheets unless a person is a regular attender at the church concerned. Sometimes copies are placed in the church's own records, but in many cases, the spare copies are disposed of after a few years.

Soceity ephemera

As well as churches, societies also produce much material that is ephemera. It does not matter whether these are professional societies or bodies, or societies for people's individual interests and hobbies. Mention has already been made of membership cards, programme cards and newsletters which are issued to members and which tend to be discarded after their validity or usefulness has passed. Some of this material might reach the society's records, but often no-one thinks about this until it is too late. However, in addition to the usual material, many societies also produce what one might call background material and provide information which is not obtainable elsewhere. For example, a leaflet[125] issued by the Special Interest on Ageing, which is part of the British Association of Social Workers, explains why the group exists and its objectives. In addition, there is information on its recent conferences and the areas where the committee has been active. Although it is only a small item, it does provide useful information on the group and its activities which the members might not appreciate for they have no copies of earlier leaflets in their records.

A more imposing type of society leaflet is that produced by the British Association of Social Workers as its recruitment material. This consists of a folded sheet, with application form for membership, a list of publications, policy documents and objectives as well as a message from the chairman, conditions for membership and its address. Again, a useful document, but it is doubtful whether any library has been able to obtain a copy let alone preserve one to be consulted by a member of the general public in the future.

The production of background material is not confined to professional bodies. Some societies also do this type of publicity work. For example, the Peterborough Mediaeval Society has published a leaflet explaining when it was formed and its objectives and how it can be booked for events[126]. Similar leaflets have been produced by the

17   Commerical ephemera, 1983 (Author)

Manchester Arts Society[127] and the Lancashire and Cheshire Anti-quarian Society[128]. Societies also produce posters to advertise their activities which could also be said to form part of a society's collection of material. These will be displayed in libraries and discarded when finished with, without a second thought being given to their permanent preservation even if they are of local interest. These posters can be informative and give the name and address of a member of the society to contact if someone is interested in joining. For example, in 1982 a very attractive poster was issued for the final public day-excursion of the T. S. S. Manxman which included attractions of the trip, where bookings could be made and a drawing of the ship as well as the information that there was a Manxman Steamer Society[129].

Stamps

Stamps have long been collected by those interested in them. Although they might not be regarded as ephemera, they do fit the definition in all ways. It is, however, rare for a local collection to include stamps in its ephemera collection unless there is some local significance in them. However, an arts library might collect special issues as examples of art.

Stocklists

Stocklists can be useful sources of information as to what a particular shop or factory has available to offer to potential customers. Sometimes they will also contain the price of the product whilst other lists may contain illustrations of the products. For example, Plant's hat block works in Manchester produced at least two lists of the products it had in stock entitled 'Exclusive millinery shapes' and 'Latest millinery shapes'[130]. As with many other examples of ephemera produced by industry and commerce, stocklists are usually to be found amongst the records of the company rather than in general circulation, although there are copies which are sent to potential customers and which find their way either onto the market or into the library as a donation.

Subscription lists

Subscription lists are much rarer today than they were in the nineteenth century. They were compiled for numerous purposes where members of the public were being asked to contribute to a cause, such as a statue of the Queen or some local dignitary, or for a new publication or a new public building. Often such lists will give the name and address of the subscriber and in the case of those making substantial donations, the amount donated. Today, although members of the public are asked to donate to such projects, the publication of separate subscription lists is not common and if they are published, are usually incorportated in a publication of some kind.

Telegrams

Telegrams and telex messages are forms of ephemera which should be collected as they may contain information that is not available elsewhere or it may be the original message relating to some major event. Although the information on such items may be very brief, it will give the bare bones on which news stories are based.

Tickets and admission cards

Tickets and admission cards are an every day part of life. To travel by bus, rail, air or sea requires the issue of a ticket as also does the parking of a car in a car park. Tickets are amongst the items of ephemera which the general public come into contact with most frequently and are usually discarded when the journey is completed. Even if the ticket is kept by the user, it is normally only a portion of it. For example, theatre tickets are normally torn in half and one portion returned to the purchaser when the seat is taken. Railway tickets, on the other hand, are normally collected at the end of the journey, although with the increase in unmanned stations, there is an increased possibility that travellers will leave the station with part of the ticket in their pockets, although it may have been clipped by the guard or ticket inspector during the course of the journey.

Tickets are to be found in many shapes and sizes and even those issued by the same organisation can vary widely. Railway tickets, for instance, can vary from computer-printed tickets to ones which are printed when there is a demand for special ones, such as awayday excursions. With railway tickets, there is no carbon copy for the traveller to retain, but with airline and sea crossing there is often a carbon made, which is retained by the traveller. This, incidentally, also applies to railway journeys on the continent when the ticket is purchased in England.

What information can be obtained from tickets and admission

cards? In the case of those issued for railway journeys, it will give the starting point of the journey, the destination, the class the traveller is entitled to use, the date the journey commenced, the period of validity and the fare paid. Wherever possible, the library should try to obtain copies of some local tickets as they do provide information on the fare between two places as this is often not easily available elsewhere. If the library is fortunate enough to have a series covering the journey between two stations and spanning a period of time, it might be possible to trace how the fares rose. For example, Manchester Local History Library has a collection of season tickets for the journey from Heald Green to Manchester covering a span of four or five years and these clearly show how the fares rose in the early 1970s.

Bus tickets, on the other hand, are not so informative. They will indicate the fare that has been paid, the stage the journey commenced and perhaps the route, but it is not possible, except on long distance coach journeys, to identify between which two points the journey was made.

Airline and sea crossing tickets will provide details of the flight or crossing, the fare, the names of the passengers and possibly the flight number or time of departure. As with many other tickets, travellers tend to discard them once they have been used. However, it is always a good idea to try to get one or two samples relating to the local airport or seaport from people who have used the facilities so that there is an example available for the future.

Theatre and concert tickets will survive as half is returned to the person attending the performance. Although many people throw them away when they get home, some do survive, often tucked inside programmes. Theatre tickets will provide information on the name of the theatre, the date of the performance attended and the time of curtain up, the name of the production is sometimes given, the seat number and the price paid. This information may appear to be insignificant on its own, but if it is used in conjunction with programmes and playbills, it can provide additional information which is not available elsewhere. With some amateur productions, the ticket may be the only information which survives to show it actually took place. Sometimes, where a special performance is held, the reason for this might be printed on the ticket together with the conditions of sale appertaining to the ticket. For example, in 1983, Michael Roll gave a recital in Manchester in aid of the Manchester Jewish Museum and this was printed on the face of the ticket together with all the other information.

Another sort of ticket is that issued for car parks. This will tell you who runs the car park, the date the ticket was issued, the price paid and the time of arrival. Sometimes, on the reverse, there are advertisements. For example, one issued in the car park at Wilmslow in Cheshire shows that the car park was administered by Macclesfield Borough Council and on the reverse is an advertisement for Moss Rose Motors at Macclesfield. As with other tickets, possibly only one from each car park might be enough to collect, although if it is noticed that the advertisement has changed or the information on the front is different, then a second example should be acquired.

Admission tickets to places like historic houses and national monuments also form part of ephemera. Some of these are more informative than others. For example, the one for the Greg Mill at Styal includes a cross section of the building. That issued at the Gladstone Pottery Museum has a view of the works in which the museum is situated on one side together with details about what can be seen. On the reverse side there are details about opening times, party books and facilities. Often, the only way to acquire this type of admission ticket is to actually visit the place itself.

Tickets are not only collected by libraries, record offices and museums, but also by private collectors. Railway tickets are a good example of this and hence it might be difficult to obtain copies of older ones, but it should not be so difficult with the more recent ones and those currently being used. The researcher may use tickets to fill in the detail which is not to be found elsewhere although those engaged in research for documentary productions for television may also find them valuable in ensuring that the props used are accurate for the period.

Timetables

Timetables come in many shapes and sizes. In the case of railway timetables, there is the large national volume, but there has been a trend recently to issue small timetable cards for specific lines or routes, such as London to Manchester or the local services between Plymouth, Torbay and Exeter. These timetables are designed to fit into someone's wallet and give the details of the principal services and the dates of the validity of the timetable. Similarly, bus and airline companies also issue timetables either for specific routes or from a particular airport.

To obtain copies of timetables, particularly the smaller type which are designed to fit into the pocket, it is often easiest if someone from the staff visits railway and coach stations regularly as well as local travel agents as the material is displayed for members of the public to pick up and take away. The important thing to remember is that most timetables change at least once a year so that visits should be made on a regular basis as there is often other material on display which will be suitable to add to an ephemera collection.

Railway leaflets and timetables (Author)

Trade literature

Although trade literature may be part of advertising, it is material which is designed to have a limited circulation, normally only to those who might be interested in using the product. Often, there is factual as well as technical information included which enables the person using the literature to decide whether the product is suitable for the purpose for which it is required or not. Sometimes, the material is more general in its approach. For example, the leaflet produced by Cheshire Reclaimed Building Materials Ltd[131] is more advertising than trade literature, but it does give the basic information on the type of brick that it has in stock and the sizes. As with much of this material, it is sent only to particular groups of people and it is necessary either to persuade the company, if it is local, that it would be a good idea if the library had some information on its files to preserve for the future or to get someone who receives it to pass it over when they have finished with it.

Wage slips

Wage slips are personal documents, but can be very useful for researchers if examples can be acquired as they will give the take home pay of a person as well as the gross pay and various deductions. It will not tell you how the money was spent, but can provide additional information to that which has been obtained from other sources. Usually such material is to be found in a person's private documents.

Window bills

These are items which might be specially produced for a shop giving details of special offers or goods available during a sale. Often, they are one-off items and the only way that a record can be obtained, unless the shopkeeper is prepared to keep them once they have been taken down, is to photograph a selection and add it to the collection of posters.

Conclusion

It can be seen that there are a great many different types of material which go to make up ephemera. Some types have different varieties, but the use that can be made of them is the same. As has been said, the

9

most successful way to discover the range of ephemera is to look through the material housed in the library or in books like those by Anderson[132] and Lewis[133], which have many illustrations of the wide range of material that constitutes ephemera.

4

The collection of ephemera

Introduction

Having indicated the various types of ephemera that can exist either in public collections, official records or personal records, it is important that the problems associated with the collection of this material and its preservation for the future by libraries, record offices and museums is investigated. It will be obvious from the types of material mentioned in the preceding chapter and in the Appendix, that ephemera is all around, although much of it is not called by that name and it may not always be collected together to form an ephemera or miscellaneous material collection.

Where a collection of ephemera exists, it is not necessary for the owning body to pursue an active policy of enhancing the collection, but merely to rely on donations and accidental acquisition of material rather than spend time and money on making new acquisitions of historic or contemporary material. Other bodies may be selective in what they collect. For example, there is one library which reportedly receives copies of all theatre playbills and cinema posters, but since it is only interested in the theatre, the material relating to the cinema is discarded, presumably without a thought being given to future usefulness, the basis of the decision being that it has not been collected in the past and therefore will not be collected in the present. However, there are many libraries, particularly in local studies departments, which do pursue an active policy of increasing their holdings of ephemera, irrespective of whether it is historic or contemporary and preserving it for the future.

If a conscious decision is made to collect ephemera, there are certain problems to be resolved which arise from the nature of the material that is being collected. Ephemera is to be found in a variety of formats, shapes and sizes, published by and obtainable from a variety of sources, many of which are obscure. Irrespective of the size, format and origin, there are three factors which relate to all forms of ephemera.

Firstly, there is the difficulty in tracing, collecting, classifying, cataloguing and storing the material. Pemberton commented that 'There is no doubt that the collection of ephemera requires different techniques from those associated with the acquisition of conventional library material'.[1] Secondly, there is the fact that it is almost impossible to provide a comprehensive collection of material due to the lack of information on what has been published and where it is obtainable from. Finally, there are the problems associated with the need to make it easily accessible to potential users whilst at the same

Some local authority ephemera relating to a particular area

time providing adequate security to prevent loss through theft and pilferage.

The first and last of these problems are ones which face any organisation with ephemera, irrespective of whether the collection is being added to or where it is one which is virtually static with new material being added only infrequently. The second problem is one which faces any collector of ephemera, irrespective of whether it is historic or contemporary, public or private, but which is more serious in the public collecting sector. Decisions on cataloguing, classification, storage and conservation have to be taken at an early stage, otherwise problems can arise with the material, once acquired, being left unsorted and therefore unusable for some time. If this occurs, the problems are compounded by the amount that has accumulated.

Before this stage is reached, however, a conscious decision will have been taken to collect ephemera and as to whether the collection will be comprehensive or representative and on the subject area to be covered. Where a collection relates to a specific field or subject, it is probably easier to build up a relatively comprehensive collection than if the collection aims to cover a large subject area. For example, it would be easier for a library specialising in theatre to achieve a greater degree of comprehensiveness on a local scale than on a national level. The wider the subject field, the less comprehensive the collection will be in its scope and content.

This chapter will look, in general terms, at the methods that can be used to acquire ephemera for the library, record office or museum. It will also consider the question of comprehensiveness and which is the most satisfactory collection – a comprehensive one or one which is purely representative of the type of material that might be found on a subject.

Comprehensive or representative?

The extent to which a collection of ephemera is comprehensive is to some extent governed by the fact that such a vast amount of ephemera is produced that no-one knows for certain exactly what is being published, by whom and for what purpose. Although attempts have been made to quantify the amount of ephemera produced, most notably by Alan Clinton[2], no satisfactory answer has been reached. Clinton looked at specific subject areas, but difficulties exist in trying to draw parallels between them as each organisation produces different types of ephemera, for different purposes, circulates it in a variety of ways and retains it for different reasons. In addition, there is a great difference between a special library or organisation collecting material within a limited subject field and the collecting policy of a library or museum or record office, whose fields of interest are much wider. What the survey did, however, indicate was the type of material which might reasonably be expected to be found in existing collections associated with the bodies he looked at and provide, as a result, a clue to the type of material which other collecting agencies might expect to find and to look out for. Although librarians and others like to compartmentalise things, ephemera belongs to that type of material which it is difficult to put into separate, clearly identified categories.

The survival rate of ephemera must affect the comprehensiveness of any collection of this type of material. To many people, the material described by the librarian, archivist or museum curator as ephemera and having an 'interest value' as opposed to a 'monetary value', is purely rubbish to be thrown away as soon as it is received or finished with. For example, many people throw out election literature as soon as it is received and the same applies to much of the unsolicited mail that is received from organisations like the *Readers' Digest*. On the other hand, a leaflet giving the name and telephone number of a new plumber in the area might be retained a little longer just in case one is needed in an emergency. Other items, however, may be retained for much longer periods. For example, guarantees, instructions on how to use equipment, receipts for bills or receipted bills may be retained for several years, but sooner or later these too will be discarded when someone has a clear out. Even in the commercial and industrial field, paper more than seven-years-old is very likely to be thrown away unless there is a legal obligation to keep it longer. Advertising literature is probably discarded by the average person very quickly. Leaflets thrust into a person's hand in the street are more than likely to be thrown into the nearest waste-paper bin or stuffed into a pocket or bag until the person returns to the office or home and to be discarded then. There is often little thought given for the archival or historical importance of an item that has been thrown out until it is too late. Often, when a history comes to be written or something requires a piece of quick research, it is realised that the piece of paper discarded many months before might have been of assistance. Pemberton quotes several examples of material that have been rescued in the nick of time from destruction[3].

It has to be accepted that it is virtually impossible for a third party to build up a complete, comprehensive collection of ephemera relating to a specific subject, organisation or area if there is no accurate information on what has been or is being produced. Dorothy McCulla in her paper to the original meeting on ephemera in 1975 commented that its collection 'depended on constant alertness and a readiness to go when required to fetch such material'[4] whilst Pemberton acknowledged that 'the collection of ephemera does . . . pose special problems even for the most highly organised library'.[5] As often as not, even the originating body will not keep a complete set of everything that it has produced in non-book form. Even where a conscious effort is made to try and keep a copy of everything, invariably some items will escape the net. It is only in the very smallest of organisations, where material passes through relatively few hands, that effective control can be exercised and material collected together. The more people there are involved in handling the material or producing it, the less chance there is of everything being kept because there will always be the one person who does not see the point of keeping something and filing it away with no apparent use in the foreseeable future. Even with the smallest organisation, the person responsible for the task of maintaining the archive may forget to add something and allow it to be destroyed, thus creating a gap in the record.

The inability of a third person to build up a comprehensive collection of material on a subject is made more difficult by the fact that there is no way of knowing what has been produced and where it can be obtained from. The means of production, distribution and the market for which it is intended vary so much that is is humanly impossible to get a complete picture of the situation. An individual printer or publisher may succeed in having a comprehensive collection of material that he has printed or published, but for a library, record office or museum, this is not possible to achieve.

The situation is further complicated by the fact that some organisations are very reluctant to allow copies of their material to be taken or even acquired by libraries and preserved, on the grounds that they are an arm of the 'establishment' with whom they may be in conflict. It can take much time and patience together with careful explanation of the functions of a library, and in particular a local studies library, to persuade them that they ought to consider letting the library have a copy and that it is not going to be handed over to the 'establishment' to be used against them. Likewise, there may be political pressure from certain quarters to prevent some material being taken, although it is of local interest. In these cases, it is a matter of convincing those involved that the library concerned with collecting local material has to collect everything and that the judges of its value will be those engaged in research in the future and not those of the present generation.

In addition to the basic problem of collecting the material once its existence is known about, there is the question of quantity. If a library, record office or museum was to obtain a copy of every item of ephemera that was produced and in which it had an interest, storage would become a serious problem, despite the fact that individual items may be very slim and not take up much space. However, it does not take long for the number of items to mount up and fill first a filing box and later a filing cabinet or other form of storage unit. If this problem did arise, it is possible to overcome it either by storing material outside the main library, which can become expensive, or by microfilming it and storing it away from the building or microfilming and discarding or sending it to a central storage point.

The decision as to whether the collection is to be comprehensive or representative is one which must be very carefully considered and must take into account the type of material that will form the basis of the collection as well as the subject field to be collected. In the case of a collecting body specialising in a particular subject or topic, such as the material produced by a firm or by the parent body, the decision is much easier to take, for in these cases comprehensiveness must be the objective. In the case of libraries and record offices, whose interests tend to be much wider, the decision on which type of collection to build up is much more difficult. The person who makes the final decision must bear in mind that no collection is going to be completely comprehensive due to the problems outlined earlier. He must also consider the type of user handling the material, their demands for specific types of material as well as the function of the library, department or section. For example, if it is a local studies library, one would expect the material to be collected to be related to the area for which that library or department was responsible or interested in and not material on an area twenty miles away, outside the local authority's area. Whatever collecting policy is adopted by the library, it must be remembered that the material which reaches the library is only going to be a small proportion of what is actually produced. By collecting only a representative sample, the librarian or archivist could be open to criticism that he or she is acting as a censor, deciding in advance what is going to be of interest and value to future researchers. Unfortunately, no-one is able to foresee what subjects are going to be 'in vogue' in the future. For example, there was hardly any indication at the beginning of the twentieth century that social and economic history were going to play such an important part in historical studies in the latter part of the twentieth century or that local historians and others were going to turn their attention to studying the 'man-in-the-street' rather than the landed gentry and the established church. This movement is very obvious in local history publications such as the Victoria County History series, started in the late nineteenth century, when the earlier volumes are compared with the most recent local history publications. It is not the job of the librarian, archivist or museum curator to act as censor and decide what is going to be used and what will be ignored in the future, that is the task of historians and others engaged in research.

Bearing in mind the difficulties of obtaining a copy of every item of ephemera that might be produced and that some items will be individual or personal copies, such as railway and bus tickets, it is to be recommended that libraries, record offices and museums aim to be as comprehensive as possible within their chosen field and leave the difficult task of deciding what is important and what is not to those using the material in the future. In the case of special libraries, where the parent body has an established field of interest, the same should apply, even if some of the material does not represent the views of the parent body. It could be argued in these cases that it is good policy to have copies of everything so that a full picture can be obtained.

The most sensible course of action for librarians, archivists and museum curators to take is to establish the parameters of their collections and having done this, to pursue a policy of collecting as much as possible within the limits that have been set, using all the means at their disposal. Material should be collected that represents all points of view, not purely that of the parent body or controlling interest or that of the librarian. It could be argued that such a policy will result in an enormous collection of material that will completely overwhelm the collecting organisation's staff when it comes to be dealt with. However, the size of the collection will to some extent be limited by the fact that it is impossible to collect everything, even on the most limited of subject fields. Even when comprehensiveness is sought, there will be certain types of material which will only be representative. For instance, one would not expect to find every railway ticket issued, but merely an example of the types that have been produced for local journeys and ones for the same journey at different fare levels. The same will apply to theatre tickets where ones for different productions and possibly evening and matinee, weekend and mid-week performances may be collected.

A collection of ephemera which is representative will only have examples of the different types of material that exist. It is, therefore, necessary to decide which items to retain and which to discard. By doing this, no attention is being paid to the use of the materials or the information it contains. It might be that a school library or a museum or college library might build up a representative collection not for research purposes, but to show the type of material which is often overlooked or which existed at a specific point in time. If the library were to establish a collection of material to be representative of the type of collections and material it had, duplicates from the main collection might be used. Similarly, if they decided to have a collection showing the material for one year, this might be representative rather than comprehensive. Representative collections are useful as teaching aids rather than as collections for permanent preservation and research as they can be changed regularly and if damaged, provided a copy is made, easily be replaced.

The final decision as to the type of collection that is built up is one which must be taken by the person responsible for the department where the collection is housed. Comprehensiveness should be the ultimate aim as the nature of the material will ensure that it is representative. If a representative collection is wanted, it should be for information purposes as to the type of material which constitutes ephemera and should not include original material where there is no additional copy in the collection. With comprehensiveness, it ensures that the difficult decision on what to keep and what to discard is one which the librarian does not have to take. The presumption should, therefore, be in favour of attempting to create a collection that is as comprehensive as far as this is possible.

Dating of ephemera

When an item is received by the library, record office or museum, it is important that a date is given to it if it does not already have one. This is particularly important for contemporary ephemera as much of it appears to be undated, or if it is dated then it is only in an obscure manner. For instance, out of 23 items picked up in Manchester at an exhibition, only five had dates which were obvious, another two had obscure dates hidden in the printer's reference and the remainder had no indication of the date they were published or the period to which they related. Even with older material, it is important to try to establish a date for the item or to check the date if it has been written on the document. For example, there is one broadsheet in Manchester Local History Library entitled 'Curtius's Grand Cabinet of Curiosities'[6] which has on the bottom the manuscript date '1791'. In 1969 Mrs Chapman from the records and archives section of Madame Tussaud's wrote to the library to say that she had been able to establish a more accurate date for the item, namely 1796. The letter was ultimately kept with the broadsheet so that anyone who consulted the item had the additional information to hand as well.

Historic and contemporary ephemera

Although there are many different types of ephemera, for the purposes of establishing and building up a collection, there are two broad categories into which all ephemera can be divided. Firstly, there are those items which could be defined as 'historic', that is, items which relate to events or activities which have passed. These items will have an historical, social and record purpose and include such items as broadsheets, tickets where the journey has been completed, timetables whose currency has expired, invitations and programmes. The second category consists of those items which are still current and

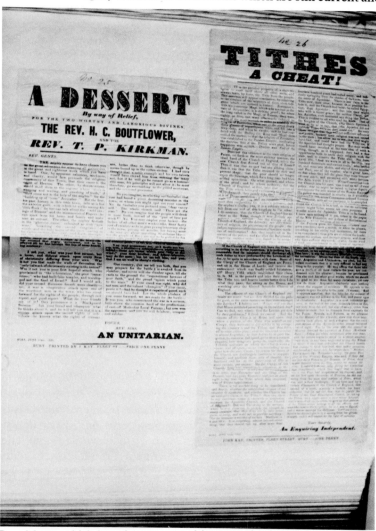

Broadsheets which have been mounted in a scrapbook and folded (Manchester Local History Library)

which are being produced at the present time relating to events yet to occur. These items could be called 'current' or 'contemporary' ephemera and include such items as tickets whilst the journey is being undertaken, tickets purchased in advance of attending an event or making a journey, technical information, guarantees before the expiry date, sales brochures and posters relating to current events. It is possible to find the same type of material in both groups as current ephemera will ultimately become historic ephemera. For example, a railway ticket becomes an historic item once the journey is complete, an invitation becomes an historic item after the event has taken place and a leaflet ceases to be current once the events advertised on it have taken place. Some items, such as technical literature and advertising material, may remain current for a considerable period of time after the machinery to which it relates ceases to be produced as there will be machinery in use for a considerable period of time afterwards and likewise, goods will be sold at the old price or at sale price.

There is a third group of ephemera which exists, which could be regarded as a subgroup of either of the main groups. This is the material which is specifically produced for the collector or for teaching purposes. For example, the various wall charts on buildings published for European Architectural Heritage Year in 1975 were intended as much for the collector as to provide information. Cigarette cards are also a good example of this type of material as when they were included in cigarette packets, it was intended to encourage the smoker not only to collect them, but also to purchase more cigarettes. Today, such items are very much sought after by collectors.

Many of the 'jackdaw' type publications contain examples of ephemera relating to the subject of the pack and intended to be used in conjunction with extracts from archival material and printed sources. For example, in the 'Princes of Loom Street'[7] out of 27 documents in the pack, there are four broadsheets and parts of two other documents which appear to have been extracted or copied from ephemera. This type of material is intended for teaching purposes and will be drawn from historic ephemera although whilst the items are still in print, one could say that they are current. In treatment, although such items may contain ephemera and the actual extracts could be said to be ephemera, libraries usually treat them as if they were a book.

The grouping of ephemera into historic and contemporary or current ephemera suggested above is not the only grouping that has been suggested. Rickards has suggested the following grouping: 'the truly transient (the ticket, the price tag, the coupon); the semi-durable (the playing card, the share certificate, the calendar), and the keep-it forever (the mourning card, the commemorative souvenir)'[8].

This grouping is equally as valid as the one which has been suggested and is designed to fit all the various types of ephemera, although it does depend on the view taken by the collector. For instance, a collector of railway tickets may not regard them as transient whilst an individual might regard a mourning card as something to be discarded once the contents have been assimilated by the recipient.

The main problem with the distinction produced by Rickards is that it does not take into account the different methods required to collect historic and contemporary ephemera and where the different types can be found. The treatment of the material once it has reached the library, record office or museum will be the same for all types of ephemera, although some of the older material might require more in the way of conservation than the more recently produced material.

It should be remembered that the purpose of the material will vary according to the use for which it was originally intended and this will also affect views as to why it should be preserved. Many people do not realise that current material will have a usefulness in the future and that what is now current will in a short time become historic. For example, a firm's technical library may include much material which fits the definition of ephemera and which will be current material whilst the machines are being produced and in service but once the machines cease to be used, the technical information will become historic and may be discarded as it takes up space. Often, little thought is given to the possible use of the information contained in the leaflets by historians of technology and museum curators in the future. Likewise, with posters and handouts which are either displayed or available within the library, it is probable that the staff of the departments where this material is available or displayed will not think in terms of passing a copy on for preservation in the local collection. One wonders how many branch libraries display posters and have leaflets available for the public to take away which are thrown out once their currency is over and for which there is no other record of the event.

How to collect ephemera

How does one go about collecting ephemera for permanent preservation in a library, record office or museum? Although the methods used will vary according to the type of material that is collected, there are certain basic ways which apply to collecting historic ephemera and other methods which are appropriate to ensure that as much current or contemporary ephemera is acquired as is feasible.

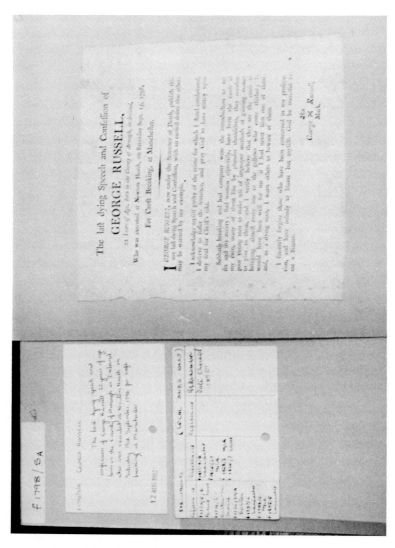

A broadsheet with index cards used in Manchester
(Manchester Local History Library)

There are two main ways of acquiring older items of ephemera, namely by purchase and by donation, although there are other methods which account for the acquisition of a smaller amount of material. The purchase of material is an accepted way of building up a collection, provided it is accepted that the library should collect ephemera to complement its book stock and other material such as maps, newspapers, illustrations and directories. Several ways exist to discover what is available at a given point in time.

Booksellers' catalogues

Libraries usually receive a large number of catalogues from booksellers in different parts of the country. Often, these are not new books, but second-hand and antiquarian books. Although many of the catalogues received will be restricted only to books, there are ones which do include items of ephemera. For example, there is one monthly list which frequently includes some items of ephemera, such as theatre playbills, posters and even collections of cigarette cards. Very occasionally, if a substantial collection of material on a specific subject has been acquired, the list may include a special section on ephemera.

Sometimes, booksellers will wait until they have a substantial amount of ephemera and like material and then issue a special catalogue related to this type of material. It must be pointed out, however, that not all the material which has been included will be ephemera, some of it will be in the nature of minor publication or pamphlet material. This arises because of the confusion which exists as to what constitutes ephemera and what minor publications. One such list was published in the late 1970s by the Tyrrell Bookshop and Gallery of Ringwood, Hampshire, which listed over 100 items which were described as 'miscellaneous items of ephemera'. These included prize cards, puzzle cards, invitations, posters, trade cards, calendars and a list of costumes and wigs issued by Abel Heywood of Manchester in about 1890 as well as material which, from its description in the listing, would be regarded as a pamphlet or minor publication.

When libraries receive trade catalogues from booksellers, particularly those from second-hand booksellers, it is to the local studies department that they tend to gravitate as this department usually pays a fair amount of attention to the contents in order to fill gaps in its stock, or to enable it to acquire additional copies for its stock. It is necessary when these catalogues are received to scan them at the earliest opportunity and if there is material of interest, to order it quickly as the library will not be the only recipient of the list. Private collectors may also receive copies and are in a position to act very quickly to order things they are interested in, things which by right should really be available for researchers in a public collection.

The fact that there are private collectors purchasing ephemera has meant that libraries and record offices have had to look at their acquisition policies for this type of material very carefully and to speed up the system used for placing orders. In addition, it has also meant that prices have risen. At one time, when the private collector was only interested in a certain type of material, many types of ephemera could be acquired by the library relatively cheaply, but as the private collector has widened his or her field of interest, so the prices have risen. In a time of financial constraints on public institutions with collections, these bodies may feel that they are not able to compete with the private sector and not attempt to purchase material which should really be in their collection. Once an item, irrespective of whether it is ephemera, a book or a manuscript, becomes part of a private collection, it is more than likely that it will be lost to those who might want to consult it for research purposes. Another point to bear in mind is that if another copy were to become available at some time in the future, its price may have risen substantially.

It is local collections in public libraries, record offices and museums which tend to collect historical ephemera and this is usually material which relates to their own particular area or subject specialism, rather than material of a more general nature covering the whole country. It is important that such collecting agencies should be given every opportunity to acquire material which relates to their particular field of interest for if they do not acquire it, it is unlikely anyone else in the public sector will do so. Books can be borrowed from other libraries or institutions like the British Lending Library, but rarely do they have material of local interest, particularly items of ephemera. If the local studies librarian or the archivist traces or finds an item which fills a gap in the existing collection or complements material already held, then every effort should be made to ensure that it is acquired, even if this means that another department is not able to purchase a second copy of a book that is in demand.

Bookshops

Another useful way of acquiring material is from second-hand bookshops. It is worthwhile getting to know the local ones as they may inform the library when they have acquired material in which they think the library might be interested, although they may also put the price up if they think they have a ready market for something. Having good relations with such booksellers may also have an important side effect in that if the bookseller is not interested in acquiring the material and it is known that the library is, someone with ephemera which they are trying to dispose of might be redirected to the library or record office. Additionally, if the bookshop is aware that the library is looking for something of particular interest, the owner may keep an eye open for it, particularly if it is required to complete a collection or complement that which the library already has.

If staff time permits, it can be rewarding to spend time browsing around second-hand bookshops and even 'junk' shops, especially where the dealer is engaged in house clearances. Many items of ephemera are kept by the individual for their own personal use and it is not realised that they may be of interest to someone engaged in research. For example, invitations, stubs of tickets and so on are examples of ephemera which may be used as bookmarks or slip behind drawers. They will usually be of little interest to anyone but the librarian and the person to whom they originally belonged. Unfortunately, in many cases, these items are destroyed before the librarian, museum curator or archivist has had an opportunity to look through them and to decide whether the material is relevant to the collection. Often, this is due to ignorance on the part of the person clearing up the personal effects of a deceased person or someone moving house. For example, on one occasion, one of Manchester's district librarians and the local history librarian were invited to a house to look at some books and, if they were of interest, to take them back to the library prior to the disposal of the property and its contents. During the course of the conversation, it transpired that there had been a large collection of invitations to civic events which had belonged to the owner of the property. On asking what had happened to them, the local history librarian was informed that they had been sent to the local tip a couple of days earlier. The relatives of the owner who were engaged in the clearing out of the house admitted that they had not realised that this material would be of interest to the library. This type of event must happen time and time again, although not necessarily with invitations, but with other material which people have saved or hoarded. The only way to overcome this is to educate the public in the type of material which local studies collections are interested in preserving.

In addition to second-hand bookshops and junk shops in the locality, it is also worthwhile looking in similar shops outside the area, for instance, in London or Brighton if material is being sought for say

Manchester or Newcastle. It is well known that many seaside postcards are on sale in the inland towns as people have sent them home from their holidays to friends and neighbours. Likewise, material from the inland towns will find its way into shops many miles from its place of origin. Occasionally, interesting items can be acquired for much less than would have to be paid locally for the same thing. For example, the menu for the Manchester Guardian's centenary dinner at the Midland Hotel in Manchester[9] appeared in a shop in London, where it was going to be used as part of a Christmas window display prior to it being sold. Needless to say, it never appeared in the display as it was purchased before it could be used for the surprisingly low price of 50p.

Donations

Donations, more often than not, are of individual items which someone has collected and decided that they no longer require, but cannot bring themselves to throw away, so they pass them to the library. For example, someone clearing out an attic may find copies of old newspapers and pass them to the library. Occasionally, someone will build up a collection of material on a specific subject and then pass it to the library rather than sell it on the open market. For instance, a scrapbook of cuttings may have been compiled on a particular subject and may not only include cuttings, but also invitations and posters. In Manchester's Local History Library, for example, there are several hundred volumes of scrapbooks which have been donated to the library. Altough a majority contain only newspaper clippings, there are some which contain invitations, *in memoriam* cards, leaflets and broadsheets. One of the finest of these collections which have been built up by individuals is of posters relating to the Anti-Corn Law League[10], whose headquarters were in Manchester in the 1830s and 1840s. More recently, the Local History Library received a series of scrapbooks compiled by a city councillor in the 1880s and which had ended up in Canada. His relatives in Canada decided that they would be of more use in Manchester than Canada and sent them over for addition to the stock of the department.[11]

The problem with people bringing in material they have found is that many of them imagine that it has some monetary value. It is hard to put a price on such items as this depends to a large extent on the laws of supply and demand. Very often, the value is in the interest of the item and the information which it contains rather than in its monetary value. This concept can be difficult to put across the members of the public, who often hope to get a reasonable price for an item. It is not helped by the media who sometimes include news items about the high prices paid for items of historic interest, such as nineteenth century photographs or unique copies of large railway posters.

It is possible for the library to encourage donations of material, but this involves educating the public as to the importance of ephemera not in terms of monetary value, but in terms of interest and value to future generations engaged in research. There are a number of ways in which the public can be educated as to the importance of ephemera as a primary source of information and the uses such material can be put to.

Talks   Talks to local societies and groups is one of the most obvious ways of educating the public about the importance of ephemera. Often, local studies librarians or archivists are asked to speak to a local society, such as a local history society or a townswomen's guild or local rotary club. If no subject is suggested or the speaker is asked to suggest a subject, it is worthwhile considering using ephemera as a topic as there is scope not only to be informative, but to use some of the more interesting items from the collection as examples. Such a talk can often galvanise a local society into action and to collect material in their own area or at the very least ensure that a copy of everything the society has produced is kept.

The media   With the increased number of local radio stations, it is now possible to use local radio, and sometimes local television, to talk about material in the library and to draw listeners' attention to specific types and its use as well as appealing for material not to be thrown away but passed to the library. Direct appeals to the public for material can have a very limited response. For example, in the early 1970s, Manchester Local History Library made an appeal for old photographs in an effort to counteract the various national appeals that were being made and to ensure that local material remained in the area. The response was poor to say the least. Sometimes, this is because the subject does not appeal to the public and sometimes, it is due to the way it is presented.

One interesting development in appealing for material through the media lies in the use of television. Several years ago, Granada Television suggested that part of one of its 'Reports Action' programmes should be an appeal for ephemera for libraries, record offices and museums. However, after investigating the subject, they decided to make a more general appeal rather than confine it to ephemera.

Sometimes, newspapers and periodicals can be used to make people aware of ephemera, especially of particular collections. For example,

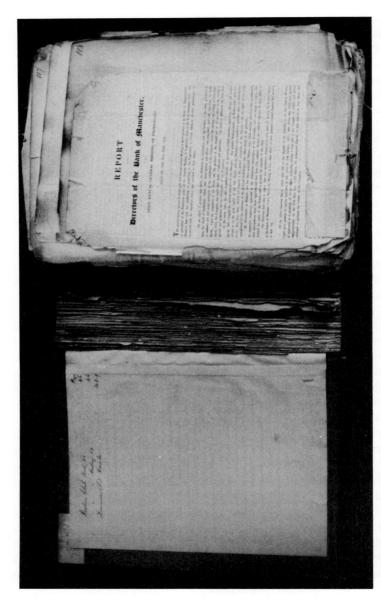

A scrapbook of broadsheets and other ephemera showing the effect of poor quality paper breaking away from the binding (Manchester Local History Library)

in 1980 an article appeared in the *Health and Social Service Journal*[12] on the Museum of Social Work. The author, Colin Harvey, argued that ephemera may be 'a means of attracting and holding the interest of uncommitted outsiders'[13]. As well as describing the objectives of the museum, he also drew attention to some possible sources of material which he regarded as ephemera – 'printed sources such as case papers, minutes of meetings, committee reports, nor should we forget non-print material especially photographs, all of which may be lying neglected and forgotten in attics and basements'.[14] Likewise, the Ephemera Society when it held its first exhibition secured good coverage in some newspapers such as *The Times Literary Supplement*[15] and *The Sunday Times*.[16]

Personal contact   Personal contact with individuals is often a useful way of acquiring material through the means of donation. Although only a relatively small number of people may be reached, it can result in some interesting and important material being acquired by the library. For example, someone clearing a house may come across material which they might have thrown out without any consideration, but if they know someone interested in ephemera, they may think twice and allow the person to take what they require as was the case with the rent books mentioned in chapter 2 or several items which were discovered relating to income tax returns of the 1890s, which were saved purely because the person into whose hands they had come appreciated that someone might be interested in them.[17]

Chance finds   The problem which often arises with the acquisition of large quantities of material rarely arises with ephemera, namely what to retain and what to discard, as often it is acquired in small amounts which have survived the passage of time more by chance than as a result of a deliberate act of preservation. An exception to this is that material which has been specially produced for collectors and is often passed from generation to generation. Chance finds of material can often be very interesting. For example, the clearance of an old building, either prior to demolition or refurbishment, may result in the discovery of material which has been left undisturbed for decades. This was the case with an old railway office block in the centre of Manchester where the architects responsible for surveying the building prior to refurbishment came across material which had been left when the railway company moved out. Amongst the material which was discovered were local railway timetables from the 1950s, excursion leaflets and a number of posters and maps. Although relatively recent in date, Manchester Local History Library did not have copies of the leaflets and posters, but now a little more of

Manchester's railway history can be pieced together with this recent find of material. In this case, the items were saved because the architect supervising the team clearing the building was instructed to look out for material and to make the necessary contacts if anything was found.

Jobbing printers and printers' workshops   Although ephemera can be produced on a wide range of equipment, a substantial amount of it is produced by small-scale printers, such as one who advertised in the *Leader and General Advertiser* in 1887. This paper circulated in east Manchester in the 1880s and 1890s and consisted mainly of advertisements for local firms. In it was an advertisement for the Sands Jubilee Print Works of 122 Oldham Road which claimed that it could print 'cards, invoices, statements, circulars, memoranda, handbills, posting bills, time notices, price lists, reports, memory cards, delivery notes and books, programmes, rules etc'.[18] Nothing is known of this firm except what appears in the advertisement, but if this firm had survived to the present day and had kept a specimen or sample of everything they had printed, it would have been a valuable record not only of the type of work they did and its changes over the years, but also would have provided a wealth of information on small businesses and societies in part of Manchester. Sometimes such collections do come to light as with that in Hartlepool Museum which was rescued by Robert Wood, a West Hartlepool teacher and amateur local historian.[19] This, however, is the exception. All too often, a small printer will only keep a sample of the type of work that is done to show clients and may be in an order suitable for this purpose and not even dated. When material is out of date or not wanted for a long time, the sample may be discarded to create space.

Local small printers should be encouraged to pass on material they have finished with to the library or record office. In this way it is preserved for future researchers but is also available to the printer to consult if the need arises in the future. Unfortunately material is often destroyed instead of being passed on. The same often applies when a firm ceases to trade. Occasionally, the material is passed on, but all too often it is left in the building and either destroyed when the building is cleared or vandals get in and use it to light fires. It is, therefore, very useful if contact can be made with small printers, especially those which have been established a long time and which are in old premises to see if they will co-operate and donate material to the library, record office or museum.

Special projects   In her paper to the meeting on Ephemera in 1975, Dorothy McCulla drew attention to an area for collecting material which can easily be overlooked, namely, the involvement of children. She argued that 'it was of particular importance to engage the interest of children. The profit was two way. The library acquired additional 'eyes and ears' and the children themselves came to accept the library as a place to come for help with whatever subject captivated their imagination'.[20] This can be achieved in two ways. Firstly, through the medium of school projects and secondly through visits to the library. It is often surprising the material which children will discover when they are set projects and if there is co-operation between the school teachers and library staff, it may be possible that some of this material will find its way, either as copies or as originals, into the library. If children are taught the usefulness of ephemera, it is a step in the direction of educating the public.

Historic ephemera in archival collections

Historic ephemera is not only found in libraries as single items or collections of material, it is also to be found in archival collections. For example, the papers relating to an estate or farm may contain, in addition to the usual material that would be expected in such an archive collection, items which are by their nature ephemera, such as posters advertising the sale of the property, trees from the estate or public notices affecting the tenants. Under no circumstances should this material be extracted from the archive in order to put it with other ephemera in the library or record office. To do so would leave the archive incomplete and take the material out of its proper context. If it is felt that there is a need to have either a reference to it with the index of ephemera in the library or to have a copy which is more readily accessible, then either a card entry directing potential users to the source or a photographic copy should be made.

Difficult historic material

Although acquiring historic material can be difficult, there are occasions when it is virtually impossible to obtain the original item. Such situations arise when the original, usually a poster or broadsheet, is discovered pasted directly onto a wall or hoarding and has been covered up for some period of time. Usually it is exposed when a later poster is taken off or an adjoining building demolished. Clearly it is not feasible to take the wall down or soak the poster off so an alternative way of obtaining a copy has to be sought. The most convenient way to do this is to photograph it as soon as the library or

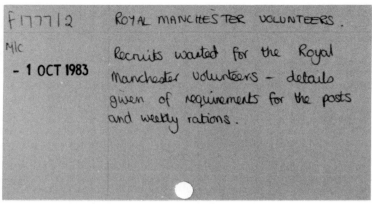

An index card giving a precis of a broadsheet
(Manchester Local History Library)

record office is notified of its existence as it will deteriorate with the weather as soon as it is exposed. For example, when the old St Mary's Hospital in Manchester was demolished in the 1970s, the exposed wall of the adjoining building had a poster on it for the Oxford Road Hotel, which must have been put up in the late 1880s or early 1890s. Once the grime on it had been washed off, it was possible to photograph it and add it to the library's collection of posters, thus preserving the information on the poster.

Similar situations can arise on advertising hoardings and public notice boards when posters are taken off, or peel off, exposing those underneath. Photography can again be used to record these before they are covered up again or removed. Similarly, photography can be used to record official notice boards, like those outside churches so that there is a record of the information they contain.

Sometimes, posters which are painted onto gable-end walls many years ago survive to the present day as is the case of one for Gillette on the gable-end of a building in Market Street, Manchester, or a firm selling pianos, which is visible on the gable of a building close to Stoke-on-Trent Station. The only way to record such material is to photograph it before the building is demolished or it weathers to such an extent that it is illegible.

With all these items which cannot be removed to safe-keeping in a library, record office or museum, photography is a useful means of recording not only the text, but also the layout, the typography used and any illustration that might be there. It may be argued that photographs are not ephemera, but in these circumstances, where there is no alternative, it is justifiable to locate them with the ephemera collection, although where there is a large photograph collection, they may be kept with the remainder of the photographs

144

and cross-referenced to the ephemera collection. Likewise, there is nothing wrong in enlarging posters and broadsheets which appear on historic photographs and adding the resultant copy to the collection.

Contemporary ephemera

The collection of historic ephemera presents problems in that it is likely to be found in unusual places and need conservation before it can be made available to the public. However, the amount that can be collected is limited as only a relatively small proportion of what was actually produced has survived to the present day. In many cases, survival has been by chance rather than by a deliberate act of preservation. With contemporary or current ephemera, a much greater problem arises. It is generally accepted that items which relate to the past should be collected and preserved, but people tend not to think of the future and the type of material which may be required for research. As a consequence, they tend not to ask the question as to why it is important for modern material to be collected and preserved or consider how it is that historic material has survived, either accidentally or deliberately, to the present day and the uses made of it. Many people still regard something that relates to their own life time as not historic, although attitudes are now beginning to change, partly as a result of television drawing people's attention to the fact that even the 1950s and 1960s are historic and that things which were accepted as commonplace or the norm in those decades are no longer so accepted. Items such as old cardboard milk bottle tops or the stiff card railway ticket are things of the past. Very often collections of contemporary ephemera will exist not only in places such as libraries, but in people's own homes, amongst their own papers, although they will not regard it as ephemera. What the ordinary person will call it will depend on why it has been retained or discarded.

Likewise, contemporary ephemera is not solely the preserve of the local studies library, record office or museum. For example, there is a great deal of ephemera to be found in a commercial library as much of the information which users of that department require will be very recent and may not reach standard book form before it is out-of-date. However, once the current value of such information is passed, usually there is little attention paid to what happens to the material itself with the result that much of it will be discarded as it is superseded. This is not always the case as there are some departments where the historical usefulness of out-dated material is appreciated and care taken to ensure that some, usually local material, is kept.

For a local studies library, record office or museum, the collection of contemporary and current ephemera will have a two-fold objective. Firstly, there will be material which is required for current awareness, such as details of meetings of local societies or of courses being held locally. The second objective will be to ensure that at least one example of as much of the currently produced ephemera is preserved within the organisation's collections as possible for use by future generations of researchers. In addition, in the department there should be an effort to ensure that as much contemporary material whose currency has passed is also preserved. It is with the collection of this current and contemporary material that decisions have to be made as to the amount that should be collected and criteria established to decide what should be retained and what discarded. The presumption should always be in favour of retention if the material relates to the department's field of interest or any aspect thereof to enable the collection of contemporary and current material to be as comprehensive as possible, for in the last resort this material will become historic ephemera. It must be acknowledged that there are other constraints which will have to be taken into account, namely space available and staff time, but this is the ideal situation which should be aimed for although not necessarily achieved.

The emphasis placed on preserving current and contemporary material will vary according to the library or department where it is housed. A commercial or technical department will rarely keep something that is out of date as this can result in the reader being given incorrect information. Some material, however, may be retained to provide background information, but usually much of it is consigned to the wastepaper basket as soon as it is replaced by more up-to-date information. In the local studies library, although there is a need to have current information relating to the subject and local events, it is more easily accepted that there will be out-of-date material in its files as its policy will be to preserve local material. For example, it is to be expected that a commercial or quick reference section will have the current railway or airline timetables, but one would not necessarily expect this to be the case with the local studies library.

What means exist to enable a collection of contemporary and current ephemera to be built up and to maintain its growth? There are several ways of doing this, but none will ensure that absolutely everything that is produced will be collected or find its way into the library's files. The means of collecting this category of ephemera varies much more widely than it does for historic material. Different types of material require different types of approach. For example, the methods used can range from asking societies and organisations to send copies of everything they produce, to systematically visiting bus and railway stations at regular intervals and picking up one of everything that is available to be taken away, from deliberately ensuring that copies of leaflets handed out in the street are collected, to asking members of staff to save everything that comes through the letter box at home and bringing it into the library. Whichever method is used, there will always be material which is relevant to the department which escapes the net. All the librarian can do is to hope that as much as possible is collected and added to stock.

Subscriptions

Probably one of the easiest ways to obtain copies of current ephemera, particularly that issued by societies and organisations, is to take out a subscription to that society or organisation. This should result in the library automatically receiving copies of everything that is issued to the membership – publications, prospectuses, membership cards, notices of meetings and visits, newsletters and agendas for general and other business meetings. However, the question of economics enters into this means of collecting material. Often, when cuts have to be made in the library's budget, subscriptions are amongst the first to suffer. The librarian has to make a strong case for the subscription to be continued, often in the face of strong pressure from larger, more prestigious departments, arguing that their case is stronger than that of the local studies library. However, it can be argued that it is the more general departments which should take the bulk of the cuts when they occur as the material which a local studies department acquires will probably be unique in the library field as probably there will be no-one else in the country taking this material. Once a gap appears in a local collection caused by the need to economise, it can be very difficult to fill it at a later date as the level of production will usually be low and if there is no other library taking the item, it may not be possible to borrow from elsewhere, as can be done with material published on a national level.

Donations

An alternative means of acquiring current ephemera issued by societies and organisations is to persuade them to donate copies of material that they publish to the library and that it is in their interests to do so. This might be on the understanding that if publication is produced, the library will purchase at least one copy and display details of the society and its programme on a notice board. Even this method can have its drawbacks as many societies are governed by financial constraints and as a result extra copies sent out when no subscription is received can eat up small surpluses which a society might have.

A similar approach can be followed for organisations, other than societies, like firms and clubs and even publishers of give-away newsheets. In some cases, they may be prepared to donate material to the local studies collection, but in others, they may say that they already send material to another department in the library and will not be prepared to send an extra copy. In these cases, it is necessary to discover which department receives the material and what happens to it when they have finished with it. If it is added to the library's stock, a check should be made to ensure that it is recorded in the department's own catalogue, but where it is not, then internal discussions should be held with the department concerned and an agreement reached whereby the material is passed to the local collection, if it is of local interest, when it is superseded.

Library notice boards

In many cases, the library can help itself to collect material. Most libraries, record offices and museums are asked to display material such as posters, programmes, handbills and leaflets on their notice boards. Once the event has taken place and the item on display is no longer current a system should exist whereby the department or library displaying the material should pass it to the local studies department for preservation or to the relevant department if there is an interest in it or if there is a collection of a particular type of material which is national or regional rather than specially local. It could be argued that the staff in the displaying department do not have either the time or expertise to decide what is worth retaining and what is relevant. This problem can be overcome by arranging for everything that is taken down to be passed to the collecting department, whose staff can then sort it and make the necessary decisions. For example, the Technical Library in Manchester displays many public notices, but until the early 1970s, the material was discarded when there was no further use for it. As a result of discussions between the Technical Librarian and the Local History Librarian, it was agreed that all local posters and so forth should be passed to the Local History Library for inclusion in that department's stock together with any other items which might have a local interest. Those posters which were not of local interest were also passed on, but to the Arts Library, who were interested in them from the point of view of the graphic arts. This system has worked extremely well, and much material which might not otherwise have been kept has now been added to the local collection.

This type of arrangement should not be restricted to the central library departments. Many branch and district libraries display material which relates to events in their locality. Sometimes, if they have a small collection of local material, they will want to add them to their own local collection. Usually, however, such material is discarded when no longer of use. Arrangements should be made to ensure that local ones are not thrown away, but passed to the local collection. It may also be argued that if a poster is unique, the original should be passed to the main collection and a copy retained in the branch.

Library information desks

In a similar vein, many libraries are asked to make leaflets and handbills available to the public by leaving them in a place where the public can pick them up. Some of this material is of local interest, such as leaflets for University Extra Mural classes in the area, information on performances at theatres, lectures at local art galleries, but other material will be of regional or national interest. Where the leaflet is of local interest, at least one copy should be kept for preservation and the same should apply to those where another department has a specific interest. For example, one department might collect material on the theatre in a region so any leaflets relating to theatres should be treated in a similar manner, namely one copy taken and added to the collection. By using this method of acquiring material, it is possible to build up a substantial collection of current ephemera for the library. In many cases, it is advisable to take two or three copies of leaflets that are on display so if one gets lost or damaged, there is at least a replacement available. For example, in 1983, Manchester City Planning Department produced a leaflet on the Castlefield area of the City.[21] The library was asked to display copies and that those sent to the library were to be left available for the public. None were specifically sent to the library for their files, but the Local History Library added several to their stock by taking them from those which had been sent to the library for the public.

As with notice-board posters, branch libraries are often asked to make material available on events and activities in their own area. Again, they should be encouraged to pass a copy to the local collection as often these items will circulate in a very restricted area and may be the only information that is available to show that an event took place. For example, the Wythenshawe Forum Library in Manchester has many leaflets on events in that area which are not available in the Central Library in Manchester.

Where a branch library has its own collection, it can be argued that it is sufficient to preserve just one copy in the branch's collection. This argument can be refuted by the fact that branch libraries do get closed down and they can be vandalised and the stock damaged. If there is a specialist department or collection dealing with local material, it is important that a copy of everything relating to the area for which it collects should be sent there so that it has as complete a record as possible of the area's history. It is also where people from outside the area will expect to find material.

The above applies particularly to the metropolitan areas where the districts are library authorities in their own right. In the shire counties, the situation is somewhat different. In 1974, a number of library authorities lost their independence and were merged with the county library. Often, these had their own local collections. In many cases, these local collections have continued to be maintained at district level whilst the county library has provided back-up facilities and advice. It is important that in the shire counties, local collections are left at district level rather than being centralised at the library headquarters, as the county local studies librarian cannot be expected to know in detail about each area and what is being produced whereas someone in an area will do so. It is often to the local library that people go for information rather than the headquarters.

Staff training

This may appear to be an unusual method of collecting ephemera, but it can be a very effective one. Library staff in departments other than that housing the local collection, and in branches, should be made aware of the need to co-operate in enhancing the existing collections. Often, this simply means basic education of staff in the use of the material and the importance of its collection. Hopefully, professional staff will be aware of the value and importance of ephemera, although this might not be the case with those who have specialised in current awareness or one of the other fields where ephemera is not dealt with except, possibly, as a source of information that is to be discarded as soon as it is out-of-date. In any library, the majority of the staff are library assistants who can be made aware of the value and need to collect ephemera by means of in-service training programmes. Where these are organised, there is usually an opportunity for the local studies librarian to talk about the department, the stock and the type of work undertaken. It is here that it is possible to

Shop window bill, 1901 (Manchester Local History Library)

stress the importance of ephemera and how they can assist in maintaining the collection by sending local material which they come across. It should also be emphasised that they should not worry if another person sends the same item in as duplicates can also be very useful. It is not very helpful if one branch thinks another will send the material in and so itself neglects to do so.

Although in-service training can make staff aware of the need for the material, this fact has often to be reinforced at regular intervals. A memo at certain times of the year or before a major event, such as a general election, will act as a reminder. For instance in the early 1970s all branches in Manchester received a memo a fortnight or so before an election asking that staff should bring in the election addresses they received. This acted as a long-stop for material which was not received as a result of a general approach to the candidates. Although the response was patchy, it did result in some material that was not received by other means being acquired.

Street handouts

Another source of current ephemera is the street. Often in the centre of towns and cities there are people on street corners and outside shops trying to thrust leaflets into the hands of passers-by. These can range from leaflets advertising the work of certain religious groups to shops advertising their products or the opening of a new wine bar or fast food shop. Many people just glance at them before

151

throwing them away. Library staff should always be on the look out for such items being given out and make an effort to receive one and take it back to the library rather than throw it away as it may supply some additional information on a firm or a shop which is not otherwise available. For example, one thrust into the hands of pedestrians in the centre of Manchester in 1983 gave the local address of the Hubbard Scientology Organisation, which might not be available elsewhere.[22]

Another place where such leaflets can be found is under the windscreen wipers of parked cars. Often all the cars parked in a car park or an area are done at one time. Sometimes, passers-by will be given them as well, but if not it is possible to take one from under a windscreen as the driver normally throws it away. For example, in early 1983, a firm in Hazel Grove which was involved in window manufacture placed leaflets under all the windscreen wipers of all the cars in Hazel Grove Station car park.[23]

The letter box

Library staff can also be of great assistance in collecting and bringing in material that is pushed through letter boxes at home. This can range from free newspapers to leaflets advertising local firms and jumble sales to church services and coffee mornings. This type of material is difficult to trace and obtain as there is no way of knowing what has been printed, by whom and when. Not only does this type of information give an indication of what is going on in a community, but in the case of firms, this might be the only information that is known about the firm. For example, a leaflet distributed in Disley from a firm called Auto Care gave details of the type of work the firm undertook as well as the address and telephone number and it also had the added bonus of the name, address and telephone number of the firm which printed it.[24]

It is not recommended that everything that comes through the letter box is retained, although a museum might keep a larger sample than a library as such items can be used to enliven displays and exhibitions. Some of the material, particularly unsolicited mail, will be of national interest and of little local interest unless it is from an organisation whose headquarters are in the area. For example, one wonders how much of the material distributed by Readers Digest is found in the local collection of the area where the firm has its headquarters. Although the material may be national, it does represent the activities of a local firm.

An interesting way to encourage material received through the letter box at home is to place a large box in a central position so that members of staff can bring material in and leave it. This will also have the advantage of showing how much is received in a given period of time as well as enabling local material to be collected and added to stock.

Information centres

Another way to obtain items of current and contemporary ephemera is to make regular visits to places where it is known ephemera, such as leaflets and pocket timetables, is displayed for the public to pick up and take away. Such places can include information offices, citizens advice bureaux, railway, bus and coach stations, theatre booking offices, tourist information offices and even shopping centres. Members of staff who visit such places either in the course of their normal duties or because they pass through them at other times should be encouraged to pick up the material they see on display. It is not a time-consuming task if the problem is approached in this way as it will only take a few seconds. If the same person checks the same place regularly, they will get to know what is new and what is not. For example, British Rail may not only display copies of pocket timetables, but also leaflets on excursions and special fares that are available. Although this system of people picking up material does not result in complete coverage of local material, it will ensure that a reasonable amount is collected.

In order to ensure that all the potential sources are visited, it is a good idea to draw up a list of the various places in the area and to check with members of staff to see which places they pass through or visit. In this way it will be noticed if somewhere is not covered and arrangements can be made for someone to go there regularly.

When this method of collecting is adopted, it can result in a large amount of material been acquired in a very short space of time. However, once the system is in operation, the amount that is acquired will diminish to a relatively few items each visit. Occasionally, there will be peaks in the availability of new material. For instance, when the railway timetable changes, a new series of pocket timetables will be issued and similarly, around Christmas, the amount issued by theatres will rise as they advertise their Christmas shows.

Household ephemera

Every household generates its own ephemera, although most people do not realise that it is ephemera. Such things as bills, guarantees and rent books may all be found in household files. If these items were all kept together, it could be said that they constitute a personal archive. However, many people throw much of this material away after a few years rather than keep it as clutter.

Although people may not want to hand over old bills and receipts, they may be prepared to hand over guarantees and instructions once they have served their purpose. Likewise, the additional material that one finds accompanying bills may be donated to the library. For example, how many libraries will have copies of leaflets which go out with the electricity bill or the rate demands? Very few have attempted to collect this type of material, yet for the future it will be of interest and use to those engaged in research into social history and living standards and conditions. Staff could be persuaded to bring this type of leaflet into the library rather than to throw it away.

Educating the public

In order to obtain as much as possible of current and contemporary ephemera, it is useful to try to educate the public into thinking in terms of the future usefulness of the material which they throw away. This can be done through the medium of talks or exhibitions. Although many members of the public might not appreciate the reason for such collections existing, it is important to try to make them understand their use and if successful, this may result in some material being received. For example, as a result of a talk to one active society, members realised that there was much current material that was not being preserved and that this would be important and useful in the future, so arrangements were made to collect as much of it as possible and to deposit it in safe keeping.

At exhibitions

Yet another way to obtain ephemera on a particular firm or organisation in an area is to collect material when visiting an exhibition. Usually, there are leaflets avaiable to be picked up, some of which will relate to local firms. If possible, copies of this material should be kept in the local collection as it cannot be said with certainty that these firms will keep a copy themselves. Not only trade exhibitions will have local material but also general exhibitions, such as the Ideal Home Exhibition or even the Motor Show may have material which relates to local firms. Again, not only is it the local studies department which may benefit from collecting material at exhibitions, commercial and technical departments may also be able to collect material which is of interest and help in their work.

Special approaches

In addition to what may be termed the obvious ways of collecting current ephemera, certain types of material may call for a special approach of their own. Usually, this involves writing letters to individuals or organisations asking for copies of material which they produce and which may only be available on a limited basis. The response to such letters will vary widely. In some cases they will be ignored, but in others, there will be a good response and material may be sent on a regular basis. Such letters should explain why the library is interested in receiving copies of the material and why it is important to ensure that the information is in a public place so that it can be consulted in the future. Sometimes, after the initial contact, which may be followed up by a meeting, the library will be placed on the mailing list. For example, a body was set up to establish a trade union centre in a building that was the first meeting place of the Trades Union Congress in 1868. Initially, the library was not sent copies of the newsletter they produced, but after the initial approach, the library got copies regularly as well as copies of earlier newsletters and other literature that had been produced because the organisers realised that it was important to ensure a record of their activities was available in the future and that having the material in the library might also draw people's attention to their aims. A good example of the specialist approach is afforded by election literature when the agents and candidates are circulated and asked for copies of the election literature they are issuing.

Local authority ephemera

One area from which it can be very difficult to extract items of current ephemera, as well as other material, is from the local authority itself. Most local authority departments tend to be very self-contained and do not think in terms of the organisation as a whole or of the need to ensure that the library has a copy. The basic problem is that many local authorities do not have a central publishing department, but each department publishes its own material and has its own means of informing the public what it has published. For instance, there may be one system used by the planning department, another by the engineers and a third by education and so on. Consequently, it is extremely difficult to discover what has been produced as no one person is aware of the full publishing programme of the local authority. Often, material reaches the library more by chance than as a result of a deliberate policy of sending material. Sometimes a particular officer will be aware of the importance of passing material on and this may result in some items being acquired. For example, in July 1983, the Manchester City Planning Department and the Greater Manchester County Planning Department jointly organised a conference on new uses for old buildings. As part of the information supplied to delegates, there was a folder containing brief accounts of the buildings that were to be visited as well as publications by the Manchester Planning Department. No one had considered sending a set to Manchester's Local History Library despite the fact that some of the historical background had been provided by that department and the sheets of individual buildings would be of assistance in answering some queries. (Ultimately, they got two sets because one of the people involved with the administration of the conference took it upon himself to ensure that copies were received by the library[25].)

One way to overcome the problem of difficulty in getting local authority publications is to write to each department and make arrangements for copies of everything that is published to be sent over on a regular basis. However, even if arrangements are made, it may be delegated to a member of staff in the publishing department and when that person leaves or moves on, the system may fall down. What has to be done is to educate members of staff in other departments of the local authority as to the need to ensure that copies are sent to the library. (This task is made all the more difficult because they may not even inform other sections within the same department about publications.)

If the local authority does most of its printing in-house, it may be possible to make an arangement with the person in charge to keep a copy of everything that they print and for it to be collected or sent over at regular intervals. It should be stressed that this not only applies to material in standard book or pamphlet format, but also to notices, leaflets and so on. If such an arrangement can be made and operated effectively, it should be possible to ensure that a majority of the authority's publications reach the library.

In cases of difficulty, the assistance of the city or borough librarian might have to be enlisted. It might be necessary for a letter to be sent to the head of each department pointing out that it is important for the library to have copies of everything their department produces in the files so that in future, there is a full picture of the local authority's activities available.

Another way in which assistance to obtain local authority material

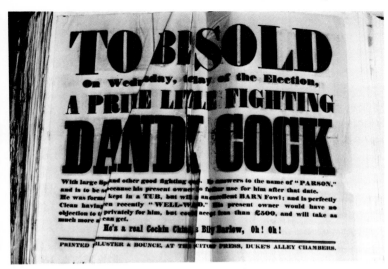

The effect of folding a broadsheet (Manchester Local History Library)

may be sought is to try to persuade a councillor of the value and importance of the library having copies of all material published by the local authority and getting him or her to raise the issue either in committees or in full council. Edinburgh District Council passed a resolution that all departments should compile a list of their publications and deposit a copy of every publication in the Edinburgh Room of the Central Library. In order to reinforce the decision, the Council made it a standing instruction and instituted a procedure whereby the material was passed to the library. This has resulted in material being received by the library which had not been known about before and which will, as a consequence, enhance the holding of local authority produced material in the local collection.[26] It is possible, therefore, that other authorities may be persuaded to pass similar resolutions and create standing orders to the same effect. Provided such resolutions are fully complied with by other departments this should overcome the problem of failing to get local authority material.

Conclusion

In many cases it is difficult to make the general public aware of the need for public libraries to have copies of ephemera, irrespective of whether it is historic or current and contemporary material. The

157

importance and use of historic items is probably the easiest to get across to the public and, therefore, can be used as a starting point in educating people into passing material on to be preserved. Once the fundamental point about the importance of current and contemporary ephemera is accepted by the public, it should be a little easier to trace this material. At the same time, commercial enterprises should be made aware of the importance of preserving material of an ephemeral nature either within the official company archives or as part of the holdings of the organisation's library or information service, provided it has such a section. Many firms will keep only the minimum amount of material on the shelves as space costs money. However, with microforms, it is possible to reduce considerably the space that is taken up.

To obtain copies of material, it is often necessary for the librarian to use all the means at his or her disposal to publicise the department's collecting policies and to educate people into thinking of an item having a use after its immediate use has been finished with. The more people who appreciate the importance of this type of material and pass it to the library, the greater the chance will be for the collection to be as comprehensive as possible. Librarians, archivists and museum curators should not be afraid to use the media to achieve this end. Campaigns have been mounted in the past to try to rescue old photographs from oblivion, with varying degrees of success, but there has not been a similar attempt to collect ephemera. Perhaps it is the thought of the amount of material which might be received that puts the professional off making such an approach. The fact that so much material does get destroyed in the course of time means that there is a form of stock control in existence, but not an ideal one.

Although it is possible to give a broad outline of how to collect ephemera, it is necessary to adapt the different methods in order to maximise the amount of material that is collected. It should always be assumed that if a library, record office or museum is the collecting agency, comprehensiveness should be the ultimate aim and not merely a representative collection. The greater the amount that is collected, the better it will be for those engaged in research in the future and the more accurate the information from which they have to work will be. It will complement material which has survived in newspapers, tape recordings and personal reminiscences. With current material, its use in the future might not be obvious today, but one cannot say what it may be in the future. Ephemera can be used to fill in gaps which other sources of information leave.

5 The storage and conservation of ephemera

Once a decision has been made to collect and preserve ephemera, there are several other decisions which have to be taken at the same time if the collection is to develop in an organised manner and to be capable of being used by both staff and members of the public as quickly as possible. These decisions relate to the storage and conservation of material, its cataloguing, classification, indexing and retrieval systems. Unless decisions on these matters are taken quickly, a situation can arise whereby material is being acquired, but nothing is happening to it except that it is piling up, and once a backlog occurs it can be very difficult to reduce it to manageable proportions. The result of a backlog developing is that only a few members of staff will be aware of what there is in the collection and even fewer members of the public and those who know about it will be reluctant to ask to use it as it may take a considerable time to obtain it and when they do, it may not be of any use to them.

The decision on where the ephemera is to be housed, the type of storage system to be used, its conservation, cataloguing, classification and indexing have to be taken at the same time. It is no use deciding to adopt one way of classifying and cataloguing the material without deciding which system of storage is to be used or ensuring that the material is in a fit state to be handled by members of the public. The question of storage is often the first to be decided as some material may have to be housed in a temporary system until there is staff time available to classify it and prepare it for use by the public. Short-term storage is acceptable provided that the conditions under which it is housed are correct and that it does not require immediate attention from the conservationist. It is important to remember that poor storage conditions such as incorrect humidity, temperature and exposure to direct sunlight can cause as much damage to ephemera as can handling by members of the public.

This chapter will look at the problems caused by the nature of the material, the question of storage and the conservation of ephemera. It must be pointed out, however, that the section on conservation will only give guidelines as to the type of work that can be done and the materials which might be used. It is important that fully qualified conservationists are used to conserve material in the correct manner, using the correct materials and methods, otherwise problems can arise which can be difficult and costly to remedy.

The causes of degradation in ephemera

The nature of the material which is used for ephemera is the cause of many of the problems associated with this type of material. As many items of ephemera are designed to have a limited life and not to be preserved indefinitely, the quality of the paper tends to be very poor and conservation is not helped by the treatment it receives from the public in general, often being pushed into pockets or shopping bags or pasted on notice boards in direct sunlight.

Paper quality

The chief cause of many of the problems associated with ephemera is the quality of the paper that is used. Often, it is poor quality wood pulp paper which can deteriorate without the aid of any outside agent, but the process of degradation is speeded up if it is exposed to direct sunlight or gets wet. This is particularly the case with much twentieth century paper, but also applies to some nineteenth century paper. One only has to look at the effect of sunlight on newsprint to realise the speed at which it changes colour. This can apply to items of ephemera as well. However, some material is produced on better quality paper, particularly if it is designed to impress the person who receives it. For instance, leaflets advertising hotels or theatrical performances may be printed on glossy paper, but even these will fade in direct sunlight. Similarly, material which is designed to be exposed to the elements by being pasted on public notice boards may be on better quality paper, but eventually this too will show the effects of the weather. The best quality paper for ephemera is to be found used for those items which have been designed for a long life, such as collectors' items where cheap quality paper would detract from its appearance and would not encourage sales.

Size

Size is another problem which faces any organisation building up a collection of ephemera. Items of ephemera can vary from a small sheet of paper no more than, say 3 inches by 2½ inches, to broadsheets and posters which may be measured in feet rather than inches. The problem is one which relates not so much to the smaller items of ephemera, up to A4 or folio size, but to those larger ones such as posters and broadsheets. In some cases these have been folded with the result that creases have been created and ultimately the item will split into several sections along the line of the creases. Consequently, repairs have to be effected before the item can be used. This problem is one which tends to affect material which has been collected by a private collector and passed to the library, or material which has been stored flat and folded to take up less space. It should not occur so frequently with material that is current or housed in libraries today as there are ways of keeping the material flat as well as there being an awareness of the effect of folding on the permanency of the material itself.

A classic example of the problems that are caused by folding large items of ephemera like broadsheets is shown by a collection of broadsheets from the 1830s and 1840s relating to the Anti-Corn Law League. These were collected by an individual and mounted in a scrapbook. In order that they might fit on a page, they were folded into four, and sometimes into even more sections. Later, the material was acquired by Manchester Public Libraries[1]. The age of the documents, the quality of the paper and the fact that they had been folded lead to a situation in the 1960s where it was impossible to issue them to the public as when they were opened up, they broke into sections along the line of the creases. In addition, corners and edges were also beginning to break off. It was, therefore, decided that they should not be issued to the public until the individual items had been conserved. There was also an additional problem in that the paper on which they were mounted was also decaying and breaking up, so not only did the broadsheets require restoration, but they also required remounting on modern, archival paper.

This may appear to be an extreme case, but it will be repeated in many libraries, record offices and museums throughout the country. It illustrates the problems which face those with collections of ephemera, namely that of the condition of the material and its preservation to enable it to be used in the future. Although contemporary ephemera should not get into the same condition as these Anti-Corn Law League broadsheets, unless they are correctly dealt with from the time of their arrival in the library, the situation will arise in the future when similar action will have to be taken to prevent their further deterioration.

Usage

In addition to the probelms associated with the quality of the paper and the size of individual items, there is another major cause of degradation of items of ephemera. This is brought about by usage by both members of the public and of the staff. Usage of material, especially that on poor quality paper, does not assist in its long term preservation. Some items will have been roughly treated before they are received by the library and their continual usage can result in further damage. For example, corners will break off and if this is not prevented, the main body of the text can be affected. Although the loss of a corner might not appear to be serious, it is the beginning of the break up of the document. Even the loss of the name of the printer can be important as this information will not only provide an example of a specific printer's work, but may also help in locating the area to which the item relates and possibly in its dating as well. Sometimes, it might be the date that is at the bottom and this could be broken off.

In addition to small parts breaking off, there is also the problem caused by grease from fingers getting on the material. In small amounts, this might not cause too much damage, but where an item is in regular use, this grease can build up and cause problems. Similarly biro, fountain pen and pencil marks might occur, albeit accidentally, on the material which will in fact deface it. It is, therefore, important to ensure that all items which are used by the public are protected in some way from accidental damage.

Conditions for storage

Poor storage conditions can be as detrimental to the material as can poor paper, folding and handling. All material has optimum conditions for temperature, light and humidity. Material which is not stored under the correct conditions will deteriorate, although this will not be serious until there is a wide discrepancy between the ideal and actual conditions. The problem relates mainly to material which has been collected by a private individual or where it has been stored by a firm in a building which is little used. Sometimes, material which reaches the library, record office or museum has been kept in an attic or basement subject to extremes of temperature and possibly damp. It is dampness which will probably have the worst effect on the material in that it will encourage mould and fungus to grow on the paper with the result that the paper starts to break down. For example, one firm in Salford stored many of its old drawings and other material for which it had little use in a disused air-raid shelter which, after heavy rain, was several inches deep in water with the result that when the material was rescued, it had to be treated very carefully before it could be made available to researchers.[2]

Dust is another hazard which faces all material which is stored for a long period of time. Creases and folds appear to attract dust with the result that it becomes ingrained in the paper and is extremely difficult to remove without causing damage. This not only applies to material which firms have kept, but also that kept in houses as well as that in the library, despite attempts in libraries and record offices to keep the dust levels down.

When the item has been designed for display out of doors, there is a further hazard in that the weather will also play its part. Mention has already been made of the effect of sunlight on paper. Rain and wind can have an equally devastating effect, as can high humidity and extremes of temperature. In addition, material can also be attacked by insects, although this problem is not as great as it is in countries with a tropical climate.

Even if it is impossible for the collecting body to undertake immediate conservation of material which is received and to make it generally available to the public through cataloguing and classification, it is important that the material should be stored under the best conditions possible as soon as it is received. It is not good practice to leave it lying on a table or desk in direct sunlight or where fluids can be spilt on it and dust allowed to settle. The ideal conditions for storing ephemera are the same as those for storing archival material, as ephemera should be regarded as a form of primary source material. Not only should the temperature be kept constant, but so must the humidity of the storage area and the amount of exposure there is to direct sunlight and dust. Ideally, both temperature and humidity should vary as little as possible. The greater the constancy, the better will be the storage conditions. The ideal temperature is about 60°F, plus or minus 5°F. With regard to the humidity, for archival material, this should be 60 per cent, although for paper it is better if it is in the region of 50–55 per cent. If these conditions can be maintained, the material will remain in a relatively stable condition and any deterioration will be restricted. A constantly changing temperature and humidity will assist deterioration and in some cases encourage the degradation of the material on which it is printed.

In addition, the place where the material is stored should exclude sunlight if this is at all possible. Likewise, storage in areas where there are pipes and other items which might burst and cause damage should be avoided if this is at all possible. Basements are not the ideal place for storage as if there is a flood it is the area which suffers first. The existence of water tanks in the storage area should also be avoided as they can increase the humidity as well as posing a threat by overflowing. Another storage area that should be avoided is the roof as roofs require attention from time to time and leaks as well as dust can cause problems.

In order to maintain a constant temperature and humidity, it may be necessary to have the storage area in a different part of the building from which the material is used, although this might not be feasible given the design of the building and the use made of it. Likewise, it should not be in an area which is accessibLE to every member of the staff such as a room which staff have to pass through to get from one part of the building to another as this will make it virtually impossible to control temperature and humidity. Some may object to the fact that it might be necessary to have the collection away from the department to which it belongs and that it is not easy to gain access to it and would prefer it somewhere close by. In these cases, it is necessary to consider the consequences of unsuitable storage on the material. If, however, it is a choice between suitable storage with the correct temperature and humidity and somewhere easy to get to for retrieval purposes, the presumption should always be in favour of the better storage facilities. With modern reprographic techniques, it is possible to make copies of particularly heavily used or vulnerable items and keep these at hand and insist that they are used rather than the originals, just as in the case where newspapers are on microfilm and have to be consulted on film rather than in their original format. Once a copy has been made, preferably by a photographic means rather than by electro-static methods, it is relatively easy to make further copies if the need arises, thus reducing the use of the original item.

The storage systems

The storage of ephemera is not as straightforward as might be expected. The wide variation in size means that it is necessary to have several different sequences or have much wasted space if the storage system is designed to accommodate the largest items in the collection. Assuming that the problems of finding a suitable location within the building with the ability to control the temperature, humidity, light, dust and access have been overcome, the next problem is to decide which system of storage to adopt. To some extent, the size of individual items is going to dictate the system that is used. Logic dictates that a railway ticket or handbill is not going to be stored in the same sequence as a large poster or broadsheet. Consequently, even in the most basic storage systems, account has to be taken of the variation in the size of items, different sizes requiring different sequences or even different storage facilities. It is, however, possible to standardise to some extent, particularly with the more recent types of ephemera as paper sizes now tend to be standardised. In addition, account has to be taken of the previous methods of storing ephemera which have been used in the library. Most libraries have got ephemera which has been in their collections for many years with the result that there may be an established system, but this may not be suitable when large quantities of more recent material are being added. For example, some ephemera might have been mounted with newspaper clippings, other items might have been mounted in guard books and yet other material might have been placed in a sequence of its own. For example, one library which has several different places for ephemera is the Local History Library in Manchester where the main collection of ephemera is to be found in the 'miscellaneous collection', but in addition there is the broadsheet collection, which is housed separately and further ephemera is to be found in scrapbooks, guardbooks and newspaper clippings as well as a completely separate sequence for theatre playbills. An attempt has been made to rationalise this with that material which was found in the newspaper clippings being transferred to the miscellaneous collection, but there still exist several different places that require to be checked by someone looking specifically for ephemera. It is, therefore, advisable to try to bring all the ephemera together to form a single collection stored in the same place.

The way libraries deal with ephemera often depends on precedent and the size of the collection. However, another factor which is taken into account when deciding on the storage method to be used will be the amount of space available to house the collection. Some libraries will use guardbooks to keep material whilst others will use boxes or filing cabinets and yet others will have vertical and horizontal systems, depending on the size of the material in the collection. No library will have a single system for its ephemera. The system or systems used will be that which suits the material in the collection.

In addition to providing adequate and proper storage for the material, there is another factor that has to be borne in mind, namely that of the security of the material. With so much of the material being small, it is very easy for items to get lost or to be taken away illicitly by readers, sometimes to be returned after a period of time and sometimes never to be returned at all. Whatever system of storage is used, it is important to remember that the less well organised it is, the greater the chance of items going astray either when being used by the public or misfiled by members of staff or even left lying around for a period of time after use and before being returned to their correct sequence and storage.

The ideal situation would be to have all items in a single sequence and capable of being stored in a single place, using the same system for everything. However, just as with books it is necessary to have several sequences – octavo, quarto and folio – to accommodate different sizes, so with ephemera it is necessary to have different sequences based on size. To mix large and small items would not only cause a waste of space, but would also allow small items to be lost amongst the larger ones. It is therefore necessary to have several sequences based on size, but the number of sequences should be kept to a minimum and preferably housed in the same room or storage area.

Having secured an area in which to house the ephemera collection, the next decision which has to be taken relates to the type of equipment which is to be used in which to store the material. There are five basic ways in which ephemera can be stored: on shelves as books are kept, in cabinets, vertically, in boxes, or horizontally.

On shelves

This method of storing ephemera is not to be recommended. Shelves are not ideal for keeping ephemera on and neither is ephemera designed to be kept on shelves. However this does not mean that shelves might not be used in conjunction with some other form of storage such as boxes or guardbooks.

Cabinets

It is possible to use filing cabinets to store ephemera. Most filing cabinets come in a variety of sizes and are thus capable of holding most sizes of material. The size of material the cabinet is designed to hold will determine the number of drawers it has. Thus, a cabinet designed to accommodate octavo, quarto or folio-sized material will have four drawers whilst those designed for the very large material will usually have only two drawers. Most items of ephemera will fit into a filing cabinet of one size or another. However, it is not recommended that the material is just put into a cabinet without any form of protection or container in which to keep it.

With many items one of the safest ways to prevent a document being damaged whilst being taken out of or returned to its correct place is to use either an envelope or a wallet and wherever possible, to mount it so that the mount takes the bulk of the handling. Mounting will also prevent items getting creased and help to flatten those items which have already been folded. There are certain items, however, which it is not possible to mount and, therefore, care has to be taken in storing and retrieving such items. The use of envelopes and wallets can assist in this, although it may not do so when very large items are involved.

Storage boxes and shelving used for ephemera in Manchester Local History Library (author)

Suspended filing used for part of the miscellaneous collection in Manchester Local History Library (author)

The use of envelopes or wallets also has the advantage in that they come in standard sizes and can accommodate items of varying sizes. Thus it is possible to have in the same cabinet, railway tickets and handbills because they will fit into similar sized wallets and can be filed together without the fear of the smaller item becoming mislaid. With the use of envelopes or wallets, it is possible to include duplicates in the same container so that less space is taken up.

Filing cabinets are usually made of metal although some may have a wooden finish to make them more attractive. However, for the purposes of storing ephemera, metal cabinets are sufficient. If it is at all possible, the cabinets should be fire resistant so that if the worst happens, the contents have a chance of surviving. In addition, the cabinets should be lockable to prevent unauthorised access and thus increase the security of the collection.

If it is decided to use filing cabinets to house the ephemera collection, it is advisable to have at least two different sizes of cabinet so that larger items do not need to be folded and, therefore, damaged. Ideally, there should be the complete range of sizes, although the majority of the items will fit into an average-sized cabinet and it will only be necessary to have one or two of the larger sized cabinets.

The advantage of using filing cabinets is that they are easily available and cheap. They also enable material to be filed and retrieved relatively easily. If wallets or envelopes are used, the classification can be written on the outside in a prominent place and not on the actual document itself although some form of ownership mark is usually required. It also provides security which can be lacking in some other forms of storage as well as the advantage of being relatively dust free.

There are, however, some disadvantages to the use of filing cabinets. One of these is the fact that if the drawers are filled to capacity, retrieval can be difficult and when it comes to inserting new material in the correct place it may be necessary to move the whole collection up, which can be a time-consuming task. The other main disadvantage is that it is necessary to go through everything in the drawer looking for something although if the classification is written on the front of the wallet, it is not such a difficult task.

Vertical filing systems

There are two methods of storing ephemera vertically, in metal chests and in cabinets with suspended filing. The former system is often used for maps and plans and requires a strip to be attached to the items to enable it to be suspended. This can result in the item being defaced or affected by the strip used to suspend it and there are also problems of the strip becoming detached and items falling to the bottom of the cabinet and consequently proving difficult to retrieve. There is also a problem with the spikes damaging the item if it is not put back carefully. The main use for such a cabinet would be very large items of ephemera which could not be accommodated in another form of storage.

The other form of vertical storage involves the use of either cabinets or units which can be fastened to walls, which may, or may not, have a front which can be rolled down. The items can be housed in pockets which are suspended from racks, but as with other storage systems, it is necessary to place the original in some form of wallet or envelope to protect it from damage.

One advantage of a vertical filing system, particularly if it is not a cabinet, is that it can be added to as the collection grows in size and if necessary can cover a whole wall, from floor to ceiling, if the space is available. It is, therefore, theoretically capable of infinite expansion. However, if there is only a limited wall space available, it might not be possible to expand at the same rate as the collection.

A second advantage of this system of storing ephemera is that in addition to putting the classification on the envelope or wallet, it is also possible to put the same information on the edge of the sling in which the item is kept, thus removing the need to hunt through looking for the correct material. It is also possible to indicate by means of slips which items are in use and who has them. Not only does it make returning material to the correct place easier, but also increases security as it should be possible to trace who has used the material if it is not returned. If a colour coding system is used for the slips, it should also be possible to distinguish which items are in use by the public and which have been withdrawn for use by the staff for one reason or another.

As with all systems of storage, there are drawbacks. One which has already been mentioned is that the size of item that can be housed in such a system is limited with the result that for the larger items another system has to be used. Another problem is one which occurs with any other system, namely that sooner or later, a section becomes overcrowded and everything will have to be moved to allow new material to be inserted in the correct place. If the material is too tightly packed, it can be damaged whilst being removed or replaced in the cabinet. The problem can be partially alleviated by leaving space to allow for expansion, but this might not be possible when space is short. If cabinets are used, it is possible to move them up to enable a new one to be inserted in the correct place, but trying to move a full cabinet even the shortest distance is no easy task.

One method of housing ephemera, used in the past and still used today, is the use of pamphlet boxes and box files which can fit into standard library shelving, as is the case with the material in the John Johnson Collection in the Bodleian Library at Oxford. If this system is used it is important that the boxes are of good quality and that the material they are made from is acid free.

On the face of it, this system might appear to be a good way of keeping the material as it does not require any special shelving or storage facilities to be acquired or made available. Boxes can be allocated to specific subjects or classes of material and it is possible to interfile them with the main stock of the library. It is also possible to create another unit of storage quickly and to interfile it in the correct position without too much difficulty. However, as with other systems, there are problems encountered in using boxes.

Firstly, there is the question of size. There is a limit to the size of box that can be made to fit on a shelf and which can be handled easily. The larger the box, the more rigid it must be and consequently, the heavier it is and the more difficult it is to handle. As a result larger material might have to be folded which does not assist in its conservation.

Secondly, there is the temptation to push too much into a single box on the grounds that a card box will stretch. Not only will this damage the box, but it will also cause damage to the material itself if it is stuffed into the box. It is also less easy to see what has been used and not returned.

Thirdly, there is the problem of those boxes in which there are only a few items. In these situations the item will probably slide down to the edge on which it is standing. After a time, the contents will develop a bend which it may be difficult to remove unless the items are subjected to pressure to straighten them out. Also items can get pushed down to the bottom of the box and be creased by other items being pushed on top of them. Although this can occur in filing cabinets, there should be sufficient space for them to become flat and therefore not to be creased.

Horizontal filing

This system of storing ephemera is one which should only be adopted where the material is too large to fit into one of the other types of system. Material in this system is stored flat, but there are problems with retrieval with the result that it can be easily damaged. If possible, this system is best avoided. An alternative is to use a vertical suspended type of map cabinet but as explained before, these too have their problems. Ideally, very large items should also be mounted whenever possible and kept in specially made large wallets.

Guardbooks and binders

This is one of the oldest methods of keeping non-book material. It usually involves accumulating material on a particular subject or a specific type of material, mounting it on special sheets of good quality paper which ideally should be acid free and fixed with a starch or other good quality paste. Normally, there will be only one item per sheet, but where the items are small, it should be possible to mount several on the same sheet provided that they are related to each other. Once a sufficient quantity of sheets has been accumulated, it is possible to bind them in the form of a book, taking care to ensure that the binders are made from acid-free board, which can then be treated in the normally accepted library manner. Birmingham Local Studies Library has done this with its collection of civic invitations.

Although the use of guardbooks has its attractions, there are problems which have to be overcome. Guardbooks will ensure that all the material is in the same place and that it can be treated as book material, but it does mean that if there is a gap in the series and it is filled, or if an item is found which fits in the middle of a sequence, it cannot be put in its correct place without pulling the book to pieces. There are also problems in making recently acquired material available quickly as the items should be kept together until there are sufficient to be bound together.

An alternative to binding the material is to use a form of ring-binder, but instead of a ring being used, a rod with one end that can be unscrewed is used. This system has the flexibility of a ring binder in that new material can be inserted in the correct place whilst at the same time, it can be treated as a book from the point of view of classification, storage and shelving. For example, the playbill collection in Manchester Central Library is kept in specially made rod binders which enable new ones to be inserted when the need arises with the minimum amount of difficulty. In order to prevent damage to the original material, it is essential that all material stored in this form is mounted on the correct type of paper and that the binders are also made of acid-free board. The mount should also be fairly stiff to make refiling easier.

This type of rod binder can also be used for smaller items of ephemera provided that they are mounted in an approved manner to protect them from handling. This system does allow for a flexibility of arrangement and the ability to insert new material in the correct place. This type of binder can usually be made to a specific size and fit library shelving. One problem is that if the classification and other details are added to the outside of the box, if the collection expands, it may be that the information given on the outside is incorrect. This can be overcome by having a system whereby the details are inserted in a panel which can be replaced at a future point in time if the need arises.

Scrapbooks

Scrapbooks are not the usual library means of keeping material which they themselves have collected, although this may have been used in the past. In the nineteenth century, however, it was the favoured means of private individuals to keep material which they had collected. The problem with scrapbooks is that it is a rigid system in that there is no way of inserting new material in its correct place and large items may have to be folded for them to fit on a page. The guardbook or rod-binder are the alternatives as both have a flexibity which the scrapbook does not have, but they can be bound and treated like books once all the material is collected together.

Summary on storage systems

Of the various systems of storing ephemera which exist, all have their advantages and drawbacks. It is advisable before making a final decision on which system to use to look at all the alternatives and if possible talk to other librarians who might have used the system which you have in mind and find out the problems they have encountered. It may that one system on its own will not be sufficient to deal with the range of material that is collected. For example, it might be decided that a vertical storage system will be the most satisfactory for the bulk of the collection whilst broadsheets and posters may be kept in cabinets. Sometimes, it may be decided to change from one system to another as the collection grows in size. For instance, Manchester Local History Library had several sequences of ephemera: boxes for the smaller items, cabinets for larger ones and cabinets for broadsheets and posters with some material also being found amongst its vast collection of newspaper clippings. In the late 1970s, it was decided to try to rationalise the system. The broadsheets and posters were retained in the filing cabinets as they were too large for the system which was to be used, namely, vertical suspended filing. Although most of the material has now been transferred to the new system, some of it has been kept in boxes, most notably the large collection of election literature where, for more recent elections, there is almost one box per election.

The existence of several sequences of material can create problems for new members of staff who will not be sure where to look and for readers who might be confused if each sequence has its own index or catalogue. It is best if the number of sequences can be kept to a minimum and that if necessary, a number if different systems are combined to provide the most suitable for the collection.

The conservation of ephemera

Conservation of material is a specialist undertaking and should not be done by an unqualified person, except under very close supervision of someone who is qualified. However, there are ways whereby the librarian can assist with the conservation of material. This does not relate so much to the actual physical side of repairing items which might be damaged or in mounting material, but by taking simple precautions. The most important is to ensure that the conditions under which the collection is housed are as near as possible to the ideal and that it is not housed in what might be termed a 'a silly place'.

Other precautions which might be taken to assist with the preservation of ephemera include ensuring that the material is replaced immediately after it has been used, or if it is not possible, as soon as is possible, and that it is not left lying around where dust can collect on it, where it can be affected by sunlight or where fluids can be split on it. These may be elementary precautions, but they will assist in helping to prevent the further degradation of the material. There are other ways of assisting such as not issuing material to the public unless it has been mounted by not issuing items in poor condition and that pencil is used rather than biro or fountain pen, that it is not photocopied if the item is too large for the machine or if photocopying will cause damage to it and that it is used on a flat surface and not in a way that can cause further damage. In addition there is the use of certain types of material which are available for conservation work and on the use of which the librarian should insist when material is sent for conservation.

Wallets and envelopes

Mention has already been made of the need to keep ephemera in some kind of wallet, folder or envelope to protect the item from damage whilst it is being retrieved or returned to its correct place. Wherever possible, these folders should be made from acid-free paper or card. If the library has its own binding or conservation section, it might be possible to get them made on the premises otherwise it is necessary to purchase them from outside suppliers, several of whom are now very much aware of the need to produce archival quality material for storage purposes and are doing so on a commercial basis. It will also be necessary to purchase folders of different sizes to take account of the different sizes of material. Usually, however, possibly three sizes will be sufficient to cover most material.

If the item is mounted and it is not intended to bind or interfile it with similar items, a manilla type wallet is ideal for storage. It will enable the item to be slipped in and out without difficulty as well as protect it whilst it is being either retrieved or returned to its correct place. It is important that where a wallet folder is used, it has a flap which will assist in protecting the contents not only whilst being taken in and out of the storage, but whilst it is waiting refiling. In addition, the wallet will also provide a facility on which the classification mark can be placed so that it is relatively simple to see where it should go. One problem with this kind of folder or container is that it is necessary to check that the material is in the wallet before it is replaced in the storage system as someone may decide to take it illegally.

Plastic or other types of 'see-through' envelopes are also available through various commercial manufacturers, but these should be treated with caution for although plastics and other similar material has been around for a considerable period of time, there is still no clear indiction of the effect the material has on paper, especially poor quality paper. In certain circumstances, it may be that the plastic can have an adverse effect on the material which it is meant to be protecting. One advantage of this type of folder is, however, that it enables the contents to be seen at a glance and could be said to act as a deterrent to potential thieves. It is necessary to try and keep upto date with developments in this field for if a suitable clear material is found and approved, it should be adopted. Plastic wallets may also have the advantage of being less bulky than card ones.

Mounting

When it comes to mounting ephemera, it should be treated as archival or primary source material. Not only is it important that the correct type of acid-free paper is used to reduce the risk of contamination of the mounted material, but the type of adhesive that is used is also very important. There are two methods that may be used for mounting material on acid-free card.

Firstly, there is the dry mounting process which involves the use of an acid-free dry mounting tissue which is fixed by means of the application of heat. Care has to be taken to ensure that the item is not damaged by heat as the process involves the melting of the tissue and its virtual permanent adhesion to the mount. Although it is possible to reverse the process, it is one which is not easy to carry out and has to be undertaken very carefully. Dry mounting is ideal for mounting illustrations, photographs, handbills and the large types of ephemera such as broadsheets and posters. It is, however, recommended that any repair work that the item being mounted requires should be carried out before mounting is commenced. Ideally, if dry mounting is the process which is decided upon, only that material which is printed on one side can be done as the reverse is lost by being affixed to the mount. Regarding the size of the mounting press that is used, this should be as large as possible to enable all sizes of material to be handled. In some cases, it might be possible to acquire a second, smaller press to handle the smaller items.

The second method used for mounting material is much older and involves the use of a flour and water paste or a specially made starch paste. This can be purchased in a ready-made-up form, prepared to an approved British Standard for use in conservation work in record offices and libraries.[3] Alternatively, the paste can be made up as it is required. Before the development of modern dry mounting techniques, this was the accepted method of mounting material and is still used for many archival items today. The use of a flour and water paste is ideal for smaller items of ephemera which require mounting, such as handbills, clippings, bill and letter heads. It is cheaper than dry mounting as no special equipment is required, only the paste and the correct acid-free card on which to mount the material.

Sometimes items which are printed on both sides may require to be mounted. It is not possible to dry mount these or to use a flour and water paste otherwise part of the text would be lost. One acceptable way to overcome this problem is to use butterfly tape, which can be peeled off if the item requires to be demounted for some reason or other and does not leave a mark as sellotape does.

The use of material such as sellotape or other pressure sensitive tapes should be avoided totally. Once these dry out, not only do they become detached from the mount and the item which is mounted, but they also tend to discolour the paper and leave an unpleasant sticky mess behind. Additionally, it is not possible to peel them off without damaging the item to which they were adhered. Also to be avoided are the commercially available glues and gloys which have chemicals added to them which can detrimentally affect the paper.

A recent development in mounting has been the introduction of spray mounts which claim to overcome the problem of mounting material. However, these also contain additives which can detrimentally affect the material on which the item is printed. The length of time these spray mounts take to have an effect on paper is not yet known as they are relatively new products. One thing that is certain is that after a period of time, the spray dries out and the mounted item becomes detached, but the spray will remain tacky on both the mount and the mounted item with the result that it can stick to something else and damage can be caused if they are not separated extremely carefully. The same applies to the sticks of solid adhesive which are now available.

Repairs to ephemera

The poor quality of the material on which much ephemera is printed, combined with the treatment it may receive, can give rise to problems in its conservation. The job of repairing damaged ephemera can be a difficult one which might involve piecing together many small pieces of fragile paper. It is not a job that can be undertaken by anyone, but should be done by a suitably qualified person who will be aware of the problems which might be encountered when carrying out the work. A qualified conservationist will be aware of the correct methods to be used in both the repair of the item and in the handling of fragile material.

When fragile or damaged material is acquired by the library or record office, a decision has to be made whether to allow it to be used in its existing condition or to send it for immediate conservation. It is always advisable to take the latter course of action as this will ensure that the item receives no further damage. It may be possible to have a photographic copy made before it is conserved so that there is a version available for the public to consult as well as a copy to act as a guide for the conservationist reassembling the document.

Some repairs, such as rejoining sections which have split along folds or creases, may be undertaken with butterfly tape. However it might be advisable to dry mount it, if this is possible. On other occasions, more extensive repair work might be necessary to prevent pieces being lost or the complete item crumbling away. Where it is necessary to insert paper to hold the item together, special papers are produced which are compatible with the original, but which are not subject to degradation.

Many large libraries and almost every record office have conservation facilities available either within the building or close at hand which form an integral part of the organisation. Some of these

The shop window of a small jobbing printers, Turner Street, Manchester, 1984 (Author)

Fly posting on a closed up building, Picccadilly, Manchester, 1984 (Author)

177

facilities are quite extensive, as in Birmingham Central Library or at the Lancashire Record Office, and are capable of dealing with almost any type of item which is sent to them for conservation or repair. However, there are many libraries which do not have these facilities available. It is not suggested that repair and conservation facilities should exist in every library, but where there are extensive collections of material which require, or which might require either repair or conservation, serious consideration ought to be given to providing facilities both in terms of qualified staff and equipment to enable most aspects of conservation and repair to be carried out. The following section aims to give an indication of the type of equipment that is required together with some of the more specialist materials which can be used.

The first requirement of any room that is to be used for conservation work is that it should be as free from dust as possible, have as much bench or table-top space as possible, good lighting as well as natural light, but not direct sunlight, and a plentiful supply of running water.

On the equipment side, in addition to ample work top space, including an area where the majority of large items can be laid flat, there will also be a need for a fumigation chamber and space for dry mounting presses and other types of press. There should also be facilities for storing sheets of mounting card and paper, which is used in restoration work, in the same conditions as those which prevail in the work room area.

In addition to the capital equipment that is required, such as dry mounting and other types of press, for a conservation section to function efficiently and properly, there is also a need for 'equipment' that is required for the day-to-day running of the department, such as chemicals and paper. Increasingly, more and more material is being produced for the conservation of material, including ephemera. For example, a special conservation board is now being produced of pure material which can be used for mounting purposes. Not only is it guaranteed to be pure, but this new conservation board also has a guaranteed length of life making it eminently suitable for use in conservation work. Similarly, special papers are being made for conservation work. Unfortunately, some, like a Japanese paper made from mulberry fibre, can only be purchased in large quantities, which might be too much for an individual library's requirements. However, if the cost is spread over a number of items and the cost per item conserved is looked at, the unit cost will probably be much reduced.

Lamination of material is a way of preventing material decaying, particularly those items which are heavily used or which are particularly fragile. However, it can be used for those items which are handled a great deal or which could be damaged or defaced. For example, the Lancashire Record Office is laminating some of its more fragile newspapers after they have been cleaned of the accumulated grime of many years usage. Lamination does present problems unless it is done properly. There is always the chance that it will turn yellow over a period of time and become brittle. This is particularly true of the older forms of lamination. Modern methods have reduced the possibility of this taking place.

Another problem which is encountered in poor quality paper is the appearance of brown marks actually in the paper itself, known as foxing. It is the result of impurities in the manufacture of the paper and not due to outside agents. As it is a stain, the only way it can be removed is by bleaching although correct storage conditions may help to arrest its spread.

Dirt is another problem with material which is received in the library, especially if it has been kept in a dusty atmosphere. Over a period of time, dirt can become ingrained into the paper and must be removed before any conservation or repair takes place. It is possible to remove surface dust first with a gentle dusting and then with the use of a rubber. Once the surface dirt has been removed, it is possible to wash the item in running water, but before this is done, it is necessary to check that the ink will not run and that the paper will stand up to being wet. Particular care must be taken with fragile items as they may disintegrate completely. Washing the item will weaken the fibres and as a result it is necessary to provide a means of permanently fixing the document either by lamination or by dry mounting afterwards.

Another problem which can occur with material, particularly historic ephemera, relates to the conditions under which it has been kept or stored prior to the library or record office receiving it. For instance, it might have been exposed to sunlight and be discoloured or faded. In these circumstances there is little that can be done to remove the discolouration or bring back the faded lettering. A more serious problem is the fact that it might have been stored under damp conditions, which will not only have discoloured the paper, but also encouraged fungicidal and insect infestation, a situation which will require the material to be treated in a fumigation chamber. The paper mite is one of the main insects that finds its way into damp paper and will be killed by treatment in such a chamber. Another problem with damp material is that it can also affect other material in that the wetness will soak through over a period of time. Damp material also has another hazard in that damp papers will stick together and may require very careful separation. Once separated, it will then be necessary to dry each item very carefully in order to stabilise their condition.

Summary

Much of the need for restoration and conservation will relate to historic ephemera. However, the general principles for storage and the type of storage to be adopted relates to all types of ephemera as it is important to ensure that modern material is preserved in good condition for the future. The type of storage system that is used will depend to a large extent on the space that is available and on previous policies. However, as the size of the collection grows, so it might be necessary to reassess how the material is housed and to look at alternative ways. Whatever system or combination of systems is adopted for storage, the need to use the correct materials and methods to conserve and restore ephemera is essential. It is important that properly qualified staff are used and that the correct materials are available in a properly fitted out area. If conservation facilities are not available, advice should be taken from an organisation which has such facilities.

6

Cataloguing, classification and indexing

Once a collection of ephemera has been established, it is important that it is properly classified, catalogued and indexed. If this is not done, then it is extremely difficult to fully exploit the collection as no-one will know what exactly there is in the collection and where to find it. The existence of a collection with no means of ascertaining what is in it makes the collection virtually useless to the researcher who might wish to consult material which may be in the collection. It might be very nice to have a collection of material which is in pristine condition, but the *raison d'être* of the collection is not to have something that is never used, but to provide information for someone undertaking research.

The key to the access of any collection of material is its cataloguing, classification and indexing. Even with the smallest collection of ephemera, it is necessary to have some form of cataloguing, classification and indexing if the material is to be fully used by both readers and staff. It is no use trying to get by relying on the memory of a single member of staff, for when that person is not on duty, that knowledge is not available and the collection cannot be properly used. Neither is it satisfactory for members of the public to be allowed to sort through large amounts of unlisted material in the hope that they might find something of use for their research. Such searching in an uncontrolled manner not only endangers the integrity of the collection from the conservation point of view, but also significantly increases the risk of individual items disappearing from the collection through pilferage. In addition, it reflects rather badly on the library if a reader has to spend valuable research time looking through a collection which has not even the most rudimentary listing to indicate what there is in it. The same will apply to staff who are engaged in answering inquiries, valuable time can be wasted looking for information and material which they think the library has, but cannot find because it is in an unsorted condition.

It is, therefore, important that from the beginning it is established that ephemera is treated like any other additions to the library stock, namely that it is catalogued and classified before it is made available to the public and as soon as possible after it is received. New books and pamphlets are not issued until adequate catalogue entries are made and some record of the existence of the item created. Yet, in the case of ephemera, much of the material is added to that which is available for use by the public without adequate records being created.

This chapter will look at the problems of cataloguing and classifying ephemera and at the need for indexing it to ensure that it can be fully exploited. It will not recommend any particular classification scheme as it is possible for libraries to adapt existing systems to cater for a collection of ephemera.

Cataloguing and listing ephemera

The nature of ephemera means that it will almost certainly be stored or shelved in several different sequences, depending on which method of storage is adopted, away from the main book stock sequences. Consequently, there has to be a system whereby the reader can trace what non-book material there is on the subject in which he or she is interested and which is related in some way to the other material in the library. As the material is often physically separate from the more usual type of material found in a library, there is a tendency to treat it as something different, not to be catalogued and classified unless absolutely necessary as there is always pressure from other departments to deal with traditional material as quickly as possible. The leaving of material can lead to problems as the size of the collection grows and backlogs develop which are hard to remove. It is, therefore, important not only from the point of view of the use of the stock, but also from a stock control angle that ephemera is properly catalogued and classified as quickly as possible.

The other major decision that has to be taken is whether the catalogue of the ephemera collection should be part of the main catalogue in the library or department or whether it should be a separate one. Ideally, there should be a single catalogue embracing all material in either the library or department, but this may not be possible as those engaged in cataloguing and classification may only have time to deal with books and pamphlets and not with material which requires classifications to be worked out and special catalogue entries prepared. This is particularly the case where there is a centralised cataloguing department for the whole library system with only one or two members of staff specialising in non-British National Bibliography material for all departments.

The alternative to having one catalogue for everything is to have a separate catalogue or sequence dealing solely with ephemera and other material which is non-standard and which might be maintained by the department's staff. This can create problems for readers in that they might look in the main catalogue and not be aware of the existence of a separate one covering other types of material. It also applies to members of staff who are unfamiliar with the system or who staff an enquiry desk in a public catalogue hall. Such a separate catalogue may also include entries for periodical articles, scrapbooks, illustrations and maps as well as ephemera. Manchester's Local History Library has a system like this whereby there is one catalogue for book and pamphlet material and another for index entries for periodicals, newspaper clippings, scrapbooks and ephemera, although it must be pointed out that the broadsides, posters and maps have their own individual catalogues or indexes.

Whichever system is used, whether the ephemera is included in the main catalogue or is part of a separate one dealing with non-book material, it is important that the material is listed in some form or other if it is not going to be dealt with immediately and shelved in its correct place. This particularly applies to historic ephemera where there may be a demand to consult the item as soon as word gets about that the library has acquired a copy. Sometimes, if a particularly large donation has been received, the donor may require a list of its contents, which could be used by the staff as an initial finding list until the material is fully dealt with and generally available for consultation. However, in the long term, the use of such lists is not to be recommended as it can complicate the search for material and create additional work for both staff and readers. It also removes some of the encouragement to provide a proper catalogue and classification for the material if there is a rough and ready way of tracing what there is in a particular collection of material.

What, then, is the ideal solution to the problem of bringing together all the relevent material on a particular subject? Probably the easiest way is through the use of a dictionary catalogue in which not only the book stock is recorded, but also the entries for all other types of material as well as index entries for periodicals and so on. This can create problems with the maintenance of the catalogue as usually only book, pamphlet and serial material is included. In some cases, where there is a centralised cataloguing department, it might not be possible to do this as staff from that department alone are allowed to insert new cards into the catalogue. This may not be feasible when there are cards not only for books and pamphlets, but also for articles and other material which they may not have catalogued and classified.

An alternative that may be adopted, where a classified catalogue is in use, is to have a separate sequence of cards for non-book material, which can cause problems if readers are not aware that this is the case and as a result miss material which they require. If this approach is adopted, and it can also be used where there is a dictionary catalogue in use and the department is not allowed to insert cards of its own making, it is possible for staff of the department to prepare the entries themselves and to file them. This does have the advantage of ensuring that the backlog is kept to a minimum, although at certain times of the year, a backlog will develop. For example, on a single day in March 1980, Manchester's Local History Library received 23 different items of ephemera for addition to its collection and for the rest of that week only one or two items were received. Admittedly, many of the items received were current, but even so it is necessary to incorporate them into the existing collection as quickly as possible as they can easily get lost or begin to build into a backlog.

Classification

Although it is possible to keep material in an alphabetical sequence, possibly under the name of the originating organisation, this method can create difficulties for those engaged in filing the material, or even just replacing it after it has been used, if the member of staff concerned is not familiar with the order of certain names. For example, problems can occur in filing *New town* and *Newtown*, which comes first? If this is not resolved at an early stage and the filing instructions adhered to strictly, serious problems can develop with material being misfiled and lost for a period of time. One way to overcome this is to classify every item received. Although many libraries use BNB classification as the basis for their own system, local collections often have a system which is specially designed to suit their own needs, as Dewey tends to be too general for such a collection, although in some places Dewey has been adapted to suit the local collection. For example, when Manchester Local History Library was established in the 1950s, it was decided to modify the existing Dewey system used by the library so that Manchester material was allocated 942.73, which was vacant at that time, and to use the various standard additions so that books on Manchester in the nineteenth century would be classified at 942.73081. This use of 942.73 was continued throughout the system so that something on Anglican churches in Manchester would be 283.4273. Not only was this system applied to conventional library material, but it was also used for the illustrations collection, maps, the miscellaneous or ephemera collection (excluding broadsheets) and the newspaper clippings files.

There is, however, one problem that arises when adapting a general system to deal with a local area. If the general classification system is revised, as Dewey is from time to time, the classification that has been adapted for local purposes might be allocated to another subject. If this happens, a decision has to be taken on whether to revise the system to meet the new circumstances or to leave it as it is. Whichever approach is taken, difficulties will arise as well as confusion. This problem, however, will not arise if the local collection has its own specially designed classification, independent of that of the rest of the library. Even with its own system, problems can arise, particularly with those items which have both a local and a general interest. For example, the history of Beyer, Peacock & Co, locomotive builders in Manchester[1], is of local interest to Manchester as well as for those interested in the technical side of railway engines and those with an interest in company history. The question arises, if only one copy is purchased, of where it should go and what its classification should be – the main library one or that used by the local collection. This is a question that can only really be answered by the library where the problem arises, but whichever approach is taken, the result is going to be out of step with one department, unless some special provision is made to overcome this. The best guidance that can be given is to suggest that it is added to the stock of the department which thinks it will make the most use of it. The real answer would be to purchase a second copy, if the budget permits. This problem might appear to be one which affects only the book and pamphlet stock, but this is not the case as it is one which affects the whole collection because in an ideal situation the non-book material will use the same classification as the rest of the department's stock.

Where a general classification has been adapted to serve a local collection, not only is there the problem of those areas which have been adapted falling out of step with the rest of the classification if it is updated, but there is also the question of it being specific enough to cater for local needs. For instance, if the case of theatres is taken, a general collection might not need to arrange the material according to names of specific theatres, but a local collection might want to do this. In these circumstances, it might be necessary to use the accepted class number, to add a series of letters to indicate which theatre it is and so to bring together all the material on a specific theatre. Thus, for instance, all the material on the Theatre Royal might have the letters TR after the classification. If this system is used, it can easily be adapted to deal with non-book material.

In the case of an ephemera collection where a thematic approach has been adopted, it may be necessary to develop a separate classification or arrangement to suit the material. For example, in the case of stamps, a country by country approach is usually followed, or in the case of a collection of material relating to railways, a company by company or line by line approach may be used. Often, with a thematic collection, the classification will not be as important as in a general collection of ephemera, as the arrangement may be by type of material rather than by subject.

A similar situation will probably exist in a firm's library where material on specific products will be arranged by product rather than by firm or manufacturer. Very often such material is not classified, catalogued or indexed as it is required only when current and discarded when it is out of date. An alphabetical sequence suffices for such collections of material as it is simple to understand and easy for the user to find material without having to resort to catalogues or staff assistance. Material which is kept for archival purposes will probably be arranged either under the name of the product or in date order, depending on what has been done previously.

Wherever possible, the classification used for an ephemera collection should be that which is already in use in the department. It is no use trying to adopt a completely different classification from the book stock as this will only create confusion for both readers and staff. If the local collection is just being established, careful thought should be given to having a classification that is separate from that of the main library stock and which is capable of being adapted to suit all types of material. There might be reluctance to do this if computer cataloguing, using one of the established systems is used, as it will mean that the local material will have to be treated separately, possibly manually catalogued and classified.

Non-local material

Local collections are not the only ones with ephemera. Departments like those which deal with technical and commercial subjects will also have ephemera in their collections in one form or another. In many cases, it is material which is required for current awareness purposes and only a small proportion of it is preserved permanently as part of the department's stock. In many cases, this material is neither classified nor catalogued in the conventionally accepted manner. In some cases, it will be merely filed under either the name of the product, firm or subject it relates to and kept in a filing cabinet to be discarded when its currency is over. For example, information on a new computer firm in an area might be filed under computer firms until the company is recorded in various trade and commercial directories. However, if it is a local firm, the information might be retained or passed to the local collection. If it is catalogued at all, it is with the simplest of entries, usually giving the basic information and its location.

A similar alphabetical approach may be taken in special libraries whereby an alphabetical approach is adopted under a recognisable name rather than under a complex classification scheme which users may not remember and which requires time to look up to find whether an item is within the library or not. For example, a firm dealing with patent medicines may keep trade literature according to the name of the manufacturing company or file it under the name of the product. Which method is used will depend on the approach the company takes in keeping its material.

Indexing

If a dual approach is adopted for local material, that is separate catalogues for book and pamphlet material and for other types of material, the entries in the latter may be in the form of index entries rather than full catalogue entries. With index entries, it is the subject content of the item which is indexed which takes precedent over the author/title of the material. Often, there will be several entries for each item so that every possible approach can be catered for. This can be best illustrated if the following example is studied:

> HIGH TREASON
> FORTY POUNDS
> REWARD
> Whereas, Joseph Fletcher, late of Park-Street, Birmingham, in the County of Warwick, CABINET-LOCK-SMITH, stands charged before William Hicks, Esquire, one of His Majesty's Justices of the Peace for the said County, of the Crime of High Treason, in Counterfeiting the SILVER COIN of this realm.
> The said Joseph Fletcher is about 28 years of Age, 5 Feet 6 inches high, smooth pale Face, long Nose, thin Visage, frowning, slender made, rather bow-leg'd, and generally wears a black Waist coat and Leather Breeches.
> Whoever shall apprehend the said Joseph Fletcher or give such information as may be the Means of his being so apprehended, the Person or Persons, so apprehending him and giving such Information as aforesaid, shall, on his being taken before any of His Majesty's Justices of the Peace, and delivered up for the Purposes of Justice, receive a Reward of FORTY POUNDS on Application to John Vernon, Esquire, Solicitor to His Majesty's Mint, Lincoln's Inn, London, or or to Mr William Spurrier, Soliciter at Birmingham.
> April 6th 1805.
> (Downes, PRINTERS, STRAND, LONDON.)[2]

In a normal catalogue entry, this item might have one single entry, possibly under *High Treason*, but this would leave much useful information missing from the catalogue. The classification might help to identify the subject. However, to enable the full use to be made of this item, there are a number of entries required to be made. It might be that one card is prepared and the rest are treated as added entries so that the amount of time taken in preparing the entries is reduced. To make full use of this item, to cater for every possible approach, it would be necessary to have the following entries: *Counterfeiting; Fletcher, Joseph; Treason; Coinage-Counterfeiting; Spurrier, William; Coinage-Silver* and possible one under *Downes*, the printer, and *Park Street, Birmingham*, as the place where Fletcher once resided. It might also be decided to have an entry under the title of the item, such as *High Treason: Forty Pounds Reward*. If such entries are made, it will then be possible to approach the item from several different angles.

This need for detailed indexing does not only apply to broadsheets like the one quoted above, but applies to all other types of ephemera. For example, a railway ticket may only require entries under the destination of the ticket, the assumption being made that all the tickets in the collection are issued by the station in which the library is situated, but where there are several stations, these will have to be identified, and possibly a general entry under *Railway Tickets* made. However, some items, like the handbill quoted below will require a great many entries to ensure that the fullest use is made of it:

BARM GIVEN AWAY!

To all purchases of 10lbs of our well-known qualities of Flour we will give, during the next fortnight, Quarter lb. of Barm.

FLOUR	Per 20lbs.	SUGAR	
Finest Snowflake	2s 4d	Small Crystal	2lb for 3½d
Finest Biscuit	2s 2d	Medium Crystal	2lb for 4d
Finest Bread	2s 0d	Tate's Superfine granulated	2lb for 4d
		Sparkling Lump	2lb for 4d

Finest MARGARINE	5d per lb
PURE LARD	6½d per lb
Finest CANADIAN CHEESE	7½d per lb

Finest LANCASHIRE	9d per lb
Home Cured BACON, own rolling, sliced	8½d per lb
2lb Jar New MARMALADE	6½d

WAX CANDLES	3d per lb or 3lbs for 8d
WATSON'S MATCHLESS SOAP	3lbs for 8½d
CAPTAIN WEBB MATCHES	2 doz. for 3½d
SAFETY MATCHES	1½d per doz. or ⅓ per gross
BORAX 2½d per lb.	STARCH 2½d per lb

Irish Eggs always Fresh

LOWE'S,
    45 MOSS STREET, ROCHDALE
Printer G Stott, Rochdale [3]

Not only would this handbill require entries under the name of the firm and possibly under the name of the printer and the address of the shop, but also on the prices given, as information on prices is always hard to trace and therefore the very minimum entry. Ideally, there should be an entry for each item mentioned in the list so that anyone wanting to trace prices of a particular foodstuff could do so without difficulty.

It may be argued that to index something as closely as has been suggested is excessive, but if the fullest use is to be made of it by both readers and staff, then this is very necessary. It is no use relying on the memory of a single member of staff that such information is contained in a handbill as that person may not be on duty when it is required or may leave and take the information with him or her.

Not only should historic ephemera be indexed before it is made available to the public, but current or contemporary material should also be indexed before it is added to stock, otherwise a backlog will build up of unindexed material and no-one will be sure what has been indexed and what has not. As with historic ephemera, indexing should be as detailed as possible to enable all possible approaches to be adopted in the future and should not only include the subject of the item, but also any advertisements which might be included.

If the approach is taken of having a separate index for the non-book material, then it should include information not only on ephemera, but also entries for periodicals, newspaper index entries and the like. The fewer the places which have to be consulted, the easier it is for both readers and staff to check whether the library has any information on a subject. It is often in ephemera that there are references to events, firms and organisations which might not exist elsewhere and the only way to ensure that this information is available and known about is to have it properly indexed.

The card entry

It is important to ensure that the card containing the entry gives as much information as possible so that the person consulting it can tell from it whether it might be of some use or not. In addition to having the heading, it is helpful if a *précis* of the contents of the item can be given, together with the date, the type of material it is and a classification or locational symbol. For example, the advertising leaflet produced by Books for Students Limited[4] might have an entry similar to the following:

Books for Students Limited

Statement of facilities offered by the company, location plan, address and telephone number, opening hours and photograph of display area. Advertising brochure. Relates to a Leamington Spa firm. No date.

In addition, there may be a class number or some other means of locating it on the shelves or in the file.

One problem which has to be faced when producing such an index is to decide which headings should be used. For example, in the broadsheet on counterfeiting, should the entry be under *Treason* or *High Treason*. The decision as to which to use will be made in the light of precedent in the library, but which ever is used, it is necessary to draw up carefully rules to overcome this problem, particularly if several people are involved in preparing entries for such an index. Similarly, with names of organisations, it is necessary to provide guide lines as to which name is to be used especially if the name which is normally used is not the full name of the company or is one which is not known to the public. For the sake of convenience, the entry should be under the more commonly known name of the organisation or firm and an entry under its proper name referring to the version which is used. Similarly, if an organisation changes its name, there should be provision made for the user of the index to trace either the old or the new name, depending on which is being looked up. Gradually, as the size of the collection grows, so a list of subject and other headings will be developed which should overcome many of the problems.

Special cases

There are certain areas which might be considered as special cases from the point of view of cataloguing, classifying and indexing ephemera. This situation can arise either because the format of the material enables it to be dealt with as a special case or because of the bulk of the material involved. Although it is not a good idea to have special cases, certain types of material, however, do lend themselves to be considered for a specialist form of treatment.

Broadsheets and posters   This group of material is one of the most obvious areas which can be treated separately because their size is such that they are often filed in a separate sequence from the rest of the material in the department. The logical way would be to index them in the main information index, but sometimes, because they are filed separately, they are classified and indexed separately also. For example in the Manchester Local History Library broadsheets and posters have their own special arrangement and index. They are not classified, but arranged in date order, their filing arrangement being determined by the date of publication and a running number. For example, a broadsheet with the opening words 'At a numerous meeting of the Gentlemen, Clergy, and Freeholders of the Parish of Saddleworth . . . '[5] has the reference f.1796/1. The first element 'f' denotes which sequence it is in, namely the folio one. The second part, 1796, is the date and the last part, after the stroke, indicates that it is the first item in the series for that year. Where there are several items on the same subject, a further letter is added at the end so that all material on the same subject is brought together. Thus, all the broadsheets relating to Peterloo will be f, or ff if they are very large, 1819/2/A to whatever letter is required.

This is a relatively simple system, but it does provide a filing order as well as a means of classifying the material. In addition, it is possible to give a running number to those broadsheets which have been mounted in volumes so that they too can be incorporated into the index. There can be a problem with that material which is not dated or which is undatable. Research may have to be undertaken in order to try to establish a date for it but if no date can be found, Manchester has adopted the suffix 'n.d.' followed by a running number. If, at some later date, the undated item can be given an accurate date, it is possible to do so and relocate it in its correct place in the date sequence.

In order to trace what exists in the collection, Manchester has provided two separate indexes for its broadsheets and posters. The main index consists of a card for each individual broadsheet on which is given the item's own reference, the title, a *précis* of the contents, publisher and place of publication and its date. There is also a note of its location and call number if it is a broadsheet that is to be found in a known volume.

The second index is a subject one in which individual broadsheets are listed under the subject to which they relate. Thus, someone wanting to look at broadsheets and posters related to counterfeiting in the library would only have to look up 'Counterfeiting' in order to find a list of relevant items and then refer back to the main card for a *préis* of the item.

This approach to indexing and listing broadsheets is one which can be best adopted if there is a substantial collection of them. Ideally, the cards made for broadsheets should be interfiled with the cards made for other items of ephemera and index entries for information in periodicals. To be completely successful, it is necessary to fully index each item. In the case of Manchester Local History Library, only one entry is made per broadsheet, except in the odd case. Consequently, there is material which is overlooked. For example, the following broadsheet has only one entry, under the Rochdale Canal, whereas it would be helpful if there were several covering other possible lines of approach which might be taken by potential users of the item:

CONVEYANCE OF GOODS BETWEEN MANCHESTER AND ROCHDALE MAY 1808

The Committee of the Company of the Proprietors of the Rochdale Canal, have undertaken the Conveyance of Goods on their Canal, between MANCHESTER and ROCHDALE; and have procured a Set of proper Vessels for the Purpose, in which they propose to carry Goods at the FOLLOWING RATES:

GROCERIES,	4½d per hundredweight
SALT	9d per load
MALT	9d per load
HOPS	8d per pockets
DO (in bags)	4½d per hundred
PORTER and ALE	12d per barrell
Do	6d half barrel
TIMBER	6s per ton
FLAGS	4s per ton
PARCELS,	3d each, if not exceeding 56lbs
Do	4d if above 56lbs and not exceeding 80lbs
Do	6d if above 80lbs
CHEESE	10d per packet

MEAL and POTATOES	10d per load (not exceeding 13 score)
WOOL (but if more in proportion)	11d per sheet
TEA	6d per chest
SPIRITS, WINE etc.	6d per five gallons
Do	8d for five gallons and not exceeding ten.
Do	12d, ten gallons and not exceeding thirty.
Do	6d per hundredweight, if the whole amount exceeds thirty gallons.
HAT BOXES	6d each
Do CHESTS	10d each

192

The above Goods will be delivered at or taken from any Place, not exceeding half a MILE from the Wharf, at the above Prices; and for Goods delivered at or taken from Places above that Distance from the Wharf, a reasonable Charge will be made, in addition.

A Vessel will sail from Rochdale,
Each MONDAY, WEDNESDAY and FRIDAY, at ONE
O'CLOCK in the Afternoon;
And from Manchester
Each TUESDAY and SATURDAY at the same hour, and each THURSDAY morning at Six o' Clock.
N.B. The vessels are furnished with Cabins for the Accommodation of Passengers, at 1/6d the Fare; will be punctual to the Time of sailing; and are expected to perform the Passage in about seven hours.

By order
RALPH SHUTTLEWORTH
Clerk to the Company

(Hartley, Printer)[6]

If this item was fully indexed in the subject index for the broadsheets, there would be a number of entries and not just *Rochdale Canal*. The others might include *Canal Transport – passengers; Canal transport – freight; Canal Transport – freight rates; Canal transport – passenger fares; Canals – Manchester; Canals – Rochdale* and if further detail was required, it would be possible to index the various goods which the broadsheet lists.

Newspaper clippings   Although newspaper clippings fit the definition of ephemera, they are frequently not regarded as such. In many libraries, particularly local studies libraries and those which require current information to be available to its readers, there are collections of clippings. Often, the extent is such that they are regarded as a separate type of material with their own classification and sequence, indexes and storage systems. Usually, they are arranged so that they can be consulted quickly and easily added to when more information is available. Often, such mateiral is filed in binders which enable new material to be added in the correct place and in the correct order, although sometimes the clippings are kept in wallets or folders until there are sufficient to mount into guardbooks or scrapbooks, which can then be treated as a normal book from the point of view of cataloguing and classification.

Where newspaper clippings are kept as a separate sequence of material, there may be a separate classification scheme or the one which is used for the remainder of the stock may be used. Manchester, for example, started off its newspaper clippings by using the same classification as was used for the rest of the stock, but later abandoned it and developed one specifically designed for the newspapers. This involved dividing everything into a number of broad subject fields and then further sub-dividing and if necessary, further sub-divisions could be used. For example, Transport is divided into Transport – General, Air Transport, Railways and Roads. Each of these sections is then further subdivided so, for example, there is a section under railways on stations and within each subsection, the arrangement is alphabetical.

The problem with having a separate sequence for newspaper clippings is that it creates another place to be searched for information. If the various sections are indexed, possibly only in general terms, and the index cards incorporated within the main information index, this problem should not arise. However, the situation with newspaper clippings can be further complicated by the fact that some material in this format will be in one system of storage and other material may be in another and treated quite differently.

Ephemera in archival material   Archival material requires separate consideration as ephemera which is found in an archive will remain with that archive and not be separated from it. In the case of this material, it will be listed in the calendar relating to the archive in the same amount of detail as other material. Its classification will relate to the classification, or numbering, given to the archive and not to that used by the library or record office for the remainder of its material.

The archivist is a leading exponent of providing very detailed descriptions of material as can been seen in the archive calendars which they produce. Some of the detailing which librarians use for their indexes derives from the archivists' practice of making detailed entries for their calendars. They, that is archivists, have been forced by the nature of the material which they handle to provide detailed entries as some archival collections amount to many thousands of documents and the archivist will not want to get out the complete archive when only a small portion of it is required. Consequently, to assist the user in deciding whether an item will be useful or not, detailed, analytical entries are used. It may be very helpful to the librarian with a large or growing ephemera collection to adopt this practice so that potential users can decide whether it is necessary to see the document or not. This not only saves the user time, but can also prevent excessive wear and tear on the original item.

One problem for someone trying to trace particular examples of ephemera in an archive office or record office is the fact that it may be necessary to go through a large number of calendars in order to trace a few items. There is no way of overcoming this unless a decision is taken to provide a separate list or index of such material. If this was done, it would probably be for internal use only, but compiling it would take up valuable time which could be spent in calendaring further archival collections.

In addition to collections of archives, record offices and archive repositories will acquire, in the course of time, miscellaneous material which is not part of an archive and which does not fit into any particular grouping of material. Sometimes, these may be treated as an archive in their own right, but often they will be treated as miscellaneous items, kept in a separate sequence and indexed separately. For example, a bill for furniture or an isolated invoice for goods supplied by a firm may fall into this category. This type of material may have its own card index, but as with material in large archival collections, it will doubtlessly be given a detailed description on the card.

If the record office or archive repository is part of a library, it may be that an arrangement can be reached between the archivist and the librarian whereby certain types of ephemera can be indexed and included in the library's indexes. If this is not possible, the attention of readers should be drawn to the fact that there may be relevant material in the archives section and that they should consult the archivist as well. Usually, however, in organisations where the two bodies exist side by side, the library has copies of the archive calendars and it is possible to go through them looking for items of ephemera and making general references to the material in the department's indexes and indicating where they can be consulted.

Scrapbooks   Scrapbooks form another special case for the librarian. Often they contain only newspaper clippings, but sometimes they will also include items of ephemera, such as cards, *in memoriam* cards, letter and bill headings and handbills, items which may have interested the compiler or which have accidentally found their way into the scrapbook. It has to be accepted that it is not possible to incorporate this material into the main collection of ephemera, unless the scrapbook is disintegrating and the material is taken out for conservation. If this happens, it is possible to incorporate the material into the main ephemera collection, although it must be remembered that when this takes place, it is necessary to amend all entries for those items which are removed so that they are not 'lost'.

Usually, scrapbooks are treated as book material as they are able to be catalogued and classified and shelved as books, but in order to make full use of their contents, it is important that they are fully indexed, especially that material which relates to the department.

Photographs Although photographs are excluded from coverage in this book, it has to be accepted that photographs can contain items of ephemera as part of the picture. Usually these are incidental to the main subject of the photograph rather than being the reason why the photograph was taken. The fact that items such as broadsheets and posters occur on photographs should not be a reason why the information is excluded from the index of ephemera as the one which appears in the photograph may be the only record of it that exists. Sometimes, it is possible to enlarge the photograph so that the poster or broadsheet becomes an illustration in its own right and thus capable of being incorporated with other posters and broadsheets. However, where this is not feasible, an attempt should be made to read the text and make an entry in the index drawing attention to it and where it can be found in the illustrations collection.

It is not only historic photographs which can contain ephemera such as broadsheets and posters, but also modern photographs, particularly those where there are advertising hoardings or where there is fly-posting or where shops have many window bills. These, too, should be included in any index which is created so that they will not be overlooked.

Bibliographical citation

When it comes to preparing a bibliography which consists solely of items of ephemera or includes some ephemera, difficulty can be experienced in making an adequate entry. With books and pamphlets, it is normal to have author, title, date and place of publication, number of pages, whether it is illustrated or has maps and diagrams and so on. With ephemera, some of this information may not be present. Few items of ephemera can be specifically attributed to an author although it is possible to use the name of the organisation responsible for its publication.

The attribution of a title can also cause problems, but it should be possible to find a title or sort one out, although in the case of some items, like tickets or bill headings, this might not be so easy. In cases where there is no obvious title, it may be necessary to make one up which is suitable for the item. For example, a railway ticket may be under the heading of British Rail, but for a title it might be necessary to simply describe it as 'Ticket: Manchester to Torquay' and likewise, with a billheading, its title may be simply 'Billheading'.

Regarding the publisher and place of publication, it should be possible to discover this from the item itself without too much difficulty. However, it might be necessary to assume that the place of publication is the same as the place where the publishing body is located. Sometimes, the date can cause a problem as often ephemera is undated or merely the day and the month given and no year. This can be overcome if all material is dated when it is received, particularly the current material. In a bibliography, some means can be adopted to indicate that the date is one given to it by the library and may not appear on the item itself. Sometimes the date will appear as part of the printer's reference and sometimes it can be ascertained from the text itself.

The most difficult part is the pagination. Where it is a single sheet or folded once, there should be no problem, but where there is more than one fold, there is a problem of saying how many pages it has. Probably the easiest way to overcome this problem is to regard items which have several folds as a single sheet and then to indicate either the number of folds or the number of sections that have been created. For example, in a bibliography of current material on the Castlefield area of Manchester which is being compiled, much of the material is in the form of leaflets, some of which have several folds. In this case, the entry merely states 'single sheet – 3 folds'. It is important that some consistency is arrived at in this area so that when a bibliography is consulted or a reference given, there is a standardised approach and everyone knows what to expect when they consult the original document.

Conclusion

Although some items of ephemera may be catalogued, it is probably better if an indexing approach is taken as this will enable more information to be given than would be possible with a conventional cataloguing approach. Additionally, it is probably easier to make the added entries that will be required to ensure that all approaches are catered for, especially if the entries are compiled by the staff of the department who will have some knowledge of the wide variety of uses and approaches that can be made to a single item. Someone who is not in contact with the public may overlook an approach or may not be aware of the development of the interest in a particular subject field.

The classification which should be used should be one which will tie in with that used for other material in the department which has the ephemera collection. The use of a classification which applies solely to the ephemera collection should be avoided wherever possible to prevent confusion, although it may be necessary to adapt the existing system in some way to cater for what is a non-standard type of material.

If it is not possible to have a single catalogue/index for all the material in the department, then the number of indexes should be kept to a minimum not only to save time for the user and members of staff using them, but to avoid material being overlooked because it is indexed in a separate place. Where there is a separate index/catalogue for non-book material, this should include entries for ephemera as well as index entries for periodicals and other analytical entries required by the department. To be successful, it is necessary to compile a list of headings to be used by those engaged in indexing material as well as rules for dealing with names of organisations and so forth. The general rule for this should be to adopt an approach which the majority of the users will understand and which is most suitable for the department and not to engage in creating something which only members of staff can use and understand. If this latter arises, then much of the usefulness of having an index will be lost as staff time will be spent in showing readers where to find material when they might be better engaged in adding further entries to the index to enable the stock of the library or department to be better exploited.

Basically, it is important to index ephemera as closely as possible and to have as few different indexes/catalogues as possible. The fewer there are, the less likelihood there is of something being overlooked. Likewise, the departmental staff might be the best ones to make the entries for the non-book material as they often do for analytical entries for periodicals and scrapbooks.

7   The value, exploitation and use of ephemera

To some people, the idea of libraries, record offices and museums collecting scraps of what appear to be useless paper, handouts and advertising literature is a strange one, especially if it is that produced by modern society. They tend to regard libraries as places where one consults books, periodicals, newspapers, maps and obtains answers to difficult problems which require reference books to find the answer. Likewise record offices are places where old handwritten papers are to be found which help trace your family tree whilst museums are places to go to look at exhibitions, which may or may not be enlivened by the use of a few posters, notices and so on. What these people do not think about is how the material came to be available in these organisations in the first place. However, there are those people who regard the collection of other people's throw-away items as far-sighted as it will enable something from the present generation to be used in the future by those researching the late twentieth century. Even those who cannot understand why material published in the late twentieth century should be preserved do appreciate the fact that material has been collected from the past and is used in research in one form or another.

Even within the library profession there are those who are sceptical about the value and usefulness of collecting contemporary ephemera and preserving it. They expect such collections to be maintained with the minimum amount of staff time and taking up as little space as possible. Yet, how many times has a library, or one section of it, been asked for a copy of a leaflet or poster which was issued a year or so previously and of which no copy can be found? Although this might not be a common event in many libraries, the question is asked from time to time and when it is, how often does the librarian think that if only a copy had been kept, the library could have been of assistance. For example, a number of years ago, the National Coal Board issued a leaflet in which the public's help was sought in tracing old mining maps and documents which would be of assistance in locating disused mine shafts. Shortly after the campaign had ceased to be current, one library was asked by the BBC if they by any chance had kept a copy of the poster. Several libraries had already been tried and it appeared that not even the NCB had a copy handy. Fortunately, one departmental librarian had decided that it might be worth adding a copy to the miscellaneous collection which was maintained and thus was able to oblige. The importance of this example lies in the fact that someone had decided to keep a copy, not knowing at the time what use it might be put to in the future.

The purpose of this chapter is to look at some of the possible uses that can be made of ephemera in a general way, the types of user that might study ephemera and how the library, record office or museum might exploit its collection of this type of material.

The value of ephemera

Although items of historic ephemera may have a monetary value, they also have a value to the researcher in terms of the information which they contain, information which might not be available from any other source. The same interest value also applies to items of current or contemporary ephemera, although this will most likely be at some unspecified date in the future. The importance of preserving historic ephemera is in the main accepted and understood, but this is not so with current and contemporary material, except possibly by the collector and some local historians. However, not even all local historians and local history societies realise that contemporary material will form part of the basic research material used by those engaged in research in the future. For example, one local history society proudly claimed that it had photographed all the buildings threatened by a new motorway/bypass as well as the actual construction work itself, but they had not appreciated the fact that the notices which had been sent out advising residents of the threat to their homes and those notices which were posted on the line of the construction work were also part of the record of the town. Once this was pointed out to them, an effort was made to to fill the gap by obtaining copies of the various notices. They also resolved to try and collect as much of the currently produced material as possible so that future historians of the town did have some material to work from in addition to that which appeared in the newspapers and official records.

In the library, record office and museum, ephemera can form an important part of many different types of collection as well as being an important basic reference tool in some departments and sections. For instance, in those departments which deal with commercial information, ephemera may provide current information which may not be available in the more traditional book or article form which may never appear in the more accepted format because by the time it would, the information is out-of-date and, therefore, useless. In an industrial library, ephemera may be found amongst its collection of material on products produced either by the company itself or by rival companies and if the material has not been discarded, it will show the changes that have taken place over a period of time not only in the product itself, but also in marketing and advertising techniques. In a library specialising in the fine arts, ephemera can be used to show the changes which have taken place in graphic design over a period of time whilst in the local studies department, ephemera is able to add to the information that is available on the history of the locality. The same also applies to a record office, where ephemera may be found as an integral part of an archive collection, supplementing the information that may be obtained from more traditional sources of information. In the museum world, ephemera can be useful in helping to bring displays to life as well as providing historical authenticity to displays and possibly helping to solve problems of how a machine worked or was assembled. The more ephemera that is preserved from the present day, the fuller the picture of life at a given point in time will be.

The interest value of ephemera will vary from item to item as also will the use made of individual items of ephemera. This will also be affected by the level of survival of different types of ephemera. The more that survives, the greater the choice of examples that can be quoted and the larger amount of information that is available. In an ideal situation, copies of most things that have been published would survive in one form or another, but this is not the real position. A very large amount of ephemera does not survive for a wide variety of reasons. It is a question of educating people to appreciate the fact that ephemera does have a use and interest value after its apparent usefulness has finished and consequently, it should not be thrown away. For example, a firm's records should not only include its minute books, account books and other documentation which it is obliged to keep by law, but also copies of notices, house journals, advertising literature and copies of its letter and invoice headings. Similarly, societies should aim to achieve a high level of coverage of the material which they produce.

The use of ephemera

Ephemera can be used in many ways and for many different purposes. Each person who uses an item of ephemera will do so for a different purpose. Take the following example from Rochdale:

Relief of Mafeking
CELEBRATIONS

PROCESSION
Assembling
On the Town Hall Square
THIS DAY (SATURDAY)
At 2-30 p.m., will leave at 3 o'clock sharp.
headed by the
MAYOR AND CORPORATION,
BOROUGH POLICE BAND
AND FIRE BRIGADE

Other BANDS will be present.

Esplanade – Manchester Road – Drake
Street – Milkstone Road – Durham St –
Oldham Road – Drake Street – Smith
Street – Entwisle Road – Whitworth
Road – Princess Street – Sheriff Street
– Spotland Road – St Mary's Gate –
Cheethan Street – Yorkshire Street,
back to Town Hall Square

COLLECTIONS en route FOR WAR FUND.

A GENERAL INVITATION to be present is
extended
WILLIAM CUNLIFFE. Mayor[1]

This handbill will not only be of interest to those studying the history
of Rochdale generally, but also to those interested in the Boer War and
the way its events were reported and celebrated in this country and
even for someone interested in the civic pagentry. The best way to
establish what use could be made of an item of ephemera is to study it
carefully and try to compile a list of the various types of information
contained in the item and the potential uses that might be made of it.
In some respects, this will have been done if the item has been fully
indexed.

In addition to the information which can be actually obtained from
the item itself, it is important to bear in mind that this information,
however small or seemingly insignificant it may appear, may well help
to answer a query. Local research is, in many respects, like a jigsaw
puzzle with many small pieces, each fitting together to help build up

the complete picture, although some of the pieces may have been lost forever. For example, the information contained on a trade card or a bill head may supplement information that is contained in a directory or an article or an advertisement by giving details of products, telephone numbers and telegraphic addresses and possibly an engraving of the firm's premises. These sources, in their turn, will supplement any written information on the firm, which will complement any of the firm's business records which have survived.

The users of ephemera

The use made of an ephemera collection will depend to a large extent on where it is located, for whom it was collected, the use made of the department where it is housed, how much publicity is given to the collection and how easy it is to discover what there is in the collection. Ephemera that is in company archives will probably be used less than that which is found in public libraries and record offices whereas that which is to be found in museums will probably be seen by more people, but handled less than in libraries and record offices.

Probably the largest users of ephemera are those who are engaged in research where even the smallest piece of information can be of use in building up a picture or in answering a query. It is not only the student and post-graduate who will use ephemera, but also school children working on projects and amateur historians working on their own special research projects as well as members of other professions and occupations using this type of material for their specific research.

School children

Today, many schools set their pupils projects, some of which will be on their own locality and may involve the use of ephemera as well as the more usual printed sources. These projects may not aim to secure the amount of detail and information which undergraduate and post-graduate research may entail, but the ephemera which children use may throw interesting sidelights on local events and places which the child is looking up and it is this type of information and the sidelights which it throws on life in a bygone age that children may often remember rather than a series of facts and dates.

With school children, the librarian has to make an important decision on the use of original material, namely whether to allow them to use original items of ephemera or to have copies made for them to use. In order to make a satisfactory decision, it is necessary to bear in mind the importance of the item, its condition and how many children will be handling it at one time. If it is suspected that it will receive much use, it is worthwhile considering having a photographic copy made, which can be be photocopied if copies are wanted by children without the fear of damaging the original and at the same time it is also possible to replace the original or copy if it is damaged. Other points which have to be borne in mind include the fact the children will come into the library to consult individual items on their own, in which case it will not be possible to make duplicate copies to be used, but when children come in a group, where the teacher has requested specific items, it is possible to make copies. For instance, if the industrial revolution and the plight of child labour is a popular subject for school visits, it is probably worthwhile getting any particularly vulnerable material copied so that the original remains undamaged. On the other hand, if a group comes in to deal with a specialist subject, such as education in their own district, and this is not a subject which attracts large numbers of classes, it will probably be all right to allow the originals to be used, always bearing in mind that some material may be too fragile to be handled. It is always nice if children can use the original, but the integrity of the original must be paramount.

Academic research

Ephemera is also used by those engaged in academic research for both undergraduate and post-graduate work. Sometimes ephemera can be of assistance in providing information which is not obtainable elsewhere or it may even provide the basis for research or indicate a new angle of approach which had not previously been considered. Even when the material is not directly related to the subject that is being researched, some items of ephemera can provide information which illustrates a point. For instance, someone working on the household economy of a family in a cotton town in the late nineteenth or early twentieth centuries may find that posters, broadsheets or handbills will provide information on prices charged for everyday things such as groceries or footwear, although the actual item may appear to have no direct connection between the subject matter of the research and the topic of the ephemera. (This is one reason why ephemera should be indexed in full.) The academic researcher is more likely to use a large number of types of material in his or her research and not merely printed or manuscript sources.

Although it is the historic ephemera which will be the main material to be consulted, there are those engaged on research, particularly in social studies and related subjects, who will want access to the more recently published ephemera. It should also be remembered that tomorrows historic ephemera is today's current or contemporary ephemera and as such will be used in the same way in the future as historic ephemera is used today.

The 'man-in-the-street'

In any local studies collection or record office there are always ordinary people to be found who are engaged on their own personal research into a wide variety of topics. Some may be researching the history of a village whilst others may be investigating their local church or the theatres of an area. These people, like those engaged in academic research, will use all the resources of the institution to further their work and not merely one or two sources. However, in many cases, when such people start their research they have only the vaguest ideas of where to look and the potential sources of information, so that in the first instance, they will often require help and guidance around the indexes and catalogues.

Graphic designers

Not only will students and others who are engaged in research use ephemera. Many other people find uses for this type of material, some of which are not at first obvious. The use graphic designers make of ephemera, however, does not come into this category. Graphic designers and artists will take particular interest in the development of design over the ages or the use of particular type faces at particular times for specific jobs and will also be interested in the general appearance of the material, particularly posters. The information and ideas they get from looking at such material may be used in designs they are working on at present or it may be used at some point in the future when someone wants to recreate the feeling of an older type of poster or advertisement. For example, the recent revival of the Bisto kids on advertisements is a look back to previous types of advertisement for that product.

The media

A great deal of use is made of ephemera by the media, especially by television which depends very much for its effect on visual presentation especially in its drama and documentary productions. Although ephemera may be used in the background research, in television it may also be used as part of the backcloth and even handled by actors and shown in close up. For example, a set showing a nineteenth century street scene may require authentic looking posters, notices and broadsheets to create the correct atmosphere. Although original material will not be used, it is possible to study those which survive either as originals or on photographs to ensure that not only is the size correct, but also the type faces that were used are accurate in the reproduction, that the layout is correct and that any pecularities in wording are also used. The general impression of street scenes can be obtained from the study of period photographs, but it is from the originals that the fine detail can be obtained. The same is true of material which is used in stage productions. For example, if a railway ticket is used in a production relating to the nineteenth century, it is important to ensure that it is correct not only in its appearance, but also in the type used by the company in whose area the action takes place. Accuracy of detail is now very important as the use of close-up shots increases and there is always someone who is on the look out for mistakes such as the use of props from the wrong period.

The provision of current information

This usage applies to current ephemera and is really the reason why such material is published. It is intended to provide information on a specific subject which cannot be easily traced elsewhere and is often designed either for the public to take away or to be displayed in a public place. At the same time, the librarian may well keep a copy handy so that if information on current events is required, it can be found easily and there is no need to spend time going through papers looking for this information if it is requested over the telephone or in writing. For example, posters like one produced by Styal Museum for a grand textile sale[2] or the programme for the Three Choirs Festival held in Gloucester in 1980[3] or the production of *Robin Hood* at the Adam Smith Theatre in Kirkcaldy in 1983–84[4] are designed to provide the relevant informant.

Not all ephemera which imparts information will be found in libraries where it can be picked up. A vast amount of it is left in other places for the public to acquire and in some cases, the librarian would direct the inquirer to the relevant place. For example, information on London Saver fares from Manchester would be acquired from British Rail rather than the library[5] whilst advertisements for goods and services might be found only in the shop, as a price list issued by Schocoland[6] and was, or like the card for Torbay Luxury Limousines which was to be found in local hotels around Torbay[7]. Information put out by firms on their products also forms part of the provision of current information use, but again it is not found in libraries, although some of it will be very informative, as the leaflet issued by James Pringle of Edinburgh is with its history of the company[8]. Although these latter examples are not the type of leaflets providing information which a librarian might give, they still aim to inform the reader of the item and try to get a message over to them.

Commercial enterprises

In an age when nostalgia appears to be all the rage, some items of ephemera in libraries, record offices and museums, have provided the basis for a new industry – the publication of copies of items for sale to the public. Sometimes, this is done by a commercial undertaking, using library material on payment of a suitable fee, but often libraries will use material from their own stock, have reproductions made and sell them to the public. For instance, Manchester Local History Library has reproduced some of its more interesting broadsheets and sells them to the public. Sometimes, the material is reproduced on items like aprons or bags, such as one which has been done using the front page of the first edition of the 'Manchester Guardian' or a handbill for a specific product or shop.

The researcher

Ephemera is a primary source of information and as such can be used by a wide range of people for the purposes of research. Mention has been made of those engaged in academic research and the amateur local historians working on their own subjects, but there are also many others engaged in research for many different purposes. Some may be working on a book or a novel and getting 'the flavour' of the period by looking at material from that age as well as seeking additional information. For example, a person working on the history of entertainment in the north west may well be interested in a playbill from the Assembly Rooms at Leigh[9], advertising a 'Grand Variety Concert' on Tuesday 1 October 1901 which also includes the names of those appearing and the type of act they performed. One of those appearing for instance was Madam Nita Rose, who was described as 'The Great Australian Nightingale. High class Ballard and Operatic Vocalist' and it was added that 'lovers of good singing should seize this opportunity of listening to one of the finest vocalists on the Music Hall

Stage'.[10]

In addition to the person working on Leigh and entertainment, such a leaflet would also be of interest to those researching the music hall and the individual artists listed. Thus, several different researchers could use the same material for very different ends.

Sometimes, when working on a particular subject, a researcher may discover a particularly rich vein of material and decide to take advantage of it. For instance, this happened when Martha Vicinus was working on literature in the nineteenth century in the north of England and discovered that there were a great many broadsheets relating to life in the area. A series of these was collected together and published as *Broadsides of the Industrial North*[11]. This is not an isolated case, but is repeated on other occasions with a wide range of subjects.

Museums

Museums and stately homes often have items of ephemera in their own archives which they use from time to time for display purposes. Sometimes these are permanent displays, used to enhance the three dimensional objects on display, and on other occasions they form part of temporary exhibitions. For example, at Styal Mill, there is a display of letterheads received by the original owners of the mill whilst an exhibition in Oldham Art Gallery was of enamel signs, which used to be very popular at one time and have virtually all disappeared except on the stations of preserved railway lines. All the signs were three dimensional and as such could be described as museum objects, but they could also be regarded as ephemera as there was writing on them and they imparted a message to the reader, even if it was advertising the fact that those 'throwing stones at the Telegraphs will be prosecuted'[12].

Members of staff

Ephemera is also of use in answering specific enquiries received in the library either by personal visitors, by letter or by telephone. Mention has been made of the current awareness value of current and contemporary ephemera, but historic ephemera can also be used to answer enquiries as well. The number of queries that might be answered as a result of material in an ephemera collection will vary, depending on the type of material in the collection, the extent to which the information is accessible and the type of question asked. Often the value of ephemera is in providing that little bit of information in a detailed answer which turns the reply into a first rate one. For instance, a label from a company might provide information which is not available elsewhere such as one from Huttenbach Bros. and Co. of Singapore, London and Penang[13] which in addition to giving the places where the company had offices also gives an amazing illustration of a monkey hanging from a tree, and this latter point of information may well be of interest to the person asking the question.

Security of a collection of ephemera

When an ephemera collection is used regularly, there is always a threat that material will either become damaged, defaced or go missing. It is important to keep a record of who is using which items and to check that the material which has been used is returned. Hence, any collection of ephemera should not be on open access, but kept locked. (If the advice on storage is to be followed, this would automatically be the case.) Items should only be issued on request.

However, problems can arise where original material is used for a display as there is not only the risk from people helping themselves, but also from direct sunlight and uncontrolled humidity and temperature changes. For example, a temporary exhibition on the Benguella Railway at the North Western Museum of Science and Industry included not only illustrations and drawings of the locomotives and rolling stock, but also a large amount of ephemera such as timetables, tickets, maps, guides and leaflets, all of which were rare and valuable items. These were displayed in locked cases which were also able to be covered to prevent sunlight falling on them as the paper was not of the best quality. This particular exhibition had the added complication of the fact that it was to go on tour. The decision had to be made that this original material, together with the archival material which was included, should not go on the tour, but copies made of some of it and the originals returned to their owners.

The exploitation of ephemera collections

As with any collection of material, it is not sufficient purely to collect it and make no use of it. There is a view, which was held by some, mostly of the older generation of archivists, that material, once collected, should be preserved and handled as little as possible. Fortunately, this attitude has almost completely disappeared as it is realised that it is important to exploit the collection, provided that the necessary precautions can be taken to prevent fragile material being damaged by handling or being left in exposed places. The exploitation of ephemera not only means using it within the department either by members of the public or by staff, but also making the public aware of the collection's existence, the uses it can be put to and of making full use of it. There are various ways of making the public aware that the library, record office or museum has such a collection and publicising it.

Exhibitions of ephemera

Sometimes libraries organise exhibitions of various aspects of the stock of the library. One of these can be ephemera where the extremely wide range of material making up the subject can be shown. At the same time, some of the more interesting uses of the material can be shown or points which might otherwise have been overlooked highlighted.

Such an exhibition can also draw the attention of the public to the fact that much of the material that is on display will be thrown away. It should not only be the historic items to which attention is drawn but also those items of current ephemera which are being collected for use by researchers in the future.

Sometimes an exhibition on ephemera can be organised not to deal with a specific subject, but with the use that can be made of the material and some of the more unusual aspects of ephemera and its usage as well as uses which might be overlooked. For example, the following handbill from Rochdale may be of interest to someone researching early twentieth century food prices and thinks that they have covered everything.

This may not appear in an exhibition on food, but it could be in a general exhibition, and if the researcher sees it, it may set him thinking along a different line as to other potential sources of information.

Sometimes exhibitions aimed at stimulating the public's interest in this type of material can result in further enhancement of the collection. It is also possible to allow material, or copies of it, from collections to be used in other people's exhibitions provided that due acknowledgement of the source is given. For example, a gardening centre might decide to run a special promotion and try to increase interest by including some historical material on the subject such as the broadsheet issued by George Vaughan, 27 Market Place, Manchester[15], in which he advertised the seeds, bulbs and plants he sold. Although there is nothing unusual in this, he also included information on the best time to sow certain seeds. For example, he

REDUCTION IN PROVISIONS!
AT
SHEPHERD'S
137 WHITWORTH RD.

Finest PURE LARD	only 6d per lb.
Splendid Irish Roll BACON	10d per lb.
Really Good BACON	8d and 9d per lb.

Our Finest Smoked and Plain HAMS
From 11d per lb, sliced

Choice Cuts of Ham	from 7½d per lb
Good Boiling PEAS	2½d per lb.

Bake with Our Lovely FLOUR, at
2/2 and 2/4 per 20lbs

FINEST SCOTCH OATMEAL	2/6 per 20lbs or 1½ per 1lb.

We have introduced a

Delicious High Grade Margarine	1s per lb
Net weight	

We invite any Lady or Gentleman to taste it against Best Butter.

Our Well-known Special Margarine at 9d per lb
Still proves a good Seller.
Call for a Free Sample. Sold by use for over 11 years

Lyle's SYRUP	2 lb Tins only 6d each
Wax Candles	3 lb pkts, only 7½d each

For Everything you require we give
Unbeatable Value[14]

recommends that cabbage seeds should be sown in July or August for early and February to May for late and between the same periods 'cauliflower, cabbage – early dwarf, early York, Naylor's York, Early Battersea, Early Sugar Loaf, Red Dutch, Large Flat Winter, Turnip, Scotch for Cattle'. He also points out that between March and April the following 'PHYSICAL SEEDS' can be sown, namely 'carduus, scurvy grass, angelica, dill, balm, fennel, tobacco, fenugreek, cummin, anniseed, caraway, coriander'. There are also tips on the conditions required for germination and when transplanting should be carried out.

The use of such material will also point out to the general public the wide range of subjects which can be found in ephemera and hopefully start to make people think about other items they may have seen or even possess.

Publication

Ephemera is also used to illustrate books, either as specific illustrations or as full-length quotations. Broadsheets are often reproduced in full in both formats, as also are railway tickets and timetables. All this is publicity for ephemera and the use that can be made of it. The same may be said of material which is used in teaching packs when copies of a wide range of material are collected together on a particular subject. Not only are such portfolios of documents produced on a commercial level, but they have also been published by libraries and museums similar to those published by Rochdale Library on the history of the town[16] and Manchester on Peterloo[17]. Every opportunity should be taken to ensure that material from the library, record office or museum which is used is properly credited and acknowledged as this can be regarded as free publicity for the library and its collections and may result in material being donated or an opportunity being given to acquire it.

The use of material from collections of ephemera to provide publishers with illustrations is one means of exploiting a collection, but there are also occasions when the majority of the publication is taken from a collection of historic ephemera. For example, some organisations have used ephemera as the basis for the production of souvenirs as the Gladstone Pottery Museum has done with the use of a handbill produced by John Lockett of Longton for a postcard[18] which is on sale at the Museum. This not only publicises the type of material which the Museum is interested in, but also provides a valuable source of income.

Publicity

It is always useful to be able to publicise a particular collection of material which the library, museum or record office has in its custody and ephemera collections are no exception to this. The use of the local newspaper to draw attention to exhibitions or when a particularly important collection of ephemera is acquired can be very helpful in making the general public aware of the existence of the collection and the importance of this type of material. Sometimes, local newspapers

212

will run a series of articles on particular aspects of the library's stock or publish a list of new acquisitions. Another useful way of publicising what has been acquired is to issue a list of newly acquired material at regular intervals, similar to that produced by Newark Museum, which might be sent to the local newspaper.

For the collection and exploitation of any collection of material, and especially that of an ephemera collection, the librarian, archivist and museum curator must use all the means at their disposal to tell people about its existence and this should include local radio, television as well as the press and periodicals which might have an interest in the subject or the information which it contains. Whenever an item is used, it is important to ensure that it is fully acknowledged where the original is to be found. If people become aware of the type of material which libraries and so forth are interested in, they may begin to think about the subject and, hopefully, instead of discarding items of ephemera, pass them to the library, record office or museum.

Conclusion

It is not possible to enumerate all the various categories of use to which an ephemera collection may be put, nor is it possible to list all the many types of user who might find one particular type of material useful. Different users will make different uses of the same type of material and even the same individual item. The important point is that the public are made aware that such material is collected and that it might have some bearing on work they might be undertaking. To ensure that the public know of the existence of the collection, it must publicised as widely as possible.

8 Who has what and where

For the user of ephemera as a source of information or for the person who is interested in the different types of ephemera from the point of view of type rather than subject content, difficulties can be experienced in trying to establish where collections are to be found, the extent of the area covered by the collection and the type of material which is in it. This final chapter looks at the problem of trying to locate material and suggests some ways in which it might be overcome.

The problem

The problem of trying to ascertain what material has been preserved and where it can be consulted is one which is not peculair to ephemera, but as the number of guides to different types of material increases, so it becomes increasingly apparent that ephemera collections as such are an area where no such guide has been attempted. Even in West's recently published book on town records[1] there is no attempt to include a list of libraries and record offices with collections of ephemera although there are lists of places with collections of illustrations, newspapers and census enumerators' returns. It is a pity that the opportunity to include such a list was not taken as it would have considerably lightened the task of the researcher who wanted to consult items of ephemera. The only way at present to discover whether a library has any ephemera is to write to the library concerned, but this means that material which is to be found in another area, but relating to this area of interest may be missed. It is probably easier for the person working on a locality to trace what there is than it is for someone working on a wider national theme. It is easier to discover what historic ephemera has been collected than it is to discover where contemporary material is to be found. What is required is a system whereby information on collections can be gathered together centrally and made available to those who are interested, a task which should not be too difficult in the computer age once all the information has been collected and processed.

For the researcher working on a particular theme, the problem of ascertaining who has what and where it can be consulted is much easier than for someone who is interested in a particular type of material. Few collections of a general nature will list the material by type as this approach is not the most usual. Usually collections are listed by subject content of the material. For example, a person interested in railway posters may have to write to every library, record office and museum in the country and still get a poor response as the material may be listed under the subject of the poster and not under railway posters. Can anything be done to assist in making information about collections more easily available? It can be, but only at a generalised level. A distinction has to be drawn between material which relates to a locality and that produced for national purposes.

What has been suggested in the past

Both Pemberton and Clinton in their reports on ephemera make suggestions as to how the coverage of ephemera in libraries can be improved. Pemberton recommends a National Documents Library with a strengthened Copyright Receipt Office to actively pursue the collection of material and that it should be able to accept material from both individuals and libraries[2]. However, Pemberton was primarily interested in ephemera relating to the social sciences and not in the complete range of ephemera as local studies librarians see it. One criticism of Pemberton's proposal is that local material might be lost to the locality to which it relates and consequently lose some of its significance as well as making it more difficult for the amateur researcher to consult the material. Pemberton appears to be expressing the views of the academic world, who would probably like to see as much as possible centralised to enable them to carry out their research without a great deal of travel.

Pemberton also suggests that the National Documents Library should also compile a

> national register of collections of research material in the social sciences, for publishing a newsletter and operating a referral service based on this register, and for advising the National Central Library on the most appropriate libraries to which material offered for deposit might be directed. Compilation of such a register is, indeed, a matter of urgency and could be initiated in anticipation of the recommended institutional changes[3].

This idea of a national register is also taken up by Clinton in his report to the British Library and in his subsequent book. Clinton suggests a National Register of Collections which would 'compile lists of collections of non-book printed material . . . The list would be built up best by concentrating on individual subjects . . . or else by working in particular local areas.'[4] In addition, Clinton believes that such a body should also be involved in helping to ensure that bodies and short-lived organisations to find a suitable home for their records and ephemera, very much in the way the National Register of Archives offers advice on the best location to deposit archival material.[5]

Clinton's suggestion is one which is worth considering as it would enable researchers to establish whether a particular library has material of a particular type or relating to a particular area or subject. To undertake the compilation of such a register would in itself be a large task and be time consuming, especially if it was to include the contents of existing collections. However, the compilation of such a register could be made a little easier if existing collections were divided into two groups – those relating to local material and generally housed in local studies collections, record offices and some museums and secondly, those collections of material which relate to national events or activities and where the material is not necessarily held by a public institution. This latter group could be subdivided into two, that material which is national in its outlook which is held by a public body and that material which is held privately by companies and even individuals.

Local material

Local material is probably the easiest of all ephemera to trace, as in an ideal situation it is to be expected to be found locally in local studies collections which will include both historic as well as contemporary and current ephemera. However, there are ocasions when non-local material may be found in such collections, which can confuse the issue. For example, in the broadsheet collection in Manchester, there are broadsheets relating not only to Manchester, but also to Birmingham, Sheffield, Eccles and Scotland as well as other towns and cities. One way information on these stray items might be passed to the relevant local collection is for the holding library to inform the others that it has material in its collection and to give brief details of the item. It is then up to the library to order a copy if it feels it is worthwhile doing so. In some cases, it may be possible to pass the original item over to the recipient library in the area to which it relates, especially if it is a distance away and there is no local connection.

The discovery of non-local material in collections is one which chiefly affects collections of historic ephemera. However, there are times when current or contemporary material finds its way into other areas. For instance, someone may have gathered leaflets on a subject or kept invitations that have been received and may pass them to the library with the instruction that they should be sent to the relevant authority if they are of no local interest. There is nothing wrong with this unless they specifically form part of a personal archive, in which case they should be kept together, but information on their existence should be passed to the area to which they relate.

It would be a relatively simple operation to establish which libraries have collections of ephemera, whether they are actively being added to or whether they are 'dead', the area or subjects covered and the type of material in the collection. Such a list or register would not give details of every individual item for to do so would invite non-co-operation by librarians, archivists and museum curators on account of the vast amount of work required to complete such an inventory. Rather, it would be best to circulate a list of different types of material, similar to that contained in the appendix, and ask the library to indicate which types of material it has in its collection, the area or subjects covered and whether current and contemporary material was added as a matter of policy. Such a questionnaire could be devised so that the results could be processed by a computer, which in turn could print out the results in virtually any arrangement required, provided the programme was written correctly. It would also be possible to up-date it from time to time, although if it was in general terms, this might only require minor alterations being made.

The result of undertaking the compilation of such a register would be that those undertaking research would be able to tell whether a particular library had ephemera which might be of interest to them, but it would not tell them what was in the collection in terms of material on a specific subject. It would also indicate areas where there were gaps in the coverage, such as libraries not collecting current material on a regular basis.

As for who would carry out such a survey, if Clinton's idea of a national register with its own staff were to be adopted, this would be the logical organisation, but if it is not, then another agency would have to be sought. Possibly the British Library could undertake such work or even the Historical Manuscripts Commission, but whoever did so would require special funding to get the survey launched.

Regional and national material

It is with material which does not relate to a specific locality that the problems of knowing what has been produced and where it is to be found are at their greatest. Clinton has clearly demonstrated that there is a vast amount of ephemera to be found outside the library field and that it is kept for various reasons. The problem is trying to discover what exactly there is, where it can be consulted and even obtained. The existence of such a register as that suggested by both Clinton and Pemberton would greatly increase the information available on the existence of such collections. At the same time, it could also include the material held in private and business collections. However, in the case of that held by the latter, there might be the need to 'educate' those concerned as to why they should record the existence of the material and in some cases, actually ensure a copy is preserved either in the records of the originator or by a third party. For example, how much of the advertising material produced by the car industry actually survives and how much is thrown away once a model ceases to be produced and sold? Such a register would be able to answer such a question by indicating whether the producer actually has kept material or whether a particular library has obtained such items. Such a register would also have to take into account that material which libraries, especially public libraries, have collected and preserved in addition to the local material.

What should be done?

As both Clinton and Pemberton have recommended, there should be some sort of register of ephemera collections not solely relating to a specific subject as Pemberton wanted, but covering all aspects of ephemera. It should include material which is to be found in libraries, record offices and museums, material which is housed in the records of organisations such as local and national government departments, the nationalised industries and that which individuals and businesses have retained as part of collections. Where such a register is housed and maintained is open to debate, but it should be in a national body, possibly attached to one of the general collections of material like that held by the John Johnson Collection in the Bodleian Library at Oxford, provided adequate funding could be made available. In addition to maintaining a register, such a body could also promote and encourage the preservation of ephemera, especially in those areas where there is inadequate coverage at the moment. If it was attached to one of the general collections, this could be enlarged to take that material which is produced on a national scale, but which is not preserved elsewhere. It would, in many respects, complement the work that local collections are doing in collecting and preserving local material and would ensure that important material is not lost to posterity.

At the local level, local collections should be encouraged to collect current and contemporary ephemera and not to regard it as something that is of no consequence. If possible, the widest range of material should be collected as no-one knows what is going to be of interest to those engaged in research in the future. The more that is preserved, the better will be the future's understanding of the present day and the more material there will be for historians and others to base their assessment on. It will not be easy to convince some people that it is important to collect and preserve this material, but most of it will cost relatively little. The costs involved will, to some extent, be hidden ones of staff time to deal with it and those of housing the material and making it available to be used. After all, in local collections, ephemera forms an important source material whilst in other departments, ephemera may contain the only up-to-date information on a subject and is ignored at the peril of the department specialising in that subject.

Looking at ephemera in the broadest possible way, it may be said that it provides information which may not be found anywhere else and that it helps to give an increased awareness of the age when it was produced whether it be historic, contemporary or current ephemera. After all, all current and contemporary ephemera will ultimately become historic. If libraries, record offices and museums do not take an interest in the material, the private individual will and material which ought to be publicly available to scholars and others will not be so, except possibly to a select few. Not all ephemera will survive to be preserved, but it is important to try to ensure that some of it does and that it is in a public institution where it can be consulted by all and not just a select few. Local studies collections are, on the whole, making an effort to collect and preserve ephemera relating to the area or district in which they are interested. It is now a matter of ensuring that material which is produced on a national scale is similarly collected and preserved either by a national body or by the producer organisation itself. At the same time, it is important that some list or register of collections is started so that there is a record of who has what and where, as it must be accepted that Legal Deposit will not catch much of the ephemera which is produced as much of it is purely local. If the British Library was to try and collect all items of ephemera that were produced throughout the country, there would be serious storage problems. However, if it can be shown that local libraries are collecting local material and preserving it in their local studies departments, then part of the battle is won as the material is being collected and preserved and the British Library can refer potential readers and users of this material to the relevant library, but before this can be done, a register of collections is required.

Appendix 1

It is always useful to have a checklist of items which are considered to be relevant to the subject under consideration. The list that is given below is of items which might be called ephemera. Not all of it will have been individually identified in chapter 3, where the material has been grouped in broad type order. It is not an exhaustive list in that other items of ephemera may well be discovered, but it attempts to list all those items which the author can think of, augmented by lists in some of the other published works.

Acknowledgement slips
Admission cards
Admission tickets
Advance publicity material
Advertising leaflets and handbills
Agendas
Airline tickets
Appeal leaflets
Application forms
Bank notes
Beer mats
Bills
Bill heads
Book lists
Book marks
Booking forms
Boarding passes
Bottle labels
Broadsheets
Bus tickets
Calendars
Cards
Catalogues
Certificates
Cheques
Cheque cards
Cigarette cards

Cigarette packets
Circulars
Clippings
Commemorative items
Company reports
Competition entry forms
Compliment slips
Computer print-outs
Computer programmes
Constitutions
Coupons
Credit cards
Driving licences
Election literature
Errata slips
Estate agents' leaflets
Estimates
Excursion notices
Fixture lists
Flag day badges
Gift vouchers
Guarantees
Guides
Handbills
Holiday leaflets
Hotel tariff cards
Household items
Identity cards
Information leaflets
Instruction leaflets
Insurance policies and certificates
Inventories
Invitations
Invoices
Job specifications
Labels
Leaflets
Letter heads
Licences
Lottery tickets
Match boxes
Meeting notices
Membership cards
Membership forms

Menus
Minutes of meetings
Milk bottle tops
Mourning cards
Music covers
Newsletters
Newspapers
Order forms
Personal cards
Petitions
Playbills
Playing cards
Postcards – non-pictorial
Posters
Prepaid reply cards
Press releases
Price tags
Printers' specimens
Proclamations
Programmes
Programme cards
Propaganda
Prospectuses
Public notices
Publicity material
Railway timetables – pocket variety
Ration books
Receipts
Recipes
Recruitment circulars
Removal notices
Rent books
Reports
Rules
Sales catalogues
Score cards
Service sheets
Share certificates
Shipping tickets
Society ephemera
Stamps
Stock certificates
Stocklists
Subscription lists

Sympathy cards
Telegrams
Tickets
Timetables
Tradecards
Trade catalogues
Trails
Visitors cards
Wage slips
Window bills
Wrappers

Appendix 2   The growth of ephemera collections and other approaches to the problems of such collections

Much of the material which constitutes ephemera in the collections that exist in libraries, record offices and museums has been preserved on a haphazard basis either as part of a specific collection of material relating to a particular subject or as a result of donations to the organisation by individual collectors or by the organisation itself making an effort to collect certain types of material which relate to its areas of interest and to preserve it for use in the future. Although certain types of ephemera were collected by libraries, record offices and museums in the past, it was not until after the Second World War that the importance of this type of material began to be fully appreciated and serious attempts were made to collect it. Much of the material that is to be found in collections today is the result of work undertaken in the last twenty years to bring together material which was scattered in many different places or which would not have been collected at all in the pre–1945 era. This rise in interest in ephemera by the professional collecting and preserving organisations has, to some extent, been stimulated by the growing interest shown by the private collector in this type of material. In the past, the private collector was interested in a limited number of subjects and types of material, such as railways or theatres or cigarette cards, but today, his interest is very much wider.

The problems for those engaged in the collection and preservation of ephemera were further complicated in the 1970s when it was realised that ephemera meant different things to different people and that there was no generally accepted interpretation as to what constituted ephemera. The fact that there were differing views on the matter was shown very clearly at a meeting, jointly organised by the Local Studies Group of the Library Association's Reference Special and Information Section[1] and the Standing Conference for Local History in October 1975, to consider the collection, recording and preservation of ephemera. Some speakers regarded ephemera as comprising material published by individuals, local societies and organisations in book or pamphlet form which was rarely recorded in the main bibliographical works, such as the British National Bibliography or British Books in Print as it was not produced by 'main-stream' publishers, but circulated within a limited area and usually only reviewed and mentioned in the locality to which it related. This view, however, did not correspond with that of other speakers, most notably local studies librarians, archivists and museum curators, who regarded such items as minor publications, ephemeral to the main stream of publishing but not true ephemera. To these people ephemera comprised the flimsier material which is more difficult to trace and process and which could be regarded as either primary or secondary source material. As a result of the existence of these two very distinct views, it was resolved to establish a working party to look at the whole question of what constituted ephemera and what were minor publications, the methods of collecting and recording this type of material and what national collections existed.

This working party was established two years later after a follow-up meeting held in Birmingham in November 1977. The working party, which ultimately became known as the Advisory Committee on Ephemera and Minor Publications (ADCEMP) comprised representatives of the various professions who had an interest in the collection and preservation of ephemera and the private collectors. The committee was asked by the meeting to:

(i) formulate a definition or definitions of ephemera and minor publications and to make proposals about (ii) the organisation of the collection of material; (iii) places of deposit, recognising that a case can be made for keeping copies of the same item in more than one repository; (iv) the basis on which the material might be recorded; (v) resolving storage and conservation problems; (vi) the funding required to facilitate the collection and retention of ephemera and minor publications; and (vii) the production of a directory listing existing collections of relevant material.[2]

Shortly after the establishment of ADCEMP, the British Library Research and Development Division commissioned two projects: one to investigate the extent of printed ephemera[3] and the other on minor publications[4] with a view to discovering whether it was possible to produce a national policy for collecting and storing the two types of material. The reports were submitted in 1980 and went some way to pointing out the differences between ephemera and minor publications as although only one of the reports dealt specifically with ephemera, the other had to resolve the problem of what constituted ephemera in order to undertake the study. One problem with reports of this type is that they have to be completed within a given time and consequently, may not be able to investigate the subject in very great depth. To a large extent, the work of the two research projects parallelled the work that ADCEMP was undertaking. It was fortunate that there was liason between the two researchers and ADCEMP enabling an exchange of views to take place.

The report on ephemera, undertaken by Alan Clinton, who used the results of his research as the basis of his book *Printed ephemera: collection, organisation, access*, concentrated on ephemera in three distinct areas: postal history, household appliances and housing. The three areas he chose represented three different types of ephemera: historical, pictorial and a modern social problem. After looking at the material available in the three areas, Clinton made recommendations on a future policy for ephemera collection in the country at a national level. His final recommendation was that a 'National Register of Collections should be established located within the Reference Division of the British Library'[5]. He continued that 'It is not difficult to set out how such a register would work, to outline its value to the community of learning, and to explain the reason for putting forward its particular form and location'.[6]

As interest in ephemera has grown, so also have the number of publications. These can be divided into two groups: 'coffee table' and the serious academic study of the subject. The 'coffee table' books tend to have a large number of illustrations to show the various types of ephemera that exist and give some indication of their potential use not so much in textual terms, but in visual terms. For example, two books by John Lewis deal with different aspects of the use of ephemera. In *Collecting printed ephemera*, he looks at the use of ephemera in providing information on social habits, social history, eating, drinking, travel and heritage whereas in his other book, *Printed ephemera*, he traces the changing use of type faces and letterforms in English and American printing as illustrated through ephemera. Both books are heavily illustrated and show the wide range of material which makes up the subject field of ephemera.

There are also 'coffee table' books which deal specifically with the ephemera of a particular topic. Anderson and Swinglehurst's book, *Ephemera of travel and transport*, for instance illustrates the wide range of ephemera associated with all forms of travel and transport. This well illustrated publication also includes information on why some of the material came into existence and its usage whilst current. A few minutes glancing through this type of book will indicate very clearly the extremely wide range of material which constitutes ephemera and will also give clues as to the potential usage of the material by those engaged on research in all its many forms.

The second group of publications are those which approach the collection of ephemera from either a professional angle or as a serious hobby. In addition to Clinton's book, there is a valuable study of ephemera collections relating to the social sciences by John Pemberton, *The national provision of printed ephemera in the social sciences*, which contains the results of a survey he undertook for the Social Science and Government Committee of the Social Science Research Council in 1971. Both Pemberton and Clinton refer to some of the problems which are encountered when ephemera is collected and where some collections of ephemera are housed, but neither go into the problems which the librarian, archivist or museum curator face, namely of how much contemporary material should be collected with a view to preserving it for the future, the actual mechanics of acquisition, the problems of conservation, classification, cataloging, storage and security which are areas of concern that must be satisfactorily resolved if an ephemera collection is to be maintained and fully exploited by the readership of the organisation holding the collection. In many respects, both Clinton and Pemberton approach the subject from the point of view of academics and academic research whereas many collections of ephemera are housed in public libraries and record offices where many of the demands to consult the material may not be on the same academic level as that found in academic libraries.

There is a book that is aimed at the private collector and in effect falls between the two distinct categories. This is Maurice Rickard's *This is ephemera*. Although aimed at the private collector, it is a very useful introduction to the subject dealing with places where ephemera can be found and the type of collection that might be built up. It is well illustrated and provides a useful introduction to the subject for beginners.

In addition to books on the subject, there are articles occasionally published on particular types of ephemera, such as broadsheets or playbills in journals like the *Local Historian*[7]. One publication that is devoted entirely to ephemera and its collecting is the *Ephemerist* which is the bi-monthly publication of the Ephemera Society and includes not only articles on specific types of ephemera and collections, but also information on meetings and exhibitions relating to the subject.

When it comes to the librarianship of ephemera, there is hardly any reference to this type of material in any of the standard works, which is surprising as ephemera forms a large part of any local studies collection. In books on the librarianship of local studies, there are a few passing references to particular types of material, but no detailed look at the type of material that constitutes ephemera or the problems associated with it. Carter's revised edition of Hobbs's *Local History and the Library*[8] makes no specific reference to ephemera or any of its constituent parts whilst Alice Lynes's *How to organise a local collection*[9] refers only briefly to certain specific types of material. The most recent publication on the subject by H. Nichols, *Local studies librarianship*[10] does make several references to ephemera, but does not go into details of how to collect the material nor discuss the way a collection might be organised, classified, conserved and exploited.

References

Chapter 1

1. *The Guardian* 13 August 1983 p3.
2. Richards, *This is ephemera* p9.
3. *Now* 25 July 1980 p15.

Chapter 2

1. Shorter Oxford English Dictionary.
2. Ibid.
3. Concise Oxford Dictionary, p. 399. 4th. ed. Oxford 1951.
4. P.M. Roget, *Thesaurus of English words and phrases*, Penguin, London, 1961 p. 37.
5. J.N.C. Lewis, *Collecting printed ephemera*, Studio Vista, London 1976 p. 9.
6. J.E. Pemberton, *The National provision of printed ephemera in the Social Services*. University of Warwick 1976. p. 6, para. 13.
7. Ibid., p.6, para. 14.
8. Ibid., p. 53–54.
9. *The Times Literary Supplement*, 7 November 1975.
10. Ibid.
11. Ibid.
12. Ibid.
13. M. Rickards, *This is emphemera: collecting printed throwaways*, David and Charles, Newton Abbott, 1977. p. 7
14. *Now*, 25 July 1980, p. 45.
15. ADCEMP, *Preliminary report*, 1979, p. 2–3.
16. A. Clinton, *Printed ephemera: its collection, organisation and access*, Bingley, London, 1981 p. 15.
17. Ibid., p. 15–6.
18. Sturgess & Dixon, p. 5.
19. ADCEMP, p. 3.
20. Dixon, p. 1.
21. John E. Short, *The John Gulson Story*, Leamington, Privately Printed, 1978.

22. *Birch Church: a short guide*, Manchester, St James's Church, Birch-in-Rusholme, 1962.

23. City of Manchester River's Department, *Descriptive notes on the Davyhulme and Withington Sewage Works*, 4th ed., Manchester, City of Manchester Rivers Department, 1937.

24. Ibid., p. 3.

25. Shell Nederland Verkoopmaat schappij BV, *Nederland van de weg af gezien*, Rotterdam, Shell, 1979.

26. E.D.J. Burrow, and Co., *Greater Manchester: an international conference and exhibition centre*, London, Burrows, 1982.

27. Greater Manchester County Planning Department and Rochdale Planning Department, *Rochdale Town Centre Conservation Area: preliminary report*, Manchester, Greater Manchester County Planning Department, 1981, folded.

28. *Britannia Hotel, Manchester*, Manchester, Britannia Hotel, n.d., folded.

29. British Tourist Authority, Greater Manchester Council, City of Manchester, *Britain: Manchester the city and the county*, London, British Tourist Authority, 1982, folded.

30. *Order of service for the enthronement of the Right Reverend Father in God David by Divine Permission, Bishop of Sheffield.* Sheffield, 1980.

31. Pickfords Removals Ltd, *A moving offer from Pickfords. Your business, your staff*, London, Pickfords, n.d.

32. Brushware Ltd, *The bluebook of brushware*, London, Brushware Ltd, 1930.

33. Salford Museum of Mining, *An appeal to preserve the local mining heritage*, Salford Museum of Mining, 1983, single sheet.

34. City of Manchester Publicity and Tourism Office, *Manchester Craft Village, Manchester*, Manchester Publicity and Tourism Office, 1982, folded.

35. Lincolnshire and Humberside Arts, *Diary*, Lincoln, Lincolnshire and Humberside Arts, bimonthly, 1984.

36. *Christ Church Moss Side*, Moss Side, Christ Church, 1982.

37. Vertikaseal, *It must be rotten having windows like this*, Macclesfield, Vertikaseal, 1983, folded.

38. Rickards, *This is ephemera*, p. 44–47.

39. Pemberton, *Printed ephemera*, p. 24 para. 91.

40. Hunter Penrose Ltd, *Just a reminder of our activities in catering for the stereotyper*, London, Hunter Penrose, n.d.

41. *Ephemerist*, vol. 1, no. 11, July 1977, p. 50.

42. R. Storey and J. Druker, compiler. *Guide to the Modern Records Centre University of Warwick Library*, Coventry,

University of Warwick Occasional Publications no.2, 1977.

43. Pemberton, *Printed ephemera*, p. 18, para. 67.

44. Now the Greater Manchester Museum of Science and Industry.

45. *Health and Social Service Journal*, 3 October, 1980, p. 1293–4.

46. Manchester Local History Library general election material.

47. Rochdale Public Library, P. 1.43.

48. For details on dating see C.E. Makepeace, 'Dating and identifying the location of undated and unidentified photographs' in *Proceedings and Papers of the Symposium of the European Society for the History of Photography*, Bath, 1981, p. 7–13.

49. M. Rickards, *Posters of the 1920s*, London, Evelyn, Adam and Mackay, 1968; *Posters at the turn of the century*, London, Evelyn, Adam and Mackay, 1968; *Posters of the First World War*, London, Evelyn, Adam and Mackay, 1968; *The public notice: an illustrated history*, David and Charles, Newton Abbot, 1973; *Posters of protest and revolution*, Bath, Adam and Dart, 1970; *The rise and fall of the poster*, Newton Abbot, David and Charles, 1971; M. Rickards and M. Moody, *The First World War ephemera, mementos, documents*, London, Jupiter Books, 1975.

50. K. Osborne and B. Pipe, *The international book of beer labels, mats and coasters*, London, Hamlyn, 1979.

51. 'Manchester Ballad Collection', in the *Manchester Review*, vol. 7 Summer 1956, p. 391.

52. E. Leach, 'Playbills and programmes,' in the *Manchester Review*, vol. 11 Spring/Summer, 1966, p. 7–22.

Chapter 3

These notes also include bibliographical citations for the examples given together with an indication as to where the original material is housed. Where there is no location given, it is in the author's private collection. Many items are single sheets which have been folded. Where they have been folded and open up to form a single sheet, they are described as 'single sheet, folded'. Other items are folded so that they are read like a page from a book in which case they are usually '4p.'

1. *Spar*, High Lane, 1977, single sheet.

2. *Spar*, High Lane, 1977, single sheet.

3. Dixons, *Foto-film-geluid-electronica*, Dixons, 1980, illus., 4p.

4. Britannia Hotels Ltd, *Swing in and get lit up for the brightest Christmas and New Year with Britannia Hotels*, Britannia Hotels, Manchester, n.d., single sheet, folded.
5. Britannia Hotels Ltd, *Curtain up on Special Nights at Special Prices*, Britannia Hotels, Manchester, 1983, single sheet, folded.
6. *Whitegate Taverns*, n.d., single sheet.
7. De Vere Hotels, *Manor House Hotel, Royal Leamington Spa, Warwickshire*. London, De Vere Hotels, n.d. illus., single sheet, folded.
8. De Vere Hotels, *Manor House Hotel: Conference and Banqueting facilities*, London, De Vere Hotels, n.d., illus., single sheet, folded.
9. Midland Hotel, *Midland Hotel, Manchester*, Manchester, Midland Hotel, n.d., illus., single sheet, folded with 3 sheets inserted.
10. Packhorse Hotel, *Tariff*, Packhorse Hotel, Allerford, n.d., illus., 8p.
11. City of Manchester Public Relations Office, *Manchester Air and Space Museum*, City of Manchester Public Relations Office, 1983, illus., map, single sheet, folded.
12. Manchester Local History Library f. 1807/3.
13. Ibid.
14. Gibb's Bookshop, *Gibb's bookshop is moving*, Manchester, Gibb's Bookshop, n.d., single sheet; *Gibb's Bookshop have moved! !* , Manchester, Gibb's Bookshop, n.d., single sheet.
15. Building Design Partnership, *Refurbishment and restoration*, Building Design Partnership, London, 1983, illus., single sheet.
16. Broomhall Domestic Appliance Services, *There's a new centre now open*, Broomhall Domestic Appliance Services, Manchester, n.d., single sheet.
17. M. and N. Haworth (Manchester) Ltd, *Opening of new stamp shop in the heart of Manchester's shopping centre*, Clitheroe, Haworth (Manchester) Ltd, n.d., illus., single sheet.
18. Wright & Co. *Catalogue of printers' machinery, joinery materials . . . London Wright & Co* Single sheets bound together.
19. *TAC Ltd, For a quick finish . . .* , Manchester, TAC Ltd, n.d., single sheet.
20. *Harrow Inn-Enstone*, Enstone, n.d., illus., 4p.
21. Commercial Go-Karts Ltd, *Go-Karting*, Commercial Go-Karts Ltd, n.d., single sheet.
22. Contemporary Music Network, *Steve Lacy Sextet, Keith Tippett*, Arts Council, 1982, illus., single sheet.

23. Exeter Maritime Museum, *The world's largest collection of the world's boats*, Exeter, International Sailing Craft Association, 1983, illus., map, single sheet, folded.

24. *What's on . . . ballet, theatre, music, art*, Arts about Manchester, 1982, single sheet, folded.

25. Adam Geoffrey & Co., *Conavon Court*, Adam Geoffrey and Co., Salford, n.d., illus., single sheet.

26. Royal Exchange Theatre, *Autumn at the Royal Exchange: Party Bookings*, Manchester, Royal Exchange Theatre, 1983, single sheet, folded; *Royal Exchange Theatre Company: Party bookings Spring/Summer Season 1983*, Manchester, Royal Exchange Theatre Company, 1983, single sheet, folded.

27. W.H. Shercliff, D.A Kitching and J.M. Ryan, *Poynton a coal village*, Poynton, Shercliff, 1983, illus., plan, maps, 84p.

28. British Rail, *Merrymaker E.84 York Scarborough*, British Rail, n.d., single sheet.

29. Wallace Arnold, *Excursion programme by coach to coast and country from Torbay*, Paignton, Wallace Arnold Tours (Devon) Ltd, 1983, map, single sheet.

30. George Philip, *A fascinating study of the development of the English countryside*, London, Philip Group, n.d., single sheet.

31. *Haddon Hall Bakewell/Belvoir Castle*, 1983, single sheet, folded.

32. Manchester University Extra Mural Department, *Courses for the public: certificate courses*, University of Manchester Department of Extra Mural Studies 1983, single sheet, folded.

33. Manchester University Extra Mural Department, *Courses for the public: opportunities in education and training for social workers*, University of Manchester Department of Extra Mural Studies, 1983, single sheet, folded.

34. Horncastle Residential College, *Bridge summer school*, Horncastle Residential College, 1983, single sheet.

35. Horncastle Residential College, *Japanese ribbon flowers*, Horncastle Residential College, 1983, single sheet.

36. *St Mary's Church, Disley, gift day appeal*, Disley, St Mary's Church, 1980, single sheet.

37. Michael Arundel, *Here tomorrow – with your help*, Eccles Parish Church, Eccles, 1983, illus., 4p.

38. *Albert Memorial: the restoration of Manchester's Albert Memorial 1977/8*, Manchester, Albert Memorial Appeal Committee, 1978, illus., diags., 30p.

39. Ancient Monuments Society, *Chester Roman Amphitheatre Appeal for £8,000*, Ancient Monuments Society, 1932, diag., 4p.
40. *Southern Electric Group*, n.d., single sheet.
41. *Lancashire Life*, January 1973, p. 37–9.
42. Ibid., p. 39.
43. Ibid., p. 37.
44. Ibid., p. 37.
45. Author's own collection.
46. Author's own collection.
47. Author's own collection.
48. Kent County Library, *Publications for sale*, Kent County Library, rev. edn., 1984, 2p.
49. Lincolnshire Library Service, *About Lincolnshire – a booklist*, Lincolnshire Library Service, Lincoln, n.d., single sheet, folded.
50. Stockport Public Library, *Fiction list no. 2*, n.d., single sheet.
51. *Geoffrey Clinton's Theatre bookshop*, Manchester, n.d., single sheet.
52. Ephemera Society, *First world ephemera congress registration form*, Conference Services Ltd., London, 1980, single sheet.
53. *Lyme Park Festival 23rd–31st July, 1983*, Lyme Park, Disley, 1983, single sheet.
54. Alice Lynes, *How to organise a local collection*, p. 48.
55. Manchester Local History Library f. 1791/8.
56. Manchester Local History Library f. 1721/2.
57. Manchester Local History Library f. 1791/9.
58. Manchester Local History Library f. 1812/28.
59. Manchester Local History Library f. 1790/6.
60. Manchester Local History Library f. 1796/2/A.
61. Manchester Local History Library f. 1778/2.
62. Manchester Local History Library f. 1815/6.
63. Manchester Local History Library, miscellaneous collection.
64. *City Jackdaw*, 19 December 1879, p. 47.
65. Manchester Local History Library prints collection – s. 725.8, Gentlemen's Concert Hall.
66. Manchester Local History Library prints collection – s. 725.8, Gentlemen's Concert Hall, acc no. 1916, date 1897.
67. London Transport Museum, Covent Garden.
68. Ibid.
69. Ibid.
70. Ibid.
71. Greater Manchester Spastics Society Ltd, *Greetings*, Greater

Manchester Spastics Society Ltd, Manchester, n.d., 4p.

72. Alison Adburham, introduction, *Gamage's Christmas bazaar 1913*, London, Book Club Associates, 1974, reprint, illus., 470p.

73. Royal Academy, *L. S. Lowry R. A. 1887–1976*, London, Royal Academy, 1976, illus, 98p.

74. Royal Academy, *The gold of El Dorado*. London, Royal Academy, 1978, illus., 240p.

75. Hunter Penrose, *Just a reminder of our activities in catering for the stereotyper*, London, Hunter Penrose, n.d., illus,: 36p.

76. Elizabeth Shackleton, *Exhibition of paintings by Elizabeth Shackleton*, n.d., 5p. Ginnel Gallery, *Elizabeth Shackleton*, Ginnel Gallery, Manchester, n.d., illus., 4p.

77. Manchester School of Music, *Rudiments of Music examination*, Manchester School of Music, Manchester, 1909, single sheet.

78. Manchester City Planning Department, *A civic cathedral 1877–1977 Manchester Town Hall*, Manchester City Planning Department, 1977, illus., single sheet, folded.

79. *Win the time of your life with British sausages*, British Sausage Time, London, 1983, single sheet.

80. British Rail, *Getting steam up in 1982*, British Rail, 1982, single sheet, folded.

81. Cheshire County Council, *Discover Cheshire by bus and train from Manchester*, Cheshire County Council, n.d., single sheet, folded.

82. Thomas Cook/North Sea Ferries, *Amsterdam*, Cook/North Sea Ferries, 1982, single sheet, folded.

83. Britain in Europe, *Keep Britain in Europe*, Britain in Europe, London, n.d., single sheet.

84. Levenshulme Self Serve, *Gift voucher*, Levenshulme Self Serve/Reddish Self Serve Ltd, n.d., single sheet.

85. *Christ Church, Moss Side*, Moss Side, Christ Church, 1982.

86. Manchester City Planning Department, *Castlefield visitors' centre*, Manchester City Planning Department, n.d., illus., map, single sheet, folded.

87. City of Manchester Cultural Services, *The Manchester Central Library, A floor by floor guide*, Manchester Cultural Services Department, Manchester, 1977, single sheet, folded.

88. *Black Country Museum*, Department of Leisure Services, Dudley, 1974, illus., plan. single sheet, folded.

89. Sheffield City Museum, *Abbeydale Industrial Hamlet: a souvenir*, Sheffield City Museum, n.d., illus., single sheet, folded.

90. English Tourist Board, *Manchester*, English Tourist Board, 1983, illus., map, single sheet, folded.

91. *Mersey Valley walking guide no.1.* Mersey Valley Joint Committee, Manchester, 1981, illus, map, single sheet, folded.

92. C.C. Atkinson, comp., *Castlefield canal basin*, Education Service, North Western Museum of Science and Industry, Manchester, 1978, illus, map, single sheet, folded; *Liverpool Road Station Trail*, Education Service, North Western Museum of Science and Industry, Manchester, 1980, illus., map, single sheet, folded.

93. Brian Lamb, *From pillar to post: 1*, N. W. Postal Board, Manchester, 1983, illus., plan, single sheet, folded.

94. Greater Manchester Transport, *The Ashworth Valley and Cheesden Brook*, Greater Manchester Transport, 1983, illus., map, single sheet, folded.

95. *A walk around Warwick*, The Warwick Society, Warwick, n.d., illus., map, single sheet, folded.

96. Norweb, *Customer care*, Norweb, n.d., 4p.

97. North West Gas, *Look after your gas central heating and it will look after you*, North West Gas, Altrincham, 1982, single sheet, folded.

98. *Tameside Metropolitan Borough*, n.d., single sheet, folded.

99. Manchester City Council, *Parking is simple when you're right at the heart of things*, Manchester City Council, Manchester, 1983, map, single sheet, folded.

100. *Torbay places of interest*, n.d., single sheet, folded.

101. *The best of Devon*, Devon Association of Tourist Attractions, 1983, illus., map, single sheet, folded.

102. British Library Lending Division, *International photocopy service*, Boston Spa, 1980, diag., single sheet, folded; *A brief guide to its services*, British Library Lending Division, Boston Spa, 1981, single sheet, folded.

103. Phostrogen Ltd, *Chemiculture for general garden use*, Phostrogen Ltd, Corwen, n.d., illus., single sheet, folded, Leaflet no. 10.

104. *Where to eat in Stamford*, 1982, single sheet.

105. *Please take care when approaching horses*, Ashton and District Bridle Paths Association, n.d., single sheet.

106. *Don't get left behind . . . GET TRAINED!* RoSPA Motorcycle Training Scheme, Birmingham, n.d., illus., single sheet.

107. Manchester Local History Library f. 1752/1.

108. *The Sunday Times*, 16 November 1975, p. 76–7.

109. Manchester Local History Library f. 1805/8.

110. Smithills Coaching House, *The Pickwick Room*, Smithills Coaching House, n.d., illus., 4p; *Royal wedding festivities*, Smithills Coaching House, n.d. single sheet; *Pickwick Room £4.99 menu*, Smithills Coaching Bolton, n.d., single sheet; *5 Great ways to enjoy yourself*, Smithills Coaching House, n.d., single sheet.

111. Constance, Francis, *Manchester Manuscripts 1 Orphan Annie*, Historical Association Manchester Branch, Manchester, 1969, Jackdaw type publication.

112 H Boardman, and R Palmer, ed., *Manchester ballads*, City of Manchester Education Committee Musical Department, 1983.

113. Boots Ltd., *Send away for a Furry Bunny*, Nottingham, Boots Ltd, 1983, illus., single sheet.

114. Manchester Local History Library, f. 1690/1.

115. St Gabriel's Church, *Grand naval bazaar*, St Gabriel's Church, Hulme, 1900, illus.

116. Aylesbury Music Club, *The Creation*, 1969, 4p.

117. *Centenary of electric railways committee: programme of centenary events 1979/80*, Centenary of Electric Railways Committee, Chessington, 1979, single sheet.

118. Ephemera Society, *Ephemera 80: first world ephemera congress provisional programme*, the Ephemera Society, London, 1979, 10p.

119. *The 1981 Buxton Festival*, Buxton Festival Committee, 1981, single sheet.

120. Stamford Arts Centre, *Summer season 1983*, Stamford Arts Centre, Stamford, 1983, map, 4p.

121. Friends of the Earth, *The world's whales need your help*, London, Friends of the Earth, n.d., single sheet, folded.

122. Friends of the Earth (Birmingham) Ltd, *Whales whaling*. Birmingham, Friends of the Earth (Birmingham) Ltd, 1977, single sheet; *Whale products list*, Birmingham, Friends of the Earth, (Birmingham) Ltd, n.d., single sheet.

123. Manchester Local History Library, f. 1812/22.

124. *Park House Putting Course and model boating marina*, Weston-super-Mare, n.d., single sheet.

125. SIGA, *Why join SIGA*, SIGA, n.d., single sheet, folded.

126. *Peterborough Mediaeval Society*, n.d., 4p.

127. Manchester Arts Society, *Enjoy all the Arts the convenient way – and at a discount*, Manchester Arts Society, Manchester, n.d., single sheet, folded.

128. Lancashire and Cheshire Antiquarian Society, *The Lancashire and Cheshire Antiquarian Society 1883–1983*, n.d., single

sheet, folded.

129. Isle of Man Steam Packet Co./Manxman Steamer Society, *Finished with Engines*, Liverpool, Isle of Man Steam Packet Co. and Manxman Steamer Society, n.d., single sheet.

130. William Plant, *'Latest millinery shapes'*, Manchester, Plant, n.d., single sheet; *'Exclusive millinery shapes'*, Manchester, Plant, n.d., single sheet.

131. Cheshire Reclaimed Building Materials Ltd, *It is easy to see why so many Architects and Developers are choosing reclaimed bricks to create homes of character*, Manchester, Cheshire Reclaimed Building Materials Ltd, n.d., illus., 4p.

132. Anderson, *Ephemera of travel*.

133. Lewis, *Collecting printed ephemera*; *Printed ephemera*.

Chapter 4

1. J.E. Pemberton, *National provision of printed ephemera*, p. 18, para. 67.

2. A. Clinton, *Printed ephemera: its collection, organisation and access*, London, Bingley, 1981.

3. Pemberton, *National provision of printed ephemera*, p. 29, paras 114–6.

4. Local History Ephemera, p. 3.

5. Pemberton, *National provision of printed ephemera*, p. 18, para. 67.

6. Manchester Local History Library, f. 1796/13.

7. M. Rosser, *The Princes of Loom Street*, Manchester, Historical Association, Manchester Branch, 1972, illus., 27 sheets plus two booklets.

8. M. Rickards, *This is ephemera: collecting printed throwaways*, Newton Abbot, David and Charles, 1977.

9. Author's collection.

10. Manchester Public Libraries, ff. 337, A5.

11. Manchester Local History Library, q352.042733 Sc. 1.

12. *Health and Social Service Journal*, 3 October 1980, p. 1293–4.

13. Ibid., p. 1293.

14. Ibid., p. 1294.

15. The Times Literary Supplement, 7 November 1975.

16. *The Sunday Times*, 16 November, 1975, p. 76–7.

17. Author's collection.

18. *Leader and General Advertiser*, 16 May 1887, p. 3.

19. *The Ephemerist*, vol. 1, no. 20, January 1979, p. 100.

20. Dorothy McCulla *'Local History Ephemera'*, p.3–4. published

by Standing Conference for Local History.

21. Manchester City Planning Department, *Castlefield*, Manchester City Planning Department, n.d., single sheet, map.
22. New Era Publications ApS, *Introducing dianetics*, Copenhagen, New Era Publishing Aps, 1983, single sheet.
23. B.W. Lowndes, *Glass and glazing Ltd*, Hazel Grove, Lowndes, n.d., single sheet.
24. Auto Care, *Everything for your car*, New Mills, Auto Care, n.d., single sheet.
25. Greater Manchester County and City of Manchester, *New uses for old buildings*, Manchester City Planning Department, n.d., 14 sheets in folder.
26. *City of Edinburgh District Council Committee Minutes. General Purposes Committee, City Chambers Sub-committee*, 5 August 1983, p. 24.

Chapter 5

1. Manchester Central Library, Ref ff. 337 A5.
2. Drawings of Lancaster and Tonge now in the Greater Manchester Museum of Science and Industry.
3. B.S. 4971. This British Standard is at present under revision and may be superseded in the near future.

Chapter 6

1. R.L. Hills, and D. Patrick, *Beyer-Peacocks: locomotive builders to the world*, Glossop, Transport Publishing, 1983 illus., diags.
2. Manchester Local History Library, f.1805/16.
3. Rochdale Public Library Pl 41.
4. Books for Students Ltd, *It's never too far to Leamington Spa*, 4p., n.d., illus., map. Author's own collection.
5. Manchester Local History Library, f. 1796/1.
6. Manchester Local History Library, f. 1808/10.

Chapter 7

1. Rochdale Local History Library Pl.10.
2. Quarry Bank Mill, *See Styal get weaving*, Styal, n.d., single sheet.
3. Three Choirs Festival Association, *Gloucester Three Choirs Festival 16–23 August 1980*, Hereford, Three Choirs Festival

Association, 1980, single sheet, folded.

4. The Adam Smith Theatre, *Robin Hood and the Babes in the Wood*, Kirkcaldy, n.d., single sheet.
5. British Rail, *London saver*, British Rail, 1982, single sheet.
6. R. S. International, *Beer price list*, Stockport, n.d., single sheet.
7. *Torbay luxury limousines*, Torquay, n.d., single sheet.
8. James Pringle, *Visit James Pringle woollen mill*, Pringle, Edinburgh, n.d., single sheet, folded, illus., map.
9. Author's collection. Assembly Room Leigh . . . Grand Variety Concert 1901.
10. Ibid.
11. M. Vicinus, *Broadsides of the Industrial Revolution*, Newcastle-upon-Tyne, Graham, 1975, 79p.
12. H. Aaron, *Pillar to post: looking at street furniture*, London, Warne, 1982, illus., 127p.
13. Displayed at Quarry Bank Mill, Styal, Cheshire.
14. Rochdale Local History Library, Pl. 42.
15. Manchester Local History Library, f. 1808/3.
16. *Rochdale . . . part 1*, Rochdale, Rochdale Libraries and Arts Service, n.d., illus., maps, 35 single sheets.
17. H. Horton, *Peterloo 1819. A portfolio of contemporary documents*, Manchester, City of Manchester Cultural Services Department, 1975, 5p., text + 20 single sheets.
18. Gladstone Pottery Museum, Longton, Stoke-on-Trent.

Chapter 8

1. J. West, *Town records*, Phillimore, Chichester, 1983, 366p.
2. J.E. Pemberton, 'Printed ephemera in the British Isles', *Aslib Proceedings*, vol. 24, no. 34, March 1972, p. 62–77.
3. Ibid., p. 47.
4. A. Clinton, *Printed ephemera: its collection, organisation and access*, London, Bingley, 1981. p. 89.
5. Ibid., p. 88–93.

Appendix 2

1. Now the Library Association Local Studies Group.
2. Advisory Committee on Ephemera and Minor Publications: Preliminary Report [ADCEMP], p. 2.
3. British Library Research and Development Project, S1/G/

279. The research was undertaken by Alan Clinton who used the report for the basis of his book.

4. British Library Research and Development project, S1/G/

386. Published as Report 5595 in 1983 by Loughborough University Department of Library and Information Studies.

5. Clinton, *Printed ephemera* p. 88.

6. Ibid., p. 88.

7. *The Local Historian* was formerly the *Amateur Historian*.

8. J.E. Carter, *J. L. Hobbs's local history and the library*, London, Deutsch, 1973.

9. A. Lynes, *How to organise a local collection*, London, Deutsch, 1974.

10. H. Nichols, *Local studies librarianship*, London, Bingley, 1979.

Bibliography

This is a select bibliography which lists some of the main publications and articles on ephemera together with some works on specific types of material.

General works

Clinton, A., *Printed ephemera: its collection, organisation and access*, London, Bingley, 1981, .

Feather, J., 'The sanctuary of printing: John Johnson and his collection', in *Arts Libraries Journal*, vol. 1, no. 1, Spring 1976 p. 23–33.

Lewis, J. N. C., *Collecting printed ephemera*, London, Studio Vista, 1976.

Lewis, J. N. C., *Printed ephemera: the changing use of type and letter forms in English and American printing*, London, Cowell, 1962, also republished by London, Faber and Faber, 1969.

Pemberton, J. E., 'Printed ephemera in the British Isles', in Aslib Proceedings Vol. 24, no. 3, March 1972, p. 62–77.

Pollard, N., 'Printed ephemera', in Pacey, P., *Art library manual: a guide to resources and practice*, London, Bowker, 1977, p. 316–36.

Rickards, M., *This is ephemera: collecting printed throwaways*, Newton Abbot, David and Charles, 1977.

Reports

Advisory Committee on Ephemera and Minor Publications, *Preliminary report*, ADCEMP, 1979.

Clinton, A., *Printed ephemera: its collection, organisation and access*, BLRDD Report 5593, Bodleian Library, 1980.

Pemberton, J. E., *The national provision of printed ephemera in the social sciences*, University of Warwick Occasional Papers No. 1, University of Warwick, Coventry, 1971.

Standing Conference for Local History, *Local history ephemera: a report*, SCLH, London, 1975.

Sturgess, R.P. and Dixon, D., *An investigation of local publications*, BLRDD Report 5645, Loughborough University Department of Library and Information Studies, Loughborough, 1983.

Periodicals

The Ephemerist, The Ephemera Society, bi-monthly, 1975 – –

Some publications on specific types of ephemera

Allen, A. and Hoverstadt, J. *The history of printed scraps*, London, New Cavendish Books, 1983 p. 145, illus.

Anderson, J. and Swinglehurst, E., *Ephemera of travel and transport*, New Cavendish Books, London, 1981.

Barnicoat, J., *A concise history of posters*, Thames and Hudson, London, 1972.

Dillon, A. E., 'War time information: its collection and dissemination', in *Manchester Review*, vol. 2, Summer 1941, p. 289–93.

Hillier, R., Auction catalogues and notices: their value to the local historian, in *The Local Historian*, vol. 13, no. 3, p. 131–9.

Hodges-Paul, R.T., 'Printer's specimens', in the *Amateur Historian*, vol. 3, no. 7 p. 299–300.

Horrocks, S., 'Manchester theatres: sources for research in Manchester Reference Library', in *Manchester Review*, vol. 6, Winter, 1951, p. 161–4.

Hudson, G., 'Printed ephemera and the industrial historian', in *Industrial Archaeology*, vol. 12, no. 4, p. 357–68.

James, L., *Print and the people 1819–1851*, Lane, 1976, illus., 368p.

Leach, E., 'The Manchester theatre-resources of the Arts Library', in *Manchester Review*, vol. 10, Autumn 1965, p. 217–25.

Leach, E., 'Playbills and programmes', in *Manchester Review*, vol. 11, Spring/Summer 1966, p. 7–22.

'Manchester ballad collection', in *Manchester Review*, vol. 7, Summer 1956, p. 391.

Osborne, K. and Pipe B., *The international book of beer labels, mats and coasters*, London, Hamlyn, 1979.

Page, H.R., 'Collecting Victoriana', in *Manchester Review*, vol. 8, Summer 1958, p. 161–180.

Rickards, M., *The public notice: an illustrative history*, Newton Abbot, David and Charles, 1973.

Rickards, M., *The rise and fall of the poster*, Newton Abbot, David and Charles, 1971.

Rickards, M. and Moody, M., *The First World War: ephemera, documents*, London, Jupiter Books, 1975.

Shepard, L., *The history of street literature*, Newton Abbot, David and Charles, 1973.

Thorpe, S., 'Leaflets for information' in *Library Association Record*, vol. 83, no. 9, 1981, p. 434–5.

'Trade mark registration', in *Industrial Archaeology*, vod. 12, no. 3, p. 27–51.Z Ward, P., *Cambridge street literature*, Cambridge, Oleander, 1978.

Watson, J., comp., *Bibliography of ephemeral community information materials, part 1 sources, guides*, Leeds Polytechnic School of Librarianship Public Library Management Research Unit, BLRDD Report 5221, 1979.

Wulcko, L.M., 'Fire insurance policies as a source of local history,' in *The Local Historian*, vol. 9, no. 1, p. 3–8.

Conservation of materials

Cunha, G.M. and Cunha, D.G., *Conservation of library materials*, Scarecrow Press, 1972, 2 vols.

Index

active collection; 25,
Adam Smith Theatre, Kirkcaldy; 206,
ADCEMP (Advisory Committee on
  Ephemera and Minor Publications); 7,
  8, 11, 225, 226,
admission cards, collection of; 117–119,
advertising leaflets, collection of; 22, 26,
  43–54,
Anti-Corn Law League; 138, 161,
appeal leaflets, collection of; 54–56,
application forms, collection of; 56–57,

badges, collection of; 97–98,
beer mats, collection of; 40, 58–59,
Beyer, Peacock and Co; 185,
billheads, collection of; 24, 59–61,
bills, collection of; 59–61,
bingo cards, collection of; 98,
Birmingham Central Library; 178,
Bodelian Library; 24, 218,
booking forms, collection of; 64,
booklets; 13,
booklists, collection of; 61–62,
bookmarks, collection of; 62–64,
Books for Students Limited; 190,
Booksellers catalogues; 135–136,
British Books in Print; 225,
British Library; 8, 13, 15, 16, 35, 215,
  217, 219, 225,
  Research and Development division;
  225,

British National Bibliography; 13, 182,
  224–225,
British rail; 153, 206,
broadsheets, collection of; 23, 26, 64–73,
brochures, collection of; 43–54,
bus tickets; 23,

calendars, collection of; 73,
cards, collection of; 73–74,
catalogues, collection of; 74–77,
certificates, collection of; 77–78,
cheques, collection of; 57–58,
church magazines; 12,
cigarette cards; 24, 31, 132,
cinema playbills; 26,

circulars, collection of; 78–79,
Clinton, Alan; 2, 8, 9, 125, 215, 216,
  217, 218, 226, 227,
clippings, collection of; 79–80,
Colman's; 28,
Commemorative items, collection of; 31,
  80,
commercial library; 27,
competition entry Forms, collection of;
  82–83,
compliment slips' collection of; 80–82,
constitutions, collection of; 83,
Copyright Receipt Office; 215,
Craven Brothers of Reddish; 29,

Diocesan Record Office; 12,
Disley Amalgamated Club; 31,
Dixon, Diana; 9, 11,

Edinburgh District Council; 157,
election literature, collection of; 26, 83–
  84,
envelopes, collection of; 84–85,
ephemera collection, types of; 23–24,
ephemera, dating of; 130,
Ephemera Society; 6, 7, 141,
European Architectual Heritage Year;
  132,
excursion and holiday leaflets, collection
  of; 85–87,

Fixture lists, collection of; 87–88,

gift vouchers, collection; 88
Gillette; 144,
Gladstone Pottery Museum; 212,
Gorton election campaign 1910; 36–37
guarantees, collection of; 89,
guides, collection of; 89

handbills, collection of; 26, 43–54,
Hartlepool Museum; 142,
Harvey, Colin; 33,
Hills, Dr. R. L.; 29, 30,
Historical Manuscripts Commission;
  217,
household ephemera; 91–92, 153–154,

245